THE

NEGRÒ PROBLEM SOLVED;

OR,

AFRICA AS SHE WAS, AS SHE IS, AND AS SHE SHALL BE.

HER CURSE AND HER CURE.

───────•●•·───────

BY REV. HOLLIS READ,

AUTHOR OF " GOD IN HISTORY ;" " INDIA AND ITS PEOPLE ;" " PALACE OF THE GREAT KING ;" " COMMERCE AND CHRISTIANITY," ETC.

ISBN:978-1-63923-817-0

Printed: March 2023

Published and Distributed By:
Lushena Books
607 Country Club Drive, Unit E
Bensenville, IL 60106
www.lushenabks.com

ISBN: 978-1-63923-817-0

PREFACE.

THE following pages owe their origin to an irrepressible desire the writer has felt to contribute, at this interesting crisis of their fate, something, if it be the humblest share, to the deliverance of an unfortunate race from an untold series of wrongs and degradation. The long night of their affliction seems to be drawing to a close, and the day of their redemption draws near. They come bowing unto us. They come with outstretched arms, beseeching us that we will extend to them the helping hand in this their time of need.

It is very generally conceded that the war now so fiercely raging in our country has a very important bearing on the great negro question. Whatever other results it may leave behind it, an assurance is felt that it will strike the death-blow to American slavery, putting the whole system beyond the possibility of a future resurrection. This once done, the question: "What shall be done with four millions of ex-slaves?" is one of the most practical and momentous that our nation—or that philanthropy and religion—ever had to decide. Not the welfare of 4,000,000 of emancipated slaves is alone concerned. Our duty here has a bearing on our nation, on Africa, and on the world, of momentous interest. England—all Europe—is moved to its centre, waiting in profound suspense, deeply interested in the settlement of this great question. King Cotton trembles on his throne; yet hopes, in the commotion, to enlarge his empire.

We have attempted to present Africa—her vast resources and capabilities in soil, mines, and forests— as a promising field, a field ready for the harvest, inviting capital, enterprise, intelligence, skill, civilization, and Christianity to come and ply their genial agencies for renovation and elevation among the nations of the earth; and, more than all, extending the welcome hand to her exiled sons, that they may return to her shores, laden with all the good things, which, in the land of their bondage, and in the school of a rigorous discipline, they have acquired.

We expect a good future for Africa. We reason here from what Africa and African races *have been* to what they *shall be.* God has never left himself without witness there. We take the presage, the promise, the prophecy, the pledge of Providence, that that long-neglected, suffering continent shall come up in remembrance before God—that the long outcast posterity of Ham shall yet share richly in the benedictions of Heaven. Her rising star is seen in the world-wide interest that is aroused in her behalf—is seen through the clash of arms; through the smoke of the battle-field, and garments rolled in blood—is seen in the peculiar religious character of the slaves; in the simplicity, godly sincerity, and importunity of their prayers; in their yearnings after freedom, and their beseechings of the throne of Grace for their deliverance. And it is seen in a corresponding readiness on the part of Africa, and her native population, to receive the Gospel.

Our hope for Africa lies in the prospect of a Christian negro nationality; such as an enlightened commerce and an extensive scheme of colonization, and Christian government, laws, and institutions, all baptized in the spirit of Christianity, shall produce. We rely on the unfailing favor of God to the oppressed, that Africa shall yet arise and shine, her glory being come. We have, therefore, taken the occasion to urge on philanthropists and Christians the 'duty to do what lies in their power, by their prayers and benefactions, and by all suitable means, to emancipate that long-forgotton continent, and to give her a name and a place among the nations of the earth.

In the following pages colonization is advocated, not as an adequate remedy for slavery—though its legitimate bearings on that whole system of bondage and degradation are not to be overlooked—but as a boon to the colored man, a privilege to every one who is fitted to profit by it, and the most suitable and hopeful agency by which to raise Africa from her present debasement, and to assign her an honorable place among the nations. We would most distinctly concede the *right* of the negro to remain in this country. It is *his* country as well as ours. Yet, we would not the less earnestly and kindly urge on him his *privilege* to go. Interest to himself, and duty to his fatherland and to his race, urge him, even if it be at a personal sacrifice, to go forth as the only agents that can rescue a continent from the low depths of social, civil, and moral debasement.

The reader may feel a temporary disappointment that the writer has not committed himself more unreservedly to the new order of things which are seemingly inaugurated by the present war. We doubt not what shall be the end, but we dare not be too sanguine of a *speedy* consummation. We have no expectation of peace, which shall deserve the name of peace, but in the extinction of slavery. The war will not, can not, cease, till its cause—its curse-provoking and war-invoking cause—be removed. Universal, unconditional emancipation we believe to be the first and immediate solution of the negro problem. Yet his final destiny, his attaining to a nationality, his emerging into a full manhood, involve time, events, changes, revolutions, which wait the sure, though often mysterious movements of Providence.

We feel safe in connecting the highest and best destiny of the colored man with his fatherland. If it be in his heart, and fortuitous circumstances favor, that he, like Israel of old, may quit the land of his captivity, and return to the land of his fathers and the land marked out by Heaven for his habitation, we congratulate him as favored above his fellows. Ransomed by the mighty hand of God, they shall return and come to their land with songs and everlasting joy on their heads. "Rewarded double" for their long and bitter captivity, they shall obtain joy and gladness, and sorrow and sighing shall flee away.

Could the present volume have appeared with the most befitting title, it would have been called the Hand of God in Africa, and her Races; for such, indeed, is the book. We have watched this all-controlling Hand in vain, if it be not now stretched out over that long-neglected continent, and that long-abused race. And we expect, from this time onward, more distinctly to discern there the stately steppings of Him who has gone forth to the conquest of the world. H. R.

Elizabeth, N. J., 1864.

CONTENTS.

1*

CHAPTER VII.

CHAPTER VIII.

CHAPTER IX.

CHAPTER X.

CHAPTER XI.

CHAPTER XII.

CHAPTER XIII.

CHAPTER XIV.

CHAPTER XV.

CHAPTER XVI.

CHAPTER XVII.

CHAPTER XVIII.

CHAPTER XIX.

CHAPTER XX.

THE GREAT NEGRO PROBLEM SOLVED.

CHAPTER I.

Africa little known—Ancient Africa—Plan of the Work—Africa as she was, as she is, and as she shall be.

In directing attention to Africa, I ask you to survey a very extraordinary portion of the globe.

Africa has long been known as the neglected continent, a land never destitute of interest, and in many respects a land of intense interest, and yet very much of a *forgotten* land. But this neglected, forgotten land is once more coming up in remembrance. "In a historical view, Africa is deserving the minutest investigation, as one of the richest archives of former times and of the ancient world. It guards, couched in mysterious characters, innumerable annals of man's progress from the earliest times down to the overthrow of the Roman Empire." No part of the world presents so varied a history, none a history so extraordnary. It has an ancient history of great interest, extending further back than that of any other nation; and a modern history—unwritten for the most part, and the most forbidden and melancholy. When Greece was yet young, and Rome was unknown—before Abraham was, or the Jewish Commonwealth had a name, Africa could boast of old and civilized kingdoms. When nations in Africa had made great advance in science and the arts, and had excelled all modern nations in architecture, Europe was languishing in barbarism, and America was unknown.

No portion of the world presents a more singular and interesting theme for study. The philosophic historian, especially, will here find abundant materials for endless speculations, and as abundant for the profoundest contemplation. In no portion of the world will he meet with so much to excite wonder, so much to perplex, so much to interest.

Africa is a land of the most singular contrasts. No where else do such extremes meet—fertility and barrenness—beauty and deformity—civilization and barbarism—light and darkness—human elevation and human depression. Though one of the earliest known, and the earliest civilized quarters of the globe, yet Africa has remained for the last three thousand years the least known, and the least civilized; sometimes the most blessed, but generally the most cursed of any part of the world.

The continent of Africa, though probably the most ancient field of geographical enterprise, is still the least explored portion of the globe. " Though once the nursery of science and literature, the emporium of commerce, and the seat of an empire which contended with Rome for the sovereignty of the world—the cradle of the ancient church, and the asylum of the infant Saviour, yet Africa still presents a comparative blank on the map, as well as in the history of the world. Though, according to Herodotus, it was circumnavigated by the Phœnicians long before the Christian era, and its coast was the first field of maritime discovery after the compass had inspired seaman with confidence to leave shores and landmarks, and stand forth on the boundless deep, yet to this day its interior regions continue a mystery to the white man, a land of darkness and of terror to the most fearless and enterprising traveler. Although in no country has there been such a sacrifice of men to the enterprise of discovery—of men the most intelligent and undaunted—of men impelled, not by gross cupidity, but by refined philanthropy—yet, notwithstanding such suffering and waste of human life, we are only acquainted with the fringes of that immense continent, and a few lineaments at no great distance from the shore.

"Africa once had her churches, her colleges, her repositories of science and learning, her Cyprians and bishops of apostolic renown, and her noble army of martyrs; but now the funeral pall hangs over her widespread domains, while her millions, exposed to tenfold horrors, descend like a vast funeral mass to the regions of woe. Christendom has been enriched by her gold, her drugs, her ivory, and the bodies and souls of men—and what has been the recompense?"*

But shall Africa always remain the same blank in creation as she has heretofore? She was not made for naught. She is, no doubt, yet to be as remarkably honored and blessed as she has been remarkably debased and cursed. Her history possesses, especially at this time, just that kind of interest which can scarcely fail to secure the attention of the observing, thinking, philanthropic, and Christian mind. Could the writer convey to the mind of the reader the interest he has expe-

* Moffatt's Southern Africa.

rienced in the investigation of this portion of history, quite sure would he feel of a respectful attention.

The sacred bard of Israel often calls Africa the land of Ham; and it seems very generally conceded that this grand division of the earth was given by Noah to his "younger" son. Yet the posterity of Ham seem not to have confined themselves to Africa. Late researches make it quite probable that Ham shared, at least with his brother Shem, the southern portions of Asia, extending through India and Siam, as far as Japan. The monumental history of Egypt and of India exhibit some remarkable resemblances. We trace the footsteps of the *same race* in the primitive works of Egypt, in the pyramids and temples of Ethiopia, and in the excavated temples of Elephanta, Ellora, and Kanarah in Hindostan. Strangely, indeed, has the ill-fated race of Ham, for centuries, disappeared from among the nations, and almost ceased to act any part on the great theatre of human affairs. And as strangely are they beginning to reappear. The black races are beginning to loom again above the horizon, below which they have been so long sunk, and may soon play a no insignificant part among the nations of the earth. Already have African races shared largely in the philanthropic feelings of man, and they seem destined soon to engross a much larger share of these feelings.

In what I have to say of Africa, and things pertaining to Africa, I shall speak of her as she *was*, as she *is*, and as she *shall* be—Africa past, present, and future. And whether her past, present, or future be before us, we shall make her CURSE and her CURE our prominent theme.

Our design is to present the claims of that mysterious and long-suffering continent to the prayers, the sympathies, and benefactions of all whom it may concern. And deeply indeed does it concern the philanthropist and the Christian of every name and nation. For a great wrong has been committed; the wrong-doers shall come up in remembrance before the righteous Arbiter of nations. He will take part with the oppressed. A great continent is to be reclaimed; an injured race, who have sat in darkness and the shadow of death, are about to see a great light. The Lord seems about to visit them in his mercy, and to reward them double for all their afflictions.

Before speaking of the *curse* which mysterious Heaven has been pleased to inflict on that truly mysterious continent, or of the remedy which Providence seems to be designating as the cure of her protracted woes, we shall say a few things concerning Africa herself.

1. Africa is very much of a *terra incognita*—a land of mystery and romance—quite an enigma in the world's history. From century to century she has remained the same mysterious and unknown land. With a few illustrious exceptions, the mere chronicler of historical events finds on this singular continent little to admire or to register among the annals of the nations; while the Christian and the philosophic historian find more to lament over, more to interest, and more to perplex, than in any other portion of the globe. Though she has for ages lain in sight of the most civilized and refined nations of the earth, yet she has, for the most part, remained uncivilized and unknown. Up to the present day, we know little of Af-

rica beyond her outlines; and even these outlines were not known till the fifteenth century. It is true that Pharaoh Necho had sailed round Africa more than six centuries before Christ; and, ages earlier, its eastern coast, and perhaps its western, had been navigated by the ships of the wise King of Israel; yet it remained a land of darkness, and its people covered with gross darkness. From generation to generation it has lain a *blank* on the map of nations. More was known of Africa two thousand years ago than at the present time. It was one of the earliest inhabited portions of the globe. There the scientific and industrial arts first flourished; there man, after the Deluge, first attained to a high state of civilization; and thence radiated, both eastward and westward, the light of civilization and learning. But now it is the least known and the least civilized of any. While the world has been advancing, Africa has been stationary or retrograding. While the resources of other portions of the world have been developing, and their powers augmenting, Africa has been dwindling into nothingness. So limited are her commercial relations, and so little does she contribute to the improvement, happiness, or productive industry of the world, that, if her circumjacent waters were to close over her, and her name were blotted out from the catalogue of nations, and all that pertains to her were sunk in the deep, she would scarcely be missed. Faint and few would be the tones of lament. Truth, science, commerce, the arts, would in no appreciable degree be impoverished. Nor would religion and philosophy scarcely feel the loss. Ignorance and barbarism reign almost without interruption, from one end of that vast continent to the other; and, with just exceptions enough to keep the world apprised of the capabilities of the land, and of the sons of Ham, ignorance and barbarism always have reigned. These exceptions have abundantly shown, we believe, the capabilities of the Africans, and of their soil, to reach the first rank among the civilized, the learned, and the religious, and the designs of Providence yet to elevate this unfortunate race, and to realize their capabilities.

It is our design, in these pages, after having said more of Africa herself, to present slavery and the slave-trade as the withering curse, which has so long kept Africa in her present degraded condition; and colonization and commerce as the remedy which shall, more effectually and permanently than any other, the Gospel excepted, bring relief to Africa, and blessings to her sons. The present system of colonization from this country will be brought forward, not so much as a remedy of slavery, as of the slave-trade—not so much the individual benefit of the colonists, as the general benefit of the whole continent. Yet we believe that the bearings of colonization on American slavery are by no means insignificant, and that the benefit to the colonist is immense.

What a wonderful continent is this rounded, smooth-shored Africa, known from the earliest dawn of time, yet so unknown; the granary of nations, yet sterile and fruitless as the sea; swarming with life, yet dazzling the eyes with its vast tract of glittering sand! No land presents, either in its present aspects or its past history, such singular contrasts; such fertility and barrenness; such beauty and deformity; so high a state of civilization and so low a state of barbarism. Since Africa, the mother of civilization, has grown gray and been lan‑ guishing under the decrepitude of age, mighty empires in Asia and Europe have sprung into being, and passed their youth, their manhood, their decline, and extinc‑ tion.   Unchanged, the land of Ham has witnessed the rise and fall, during a long succession of ages, of the Assyrian, the Persian, the Greek, and the Roman em‑ pires.   Asia has been again and again revolutionized; civilized Europe has, in the mean time, sprung into existence, and the sun of some of its nations has long since set; England has grown, in the mean time, into a colossal empire ; the youth, the manhood, and decline of Rome, though extending to some twenty centuries, has interposed and passed away before the dim vision of Afric's sable sons ; a new world has been discovered beyond the western ocean ; its forests reclaimed from the dominion of wild men, and the empire of freedom established.   The world has been rapidly advancing. In science, civilization, .government, religion, there has been a signal progress ; while Africa, the mother of civilization, the cradle of science and the arts, has been sitting solitary, languishing in decrepitude, and not able to rise, by reason of weakness.

The past history of Africa we have seen wrapped in a profound mystery.   Her soil has been abundantly fertile in some of the best and many of the worst of human productions.   There have mingled, for centuries, the extremes of good and bad government ; of liberty and despotism ; of freedom and slavery ; of learning and ignorance ; of civilization and barbarism ; of the gross‑ est darkness and the clearest light.   History there records some of her brightest ornaments and some of her blackest deformities.   There, in all the romance of an Eastern tale, a Hebrew slave becomes the ruler of millions. There, an outcast child, mysteriously picked up by a king's daughter, becomes the deliverer and leader of that equally mysterious people, who, after their singular wanderings during forty years in the deserts of Arabia, settle down amid the hills of Palestine, and soon expand into one of the most extraordinary nations that ever existed. The progenitors of the Hebrew commonwealth were there schooled and disciplined, and prepared for their national existence. Moses, the most extraordinary man that ever lived, than whom no mere man has left so much of the impress of his mind upon every succeeding generation, was reared and schooled in Africa. In no other court than Pharaoh's could such a man have been reared. In no other nation could the Hebrews have been qualified to form that civil polity and that church organization which now, in the purposes and arrangements of Providence, became needful in carrying on the great work of human salvation.

There, too, was the home of Dido, of Hannibal; the scene of Scipio's triumph and Jugurtha's crimes. There lived Tertullian, Athanasius, and Augustine; the romance of the Moors dwelt there; the last breath of Louis of France was drawn there. And there, too, is the home of the mysterious negro races, whose past history has baffled the most philosophic speculations of the historian, whose present condition is an anomaly among the nations of the earth, and whose destiny is evidently not yet revealed.

·And not only has Africa been the home of the scholar, the theologian, the philosopher, the statesman, and the soldier; not only was she the cradle of the arts and the nursery of the sciences, but in later ages, in the first days of Christianity, she contributed more than her proportion of the early agents for the propagation over the earth of the new religion. How many of these do you suppose were from Africa, or of African descent? More, undoubtedly, than you have supposed. The names of some, and the localities or native places of others, will enable us to judge on this subject with some degree of correctness. Luke, the beloved physician, was from Cyrene; he was an undoubted African, by birth at least, if not by blood. If Luke be not the same as *Lucius* of Cyrene, we then have here another of the first teachers of Christianity, from the same African region. Simon, the father of Rufus and Alexander, was also a Cyrenian; and, to leave no ground for mistake as to his country, he is called the Cyrenian (from Cyrene, a city in Lybia, in Africa, west of Egypt). It was this black man, this native of an African city, who was compelled to bear the cross for the exhausted Sufferer as he went up Calvary to be crucified; a coincidence not to be overlooked. Again: we meet, among the prophets and teachers, at Antioch, one Simon, who was called *Niger* (black). We have here, at least, one evangelist and four of the early disciples and teachers of Christianity, who were Africans. And, as successors to this first generation of disciples, Africa supplied her full quota of Christian bishops and teachers. Origen, Bishop of Alexandria, was an African. Julius Africanus, as the name seems most obviously to import, was a native of the same country; and so we shall venture to assume that Athanasius and Dionysius, celebrated Bishops of Alexandria, and

Cyprian, Bishop of Carthage, were of the crisped hair and the thick lip.*

No doubt an African soil is capable of producing *men*. It has been rich in such productions, and its capabilities are not exhausted. Paul chose for his traveling companion and his intimate friend, an African; Paul's Master chose that some of the first and brightest ornaments and most efficient agents and teachers of the early Christian Church should be men of the same kindred and color. Yea, the suffering Jesus chose that he who should perform for him the last act of kindness on earth, who should bear with him his cross up the hill of Calvary, should be an African. Oh! is there not a deep significance here? Poor Africa was allowed to bear the cross; and heavily, indeed, from century to century, has she borne the cross. But shall she not wear the crown? Shall that humble act, done *at such a time*, be passed by and forgotten? No! Africa shall yet come up in remembrance before her King, and she shall be rewarded double for all her sorrows.

We have a guaranty in what Africa has done, for what she may do. Native Africans have shown themselves masters, as already intimated, in every station and avocation in life, in every art and science, in genius and eminent talent, in qualities intellectual or physical, and in moral and religious character. The past history of Africa leaves no doubt of the abstract capa-

---

* And in Peter's well-known assembly on the day of Pentecost there was a large representation from Africa and the Stock of Ham; men from Egypt and the parts of Lybia about Cyrene; Cretes and Arabians; to these we may add "*Arnobius*, the African," who, in the third century, wrote a copious and powerful defense of Christianity.

bilities of Africans to become the highest type of man. Whether in warriors or statesmen, philosophers or divines, Africa has shown herself equal to the exigences of any past age. This we may receive as a pledge that she shall not be found wanting when her sons shall be called to act in a more advanced age. Her present degradation and the inferiority of her races present no argument against her equality to any other portion of the human family. Her present degradation and evident inferiority is most obviously a result of circumstances simply, of external causes, and not an inherent and original incapacity; a result, perhaps, of the malediction of Heaven. It is, at least, the fulfillment of some wise and inscrutable purpose of the King of nations, and argues nothing as to what the same race may become under other circumstances, and under the benediction of Heaven.

We have called Africa the land of Ham, and we shall undertake to show that, not only is this mysterious continent a land kept in reserve for some great future realizations in the progress of the Redeemer's kingdom, but that there remains a blessing in reserve for the poor down-trodden sons of Ham. Shem largely and for a long time shared in the rich benedictions of Heaven. Up to the advent of the mediatorial King, the descendants of Shem were the favored race. Religion dwelt with them. Here were the patriarchs, the prophets, the living oracles of God, the city and temple where God chose to place his name and reveal his glory. Here were the revelations of Heaven by types and shadows, dreams and visions. But since the advent of the great Reality, the embodiment of old truths in the more practical form of Christianity, the ark has passed from the tents of Shem to the tabernacles of Japheth. But is there no blessing for poor Ham? Shall the curse of Canaan rest upon this unfortunate family forever? We think we hear the voice of a Father's love speaking comfortably to this alienated and long-forsaken son. Shall the ark rest forever with Japheth? Shall not this other great branch of the human family come up in remembrance before the Lord, and he yet give them double for all their afflictions?

We have assumed that Africa has been *reserved* for the development of a higher order of civilization and a better type of Christianity than has yet been known. Though this be not a proposition, in the nature of the case, to be *proved*, yet by pursuing a historical argument, already casually introduced, we shall, we think, make it appear exceedingly probable. The argument is drawn very much from the *capabilities*, which Africa has already evinced, to realize all that I have here intimated. Exhibitions have already been made on an *African soil*, and *by Africans*, which, I think, we are warranted in receiving as a sort of *first-fruits* to a plenteous harvest.

I shall, therefore, ask you, in a subsequent chapter, to go over some of those enchanted grounds, and take, at least, a cursory glance of some of those monuments of her ancient greatness. We shall, in such an excursion, learn what Africa *has been*, and at the same time find some substantial ground for our inference as to *what she shall be*.

Of the interior of Africa we know very little. It has always been an unknown land. Occasionally its vast regions have been penetrated by the solitary traveler, who has sent back a report. Still it has remained an unknown land. For aught we know, great empires may have flourished there—opulent cities—commerce —manufactures—the arts and science. We know just enough about the interior of Africa to throw a sombre romance over those vast unknown regions, and to make us desire to know more. Yet Africa has been known to the world from the earliest ages of the earth's history; and she has been the theatre of some of the most thrilling events of its history. Yet, except a narrow skirting upon her borders, we know scarcely more of her than we do of the same track of territory on Mars or Venus. Evidently Africa is a grand *reservation ground*, kept back from acting any part on the great theatre of human activity and development till, in the fullness of time, she shall be needed.

What movements may have agitated her in the deep recesses of her seclusion—what human activities may have played some noble part there—what nations flourished—what kings reigned—what battles fought—what deeds of daring done—what noble deeds of love performed—what virtues cultivated—we may never know. All is as yet as if it had been done on the face of another planet. And, perchance, the history of those secluded regions shall never become a part of the world's history.

We might ask, indeed, why has Africa existed at all? What good purpose has she yet served? Or what part have the negro race yet played in the great drama of human affairs? What part are they destined to play? These are legitimate queries, more easily raised than answered.

We, perhaps, hazard nothing in saying that no principal purpose has *yet* been accomplished in connection with Africa or the negro race. Subordinate and incidental purposes have been served, but no principal and ultimate purpose. The most probable conjecture which we can form of Africa and her inhabitants is, that they are held *in reserve* for some great, and yet future purpose. We may, perhaps, form no well-defined conjecture as to what this purpose may be. Past developments on an African soil, and in African races, have, however, given certain premonitions of what that continent shall yet become. Egypt and Carthage were realizations of true human greatness. They were pledges of future realizations—the first-fruits of a full harvest. And where shall we look for nobler specimens? In Church and State; in science and the arts; in all that goes to bless and ennoble humanity, Africa has held out indications that she is not a whit behind any other portion of the globe. No land has shown greater capabilities of soil for the support of a vast population; none has indicated richer mineral wealth, and no race has exhibited greater capabilities of a high state of advancement, than certain African races. African statesmen, philosophers, artists, warriors, divines, have nobly compared with those of other nations. Christianity has nowhere had brighter ornaments or more able defenders than in Africa. We need but repeat names already referred to—the well-known names of Cyprian, Bishop of Carthage, Augustine, of Hippo, or the truly illustrious prelates of Alexandria, or Origen, a presbyter of the same city. These were mighty men for the truth; and the world has, perhaps, nowhere else had better examples of Christian piety.

2. *Africa is held in reserve for some future purpose.*

A far-seeing Providence is wont to make such provisions for the accomplishment of future purposes. Ages often pass before these purposes transpire. God created this globe of ours for the habitation of man, and for the great and lasting purposes which he would achieve for and through man; yet for unknown ages the earth remained "without form and void," before it received its human tenants, or its destined purposes began to be accomplished. And how strangely since have different portions of the world been held back from accomplishing their destined end! During indefinite ages, the whole American continent remained scarcely more than a roaming-ground for the Indian, or a grazing-field for the buffalo. Indeed, large portions of America, and also of the eastern continent, seem, till quite a recent date, to have been under water. There are unmistakable traces that the great and fertile valley of the Mississippi, and also many other large and, at present, beautiful alluvials, both in the new and the old worlds, were once the bed of some great inland sea or lake. As human affairs have advanced, as the wants of the world have demanded more room, the domains of the sea have retired, and the habitable parts of the earth have been enlarged. Native forests have then given way before the march of civilization, and the wild tenants of the woods have yielded their dominion of *the wilderness* to civilized man. The American continent has scarcely begun to fulfill its appointed mission. Some forty millions (and scarcely one half of these civilized men) hold possession of all North America—a territory sufficiently large and productive to sustain, twice told, the entire population of the globe. And South America, a territory capable of sustaining as many more, is scarcely more than roaming-ground for twenty-millions of people. We expect that, in the fullness of time, these vast reserved territories, and the exhaustless, yet, till now, mostly unemployed resources of these countries, shall be brought into requisition in the service of the great King.

And not only are large portions of the present dry land thus held in reserve for future use (now mere moral wastes), but large portions of dry land evidently remain to be created. The habitable world is yearly enlarging. Other large sections, yet to be the habitations of vast multitudes of the human race, are to be reclaimed from the ocean. Old Neptune is to yield up yet more of his domains to the ceaseless aggressions of civilization and Christianity. Bound in his adamantine chains, he waits the fiat of his God, when he shall surrender them to the insatiate demands of an all-controlling Providence, who, unhindered, works out the stupendous problem of human salvation. When the mandate comes, they will appear—appear the moment they shall be needed. Coral insects, countless millions of God's mighty architects, are at work in the Pacific Ocean, forming a new and vast continent. When, in the progress of the Divine purposes, it shall be needed, it shall appear. When sin shall so diminish and disease so abate its ravages—when death shall so lose his dominion over man as to fill the world with a population immensely greater than its present number of inhabitants, a new western continent will be needed. And it will be ready. It is in the course of a rapid preparation. We shall then be able to answer the question much more intelligibly than we now can, why so large portions of the earth's surface are covered with water? Not because so large a portion of water is *necessary*, either rightly to balance the earth, or to supply the clouds with vapor, or to facilitate intercourse between the nations, but because God adopted this method to hold in reserve territories which he would afterward use for human habitation.

Or, in like manner, we might have said our *world*, in its past and in its present condition, is held in reserve for a future purpose. All as yet has been preparatory. Incidental and subordinate purposes have been fulfilled; but no direct and ultimate purpose. It has, for the most part, been given up to waste and to desolation—surrendered to Satan, the god of this world, that it may first be seen what *sin* can do in so fair and rich a world as this. With just exception enough to keep all parties apprised of the claims and purposes of the rightful King and Proprietor, the "god of this world" has had all things in his own way. God has fulfilled, in respect to this world, none of his final purposes. He is preparing agencies, gathering resources, accumulating materials for a grand and final consummation. But the devil is allowed first to employ all his agencies and appliances; and when he shall have signally and finally failed, the Lord will make bare his arm—will take to himself his great power, vindicate his own cause, and wrest from the hand of the usurper the wealth, the power, the learning—all the rich and varied resources of the world, and will employ them in the furtherance of his own benevolent designs.

Africa is one of the most notable of these reservations. From century to century has she lain as a dark cloud on the horizon of the world's history. Many a nation has emerged from a kindred darkness and run its destined career. Africa has slept beneath the black drapery of her own protracted night. Solemn and mysterious has been her sleep. But we look that she shall yet awake; that she shall rise in her giant strength, put on her armor, and when the day of the world's redemption shall come, she shall stand in her lot, washed and clothed in the white robe.

3. But why has Africa been *reserved?* Why has a continent of such extent, of such resources, of such stupendous capabilities, been so long kept back? What is the destiny of this mysterious Africa? We can speak with no prophetic ken; we may be able to form no probable conjecture; yet the idea will cling to us that the Hand which has formed nothing in vain, has purposes to answer through the African continent, which have as yet but feebly entered into the mind of man, or been but faintly indicated by the course of Providence toward that singular portion of the globe. The aborigines of America, of Asia, and many islands of the sea, seem destined to *dwindle* and disappear before the encroachments of a more civilized race. Japheth dwells in the tents of Shem. He takes possession, dispossesses the old occupants, and becomes himself a permanent resident. But not so among the sons of Ham. While they may dwell with the Anglo-Saxons, serve them, and in their turn derive from them most substantial benefits, yet neither the Anglo-Saxons nor any other branch of the family of Japheth may dwell in the tents of Ham. An impassable barrier is set about Africa, a sanitary cordon drawn about her. If the white man pass it, he will soon sicken and die. The climate of Africa, in general, has, to a very great

extent, settled the question that Africa is not to be, like North America, another vast area open to the expansion of man in the Anglo-Saxon type. What then? We look for a different destiny for Africa; but what shall it be? Other races dwindle under oppression, and end in extermination; but there is no dwindling of the African race. Though forty millions of her sons have been feloniously extracted from her by the ruthless hand of slavery, and a vastly greater number by the villainous *means* used to ensnare her people and reduce them to bondage, yet there seems no tendency to diminution. Place the negro where you will, and he will multiply and fill the land.

The past history of Africa would seem to justify at least the opinion that, whatever is to be her destiny, that destiny is to be wrought out by herself, by her own men and resources. She may not be an exception to the general rule that nations are advanced by migrations, wars, commerce, civilization, and, more than all, by pure religion; yet, in the case of Africa, the mode is, in many respects, reversed. Instead of another and a more advanced race coming to her, her sons are involuntarily carried to them, there to live in "durance vile," till permitted to return, through their offspring, to bless their own happy land. Instead of wars waged upon her by other nations, and the victors unfurling there the standard of a higher national life, she has waged the most ruinous wars on herself; and yet these wars have been made the first links, which, though dark and bloody in the beginning, shall be bright and blissful in the end. Africa has had a *commerce*, but it has been a commerce in the flesh and blood of her own sons and daughters, and this traffic has engaged in its prosecution all the worst passions of men; yet this very traffic is being strangely over-ruled by Him who brings good out of evil, to the great good of this unhappy continent.

We shall assume—and hope to make the assumption wear the face of probability—that Africa is reserved for the development of a higher civilization and a better type of Christianity than the world has yet seen. There is nothing in the *present condition* of Africa, and certainly there has been nothing in her past condition, which makes such a supposition absurd; certainly no more absurd than it would have appeared to an intelligent Egyptian, in the days of Sesostris, had he been told that the illiterate wanderers of Greece, to whom Cadmus was then attempting to make known the letters of the Phœnician-alphabet, should produce a Plato, an Aristotle, and all for which Greece was so justly famed. The present condition of the Grebo, the Foulah, or the Berber, is not more hopeless than that of the ancient Greek. Nor is there any thing in the position of Africa, in her soil or climate, which precludes our supposition. Or, is it not quite as likely that Africa will yet produce a higher order of civilization, and a better type of Christianity; that her sons shall yet astonish the world, and bless the Church with a rich inheritance of great and good men, and with institutions which are the glory of any people, as it was that the ancient Britons should do it? Yea, it is much more likely. For neither the Greeks nor the Britons had ever shown, as the Africans have, their capabilities of that higher civilization which they afterward realized.

Yet Africa has a history—a history more varied and

2*

extraordinary than any other portion of the globe. But the history of Africa differs, in its form, from that of every other land. It is neither, except to a limited extent, a *written* history, nor a traditionary one. It is a *monumental* history. The history of Ethiopia, of Nubia, Meroe, Egypt, and Carthage, is to be read in the magnificent ruins which still bestrew those long-neglected lands; and which still rear their heads in hoary grandeur over lands now ˉdesolate, but which were once as the garden of the Lord.

Though ancient historians are not silent respecting the great African kingdoms to which I have referred, yet, from their pages we get, as is evident from the monumental history of the same kingdoms, but a faint picture of the extent, wealth, power, and grandeur of those kingdoms. Such kingdoms are incidentally mentioned in Scripture. Indeed, we are indebted principally to the inspired Word, not only for our most authentic accounts, but for nearly all we know of them. The frequent mention we find in the Bible of Ethiopia, Egypt, Lydia, and the allusions so often made to their merchandise, commerce, arts, and architectural works, furnish the best information we have respecting these wonderful countries.

In attempting, therefore, to give some idea of *what has been done* already in Africa, as indicating what may again be done there, I shall derive proof from the following sources, viz.: The condition of agriculture among the ancient Africans, fertility of the soil and productions; their commerce and manufactures; notices of their wars and munitions of war, and armies; progress of learning, arts, and science; progress in the science of government and jurisprudence; acquaintance with mining and engineering; architectural monuments, and religion and temples.

But before proceeding further, we need to disabuse our subject of an inveterate and killing prejudice. The moment we appear as the advocate of African amelioration we meet with a damper, which comes as a besom of destruction to all our hopes, and seems to render abortive all our efforts. "God is against us," the pert objector says; "heaven is against us—all the common instincts of man are against us—the united prejudices of all other races have consigned over to remediless servitude the entire progeny of poor old Ham." If there be upon them this irremediable "curse" of heaven, our task is vain. There is no hope for devoted Africa. But before we yield a point so vital to the highest interests of so large a portion of our race, and a point, which, if established, seems to cast so much dishonor on the great Ruler and Disposer of the nations, we must be allowed to challenge some inquiry into the fact and nature of this "curse."

On whom did this curse of Canaan fall? What was its import? And what application, if any, has it to the negro race? But we reserve these considerations for the next chapter.

CHAPTER II.

THE CURSE OF CANAAN—Who uttered the curse?—Its import; to whom apply?
—How fulfilled on Canaan—No application to Cush and the negro race—
Their probable future.

BUT our hopefulness meets at the very outset a singular rebuff. We are told that Africa is the hopeless
victim of a Divine malediction—of an incorrigible *curse*
which precludes all hope. Her people are a doomed
race passed all recovery—at least, such is the hopeless
lot of the whole *negro* race. Ham, the objector claims,
was a *black* man, with thick lips, and crisped hair, and
as such was doomed to a condition of debasement and
oppression passed all redemption. But lest the general
malediction over so broad a surface of humanity should
not prove sufficiently local and special, the abettors of
the curse have more especially concentrated it on one of
Ham's descendants, even on the graceless *Canaan;* that
he and all his posterity, down through all coming generations, should bear the mark of a most galling servitude. "A servant of servants should he be."

Now if the whole negro race in particular, and all
African races in general, be consigned over by an incorrigible decree to a hopeless bondage—if so dark a
cloud has settled down upon them—we may hang our
harp upon the willows, and, in fell despair, sing the
dirge to all hope to a hapless race.

But this· is too large an interest to yield without a
very serious demur. Shall an entire race—shall races
of men from century to century cry unto heaven for

deliverance, and there be no deliverance for them? Shall they dwarf their humanity and pine in hopeless bondage, and gracious Heaven not have a word of consolation and hope for them? We would not, without a most earnest demur, accept so damaging a repulse to all our hopes of a renovated and elevated manhood in *all* its different races. We believe in the renovation and exaltation of our common manhood to a vastly nearer approximation to the original type. And we do not believe the negro race shall be made an exception; at least, we will not believe it till we shall have examined that fearful malediction, and see if it is the final heritage of the long-despised and oppressed negro.

"And he said: Cursed be Canaan; a servant of servants shall he be unto his brethren." Gen. ix. 25.

Few passages of Scripture have been so sadly perverted, or perverted to abet so stupendous an evil. Because Canaan, the youngest son of Ham, was cursed by Noah as he awoke from his wine, provoked by the indignity which had just been done him by Canaan, the idea has been caught up and cherished by the whole pro-slavery fraternity that Ham and all his posterity were brought under the curse, and, therefore, rightfully doomed to a perpetual servitude—that it is right to kidnap, buy, sell, and enslave all Africans, if not all black men, because Noah, under the circumstances alluded to, said: "Cursed be Canaan; a servant of servants shall *he* be." The whole system of modern slavery, including, of course, all the horrors of the slave-trade, from the beginning to the present day, has been justified, and, indeed, gloried in, as if it might claim a Divine sanction. It has on this account been claimed as a *Bible institution*. And, by inference, all who would do away with the enslavement of the African race are, forsooth, fighting against a well-known providential arrangement. They are wise above what is written.

Does the passage quoted warrant any such interpretation? The question opens a subject of a very grave and practical character. *Who uttered the curse? What is the import of the curse?* And *to whom* does it apply, or who are the subjects of it? Having answered these queries, we shall be prepared to consider how the malediction was fulfilled on Canaan and his posterity, and how it has no application to the other branches of the family of Ham—not even to *Cush*, the progenitor of the negro race.

Who said "Cursed be Canaan?" It is not written that the *Lord* said it. It was the declaration of Noah; and under circumstances which render very suspicious the claim of inspiration which is set up for it. The circumstances were these: Noah, having taken too freely of wine, fell asleep; and during his sleep he suffered certain indignities from his grandson Canaan, the youngest son of Ham; at which it would seem that his son Ham so far connived as to report the same to his brethren. On awaking and learning the disagreeable position he had been in, Noah gave expression to his chagrin and displeasure in the words of the curse in question.

Now, we are by no means to suppose that every thing that Noah did or said was *inspired*, or said and done under Divine guidance. We should, on such a supposition, be obliged to accept as an inspired act the unhappy instance of his inebriation. The truth, we apprehend, is, Noah spoke as an irritated man; and predicted (not necessarily under inspiration) that *such* a young man—a young man who could do so foul a deed —would fall under the malediction of Heaven. Simply, as is often said of any young man of bad principles and practices, he will come to a *bad end.* He does not possess a character that will secure the blessing of Heaven, and his own consequent prosperity. It is not the result of any supernatural foreknowledge or spirit of prophesy, but the result of human sagacity, founded on experience and observation.

It must here be borne in mind that God had already blessed *all the sons* of Noah. Noah simply repeated these blessings as applied to Shem and Japheth, but mentioned neither curse nor blessing in relation to Ham. Shem and Japheth were not blessed more, nor Ham less, on account of these utterances of Noah on this notable occasion.

Or admit, for a moment, that Noah spoke by inspiration of the Almighty, and still it will follow that we are greatly wanting in a Scripture warrant for the enslavement of *the whole African race.* This will appear as we consider :

The import of the curse, and to whom it applies. We are left in no doubt who should be the immediate subject of the malediction. It was not Ham and his posterity that were now put under the ban of the curse ; nor was it either of the sons of Ham, except the particular one named. The four sons of Ham were Cush, Mizraim, Phut, and Canaan. Cush was the father of the thick-lipped and crisp-haired races, to which we give the common name of negroes ; the second son, Mizraim, was the father of the Egyptians, and of kindred nations in the eastern part of Africa ; while Canaan, the fourth and youngest son, was the father of the Canaanites, whose country stretched along the eastern shore of the Mediterranean Sea. Their country, after they had been destroyed or driven off, became the possession of the chosen tribes of Israel. The different branches of the Canaanites we know as Hittites, Jebusites, Amorites, Girgasites, Hivites, Arkites, etc. These are the people that fall under the curse of Noah. They were not the descendants of Cush, but of Canaan. Most certainly they were not *negroes*.

If we would know the real import of the curse entailed on Canaan, we must recur to the subsequent history of his posterity. No malediction seems immediately to have followed the settlement of those nations in the western part of Asia. They went out from Shinar, and enjoyed for a long time a high degee of worldly prosperity. Melchisedek, king of righteousness and priest of the Most High God, to whom Abram gave a tenth of the spoils, was a Canaanite. So was Abimelech, of whom honorable mention is made. The Sidonians, one of the earliest civilized nations; the Phœnicians or Tyrians, who extended their commerce and their arts over a great part of the known world; and the Carthaginians, the rivals of Rome, were all the descendants of this same Canaan.

But they could not continue, because they feared not the God of heaven. They were left to fill up the measure of their iniquity; and then the fearful day of reckoning came. Abraham could not have possession of the land of promise, because the "iniquity of the Amorite was not full." But, in process of time, it was done. The displeasure of heaven could endure no longer. Like Sodom and Gomorrah, they were given over to their own destruction. The difference was, the cities of the plain were doomed to suffer the immediate wrath of heaven, in a shower of fire and brimstone; the other were given over to war and bloodshed, till they should be utterly overcome and destroyed. And from this time they essentially disappeared from among the nations and are known no more., Those were exterminating wars. The miserable remnant that fled, lost all national existence, and became the servant of servants among their brethren. And so they have remained until this day. Their place and memorial among the nations are gone forever. And thus has the curse been fulfilled.

Had we the history of those nations we should be able, no doubt, to trace a more literal and particular fulfillment of the prophecy. The Gibeonites, who were of Canaanitish descent, and whose history we happen to know, were literally subjected to slavery for life. We must, at all events, take the singular dealings of God with the Canaanites as a fulfillment of the curse pronounced against them. It was the curse of war and extermination.

But is the negro race involved in this curse? Not at all. Not a word of it in the Bible. They are the descendants of Cush, and not of Canaan. And no curse is recorded against Cush and his descendants. The Canaanites were Asiatics, and not Africans at all. The remnant that escaped the general destruction and fled to other nations, fled to Europe rather than to Africa. And if, intent on pursuing them and entailing on them the curse as the doomed race, we insist on the Divine right to enslave them, we must search for the objects of our curse, not among the black men of Africa, but among the white men of Europe, and, perhaps, of America. For the same accursed Canaanites, *especially* in the branches known as Phœnicians and Carthaginians, formed colonies in nearly every nation in Eastern and Southern Europe, not excepting Spain, France, Ireland, and England. And their blood (not black) may be running in some of our veins ; and if we insist on the Divine right to enslave that race, on account of the curse of Canaan, we may find the argument coming a little too near home for our own convenience. It would fall on the European, rather than on the African.

The curse in question does not fall on *Cush,* or on any race that does now, or ever has, inhabited Africa. And we have seen how severely, and in what shape, it did fall on the posterity of Canaan. They became a notoriously wicked race ; and having filled up the measure of their iniquity, and the Divine forbearance having become, at length, exhausted, heaven abandoned them to an accomplished destruction. In vain do we now ask where is the Canaanite ? His name has perished ; and scarcely a record has he, except a record of his sin, and the sure and complete destruction which followed.

By what strange perversity, then, has modern cupidity transferred the curse from Canaan to Cush, and sought to entail on the African, or on the *present* posterity of Cush, a curse which was pronounced on Canaan in the days of Noah, and fulfilled on the different branches of the Canaanitish family more than thirty-three centuries (3,310 years) ago? This is certainly being hard pushed for a warrant to enslave Africans, or the children of Cush. Yet, far fetched and absurd as it is, it is the great and the sole argument for inflicting such servitude—the *Divine sanction* for the slave-trade and all its unmitigated abominations, and for a system of slavery and its untold injustice and wrong. Yet, when we come to inquire after the *reasons* for such a sanction, we find none at all.

And here it is worthy of inquiry, how it is that modern nations, interested in the slave-trade and the enslavement of the people of Africa, have fixed on *this form* of the fulfillment of the curse. If they will have it, that the curse pronounced on Canaan, after having first spent itself on that branch of the family of Ham, passed from Canaan, the youngest son, to Cush, the oldest, how is it that in its reproduction on the latter it should so exclusively take the form of servile bondage? And how is it that they should be agreed, from generation to generation, to inflict the heavy curse on this race? We can explain it only on the supposition, that the large classes of men interested are driven to such a subterfuge in order to furnish an excuse for their nefarious trade. And why they are agreed to kidnap and to reduce to perpetual bondage the descendants of Cush, who were not cursed, instead of the posterity of Canaan, who were, we can assign no reason—except it be the very cogent one, that the posterity of Canaan, having already expiated their sins in their overthrow and final extirpation, no longer afford the *victims* on which to prey.

But here, very naturally, arises the inquiry, if the negro race have not, in all past ages, been suffering under some woeful curse, how happens it that they have, up to the present day, been so signally degraded, abject, and downtrodden? What aileth them? How shall we account for their singularly *depressed condition?* So protracted, and so unmitigated? I do not know that we are bound to do more than to resolve it into the same mysterious Providence which controls the destinies of nations, as he does those of individuals, putting up one and casting down another, as it seemeth to him good. He has reasons, and reasons the most substantial, founded in the wisdom and benevolence of his nature, but which lie hid deep in the counsels of eternity. They are high as heaven, what can we know?

While we see nothing in the *fact* of the degradation and long depression of these children of Cush to distinguish the dealings of Providence toward them as peculiar, and unlike his dealings with any other people, yet we see something *in degree* which is worthy of notice. We know of no other people whose debasement has been so protracted and so profound. We are left very much in doubt whether the negro race has ever, prominently and for any great length of time, figured on the great theatre of nations. The Jews, the Assyrians, the Egyptians, the Greeks, the Romans, have all had their elevations and their depressions, but they never sunk so low as the Cushites have, and never remained in their prostration so long.

The rejection of this race, or the setting it aside for so long a time, is, therefore, only of a piece with God's dealings with other races. It is only more marked; and furnishes no argument for their final rejection. Nor may we receive it as any token of God's special displeasure with that race, but rather as a guarantee of their future gracious visitation and elevation. God is wont to use, as his great agency in the work of human progress, but one race at a time; and we despair not that, in the great revolutions which centuries realize,

the sceptre shall pass to the hands of the sable races
of Africa; the thick cloud, which so long settled down
upon them, shall arise, and they shall loom up among
the nations, and shall become distinguished as the
favored race by which God will work in the final renovation of the world, as they have heretofore been distinguished as the forgotten of man and forsaken of
Heaven. We shall undertake to show, as we proceed,
that this despised race are our Great Captain's *reserve*.
He uses, and sets aside, as he pleases, one and then
another. And if he shall, as possibly he may, set aside
the present Anglo-Saxon race as the grand agency by
which he works, he may astonish the world and mag-
nify his own sovereign will and pleasure, and tarnish
all human pride, by lifting up the heads which have so
long hung down; extorting from the lowest condition
of man, the honor which comes from above.

As I shall, in the progress of this volume, speak of
African races as seemingly suffering under the malediction of Heaven, I do not mean that which is techni-
cally known as the " curse of Canaan." I simply mean
that the whole race has, for many a long and dreary
century, been made to pass through a cloud strangely
dark, strangely mysterious.

I shall take occasion, in the following pages, to say
a word on the probable destiny of the posterity of
Cush, the father of the negro race. If there be resting
on them no irreversible curse—if Heaven has not decreed them outcasts from the commonwealth of civilization, social elevation, and moral and religious advancement—outlaws in the great family of man—if, as
we shall elsewhere show, there be no lack of well-attested examples of the *capabilities* of this race to reach

even a high state of advancement in every department
of human progress, we see not why we should not anticipate for them a future position which shall quite
redeem the race from the long-standing stigma which
has rested on them, and vindicate the ways of God in
his mysterious dealings with them. We discover in
the peculiarly docile and imitative character of these
people a brighter future awaiting them. It is well said
of them, they are a docile race, apt to imitate, quick
to seize, ambitious to achieve civilization. Whenever
brought into contact with Europeans, they copy their
manners, imbibe their tastes, and endeavor to acquire
their arts. Under all the circumstances of their servitude in this country, which, in general, have not been
rigorous, they have vastly improved, and at this moment the Africo-American colonist at Cape Palmas is
as far superior to the native of the Coast as the white
man here is superior to the negro that serves him.
Yet the African has never been placed in circumstances to allow him a fair opportunity to vindicate
the claims we assert for him, of a manhood not inferior
to those who now lord it over him. He has never been
fairly brought in contact with civilizing influences, except in the condition of a slave, or a condition scarcely
less menial. None but a people peculiarly imitative
and apt, and desirous of acquiring the habits, and con-
forming to the customs of civilized life, would ever
have *advanced* at all, as they are well known to have
done, in the " durance vile" to which they have in this
country been so ruthfully subjected.

We see, in the very providence which brought them
to this country, a still surer presage that a brighter
destiny yet awaits them. No thanks to the slave-

trade; no thanks to slavery, or to slaveholders or slavedealers, that, first and last, some millions of the besotted children of Africa have been torn away from their homes and kindred, and, in their cruel bondage in this country, have been brought under influences which, with their peculiar aptitudes and idiosyncracies, they are raised vastly above their original condition in Africa; and, indeed, not a few compare favorably, as we shall see, in vigor of character, enterprise, intelligence, and, especially, in religious character, with our own race. To no other nation could they have been consigned with so good a hope of their own lasting benefit. The fact that Providence chose to school them for their future destiny amid the free institutions of America—to induct them into the immunities and blessings of freedom while themselves groaning under the thraldom of slavery—to subject them to the rigorous discipline of a servile bondage, would seem to indicate a future destiny of no ordinary character. This has a significance not to be overlooked.

And we would not pass unobserved the *protracted duration* of this preliminary discipline. The bondage of the negro race—to say nothing of the previous centuries of their depression in their own country—has already been protracted to more than two centuries, a period which synchronizes with a singular exactness (perhaps exactly) with the duration of the bondage of the Hebrews in Egypt. *That* discipline was neither too rigorous, nor protracted a day too long, to fit the chosen people for the mission assigned them. So may future generations say of the race in question. Like the oak whose growth is proportioned to its long-lived maturity, we may anticipate for them a future that shall correspond in duration and magnitude with the long and severe discipline of their growth.

This, indeed, as we shall show, is but analogous with the growth and maturity of other peoples and nations. How long was the Hebrew Commonwealth travailing in pain, waiting her deliverance? And how was it with England, France, Germany? We gather confidence, that our own beloved Republic will not meet an untimely end from the long and severe preparation of the materials of which our body politic was constructed, a training first in England, then in Holland, and finally in New England. And England was yet longer in reaching her manhood. Her early childhood points back to a period long anterior to the landing of Julius Cæsar on the coast of Briton, even to the misty age of the Druids.

But we have a more sure ground for our belief in a long and good future for the Cushites. It is the sure word of prophecy, the unfailing promises of Israel's God, which we may not pass unheeded. Oppression has been the peculiar form of burden which has been laid upon the race. Hence the character of the promise of their deliverance; and hence the peculiar judgments that await them who will not "undo the heavy burdens, and let the oppressed go free." "Therefore, thus saith the Lord : ye have not hearkened unto me, in proclaiming liberty, every one to his brother, and every man to his neighbor; behold, I proclaim liberty for you, saith the Lord, to the sword, to the pestilence, and to the famine."

"Thus saith the Lord, the labor of Egypt, and the merchandise of Ethiopia, and of the Sabeans, men of stature, shall come over unto thee, and they shall be thine; they shall come after thee; in chains they shall come over, and they shall fall down unto thee; they shall make supplication unto thee." And the same cheerful obedience and ready return at the mandate of their Lord is expressed in the 60th chapter of Isaiah. When the "kings of Sheba and of Seba bring their gifts"—when the "multitude of camels shall cover thee, the dromedaries of Midian and Ephah, and all they from Sheba shall come, bringing gold and incense, and showing forth the praises of the Lord"—when all the "flocks of Kedar shall be gathered together unto thee, and the rams of Nebaioth shall minister unto thee, coming up with acceptance upon thine altar, and glorifying the house of thy glory"—the whole is represented as coming as a "cloud" borne on the wings of the wind—conspicuously, as a cloud borne on in the face of all men, and so readily do they come, that they seem as doves that flock to their windows.

But the most direct and oft-repeated prophecy remains to be mentioned: "Ethiopia shall soon stretch out her hands unto God." She shall "soon," readily, eagerly, without demur or hesitation, turn unto the Lord; shall come as soon as called. When the proffers of peace and pardon shall be made, these shall most readily accept them, and, with willing feet, shall hasten to the fold of the Great Shepherd. And so sudden shall be their acceptance of the Gospel, and their turning unto the Lord, and such its influence upon the unevangelized nations, that it is represented as the signal of the world's jubilee, in which all the kingdoms of the earth shall join. When Ethiopia shall return to her forsaken Lord, and her head, which has been so long bowed down, shall be lifted up—when "princes

3

shall come out of Egypt," then shall follow the jubilee song: "Oh, sing praises unto the Lord, Selah, to him that rideth upon the heaven of heavens, which were of old; lo, he doth send out his voice, and that a mighty voice. Ascribe ye strength unto God."

But we have yet another prognostic of a better day for them. We meet it in the successful experiments of the present day, to *colonize* Anglo-Africans—to form them into a nationality in their fatherland—to make them moral, industrious, self-reliant, and self-governed. Such experiments have been in the process of trial for some years past, and, it will suffice for the present, to affirm that they are so far successful as to give courage to our hopes, and confidence to the predictions, that the day of Africa's redemption draws near—that a glorious future is still in reserve for them who have so long been the downtrodden and the off-scourings of the earth. Enough has already been accomplished abundantly to refute the idea that there is any normal inferiority in the African race, which should render their restoration from their long degradation impossible, or their elevation to an equality with other races impracticable.

Our argument is, that enough has already been done through these colonies to indicate that the African needs only the *opportunity* and the *time,* and he will show himself a *man ;* a man, if not capable of the *same* type of civilization, and the same order of Christian development, he will show himself capable of a type and order not inferior.

But we reserve what we would say on colonies as an agency of negro advancement, to another place, and come to consider Africa, AS SHE HAS BEEN.

CHAPTER III.

Africa as she *has been*, a presage of what she shall be—Agriculture, commerce, manufactures—Wars, armies, munitions of war.

WE are first to speak of Africa as she *has been*. And here we can do little more than indicate, by a reference to a few facts, what developments certain African races have made, and to suggest that these developments are but examples and pledges of what Africa shall yet do. We may, therefore, assert and hope to show that this now despised continent, and some of its despised races, have shown themselves not inferior to any other races in all that goes to humanize, civilize, and aggrandize a race. And the inference seems very legitimate, that what any particular race *has* done, it may, under similar circumstances, do again. And much more it may be expected that the same race, under far more favorable auspices, may again, at least, attain to a degree of advancement once reached by their forefathers. If in Nubia, Abyssinia, Egypt, or Barbaria, a certain race cultivated in a high degree the arts of civilized life, and pursued learning; and possessed the higher virtues, we may not doubt the capabilities of the same race to attain to the same height again.

We will, therefore, in the present chapter, take a brief survey of some things which have been done in Africa and by Africans. Such a survey will enhance the wonder, that a people capable of rising so high should now be sunk so low; and, also, indicate what may yet be the destiny of that ill-fated continent. We can not go into lengthy details of the ancient history of Africa, but shall rather fix on a few features which shall abundantly sustain my position. We gather from sacred history, that certain African nations had attained to great eminence, in many things which go to aggrandize a people, long before the period at which commenced our profane history. We have no well-authenticated records of secular history which lead us back beyond seven or eight centuries before Christ.

From the following sources we have frequent and unmistakable hints, which lead to some just conclusions as to what was the real progress of certain African nations.

We have, ever and anon, intimations respecting the state of *agriculture and the fertility of the soil* in the eastern and northern countries of Africa, which clearly indicate what was the state of advancement in those countries. For a barbarous people are not an agricultural people. The simple fact that Egypt and Ethiopia and the northern countries of Africa were remarkably fertile and productive countries, is a *prima facie* evidence that agriculture in those countries was brought to a high degree of improvement; the fertility of a country depending, in the arrangements of Providence, very much on culture, Perhaps, in nothing have we a more satisfactory evidence of the advanced condition of the arts, and of civilization than in the great care taken to improve the productiveness of the soil by means of artificial irrigation. Canals, dikes, artificial lakes, modes of raising water from the Nile, and the various means of irrigating their lands, are the best possible indications of the advanced state of agriculture among the ancient Egyptians. The *chain pump*, which has but recently, like many other *new* inventions of modern times, come into vogue among us, was well known, and of common use among the Egyptians.

The famous Lake Mœris remains to this day—though in a very diminished form—the most stupendous monument of the zeal and devotion of the ancient Egyptians to agriculture; and, also, a most wonderful monument of art. The lake, which was 3,600 stadia (450 miles) in circumference, and 300 feet deep, was excavated in a dry and desert part of the country, for the purpose of protecting the land from the excessive inundation of the Nile, and at the same time reserving the superfluous waters for irrigating the adjacent wastes, and, also, for supplying the lack of water in the river during a dry season. The lake communicated with the Nile by an artificial channel, by which it received its supplies, and by another channel it returned its waters to the river, when needed. In the centre of the lake stood two colossal pyramids, 200 cubits above, and as many below, the water, and each surmounted by a colossal statue. This stupendous work, if there were no other, affords good evidence that, in the days of the Pharaohs, no expense, no labor, was regarded as too great, provided it could secure to the agriculturist the benefits of the Nile.

We have a good illustration of the extraordinary capability of the soil in North Africa, and the progress made in agriculture, when held by the Carthaginians, Though these Anglo-Saxons of Africa, as they have been very significantly called, were essentially a mercantile and commercial people, yet they by no means neglected agriculture. On the contrary, " the whole of their territory was cultivated like a garden," and well did the soil repay the labor and skill bestowed upon it. Historians speak, with admiration, of the "rich pasture lands carefully irrigated; abundant harvests; plantations of fig and olive trees; thriving and populous towns, and the splendid villas of the Carthagenians." No sooner was an African soil subjected to the culture of these enterprising colonists, than the desert was changed into the garden of the Lord. And what *has* been, under like circumstances, may be *again*.

This is in striking contrast with the following description of the *present* condition of agriculture. A late African traveler speaks of seeing men plowing with a crooked stick, to which was harnessed a couple of *cows*, by ropes attached to their horns. Yet, no country so abundantly rewards the scanty toils of the husbandman as Africa. Her generous soil, almost unsolicited by the hand of culture, pours her copious stores into the lap of the cultivator.

And such, indeed, is Africa at the present day. Save her deserts, the same area of no other country is *capable* of sustaining so great a population. Its spontaneous productions are amazing; while, under a meagre cultivation, it produces in the greatest abundance. "There is," says an intelligent writer on Africa, "probably no other equal expanse of territory which has so large a proportion of its surface capable of easy cultivation."

"Everywhere, in the soil, in the climate, and in the situation of the country," says one who speaks of North Africa, "are seen scattered, with a liberal hand, the elements of prosperity; and it is manifest that the plains which were once esteemed the *granary of Rome*, might again, with the aid of modern science, be rendered extremely productive in the luxuries, as well as the necessaries, of life."

We can scarcely credit what historians tell us of the high state of cultivation which once adorned some portions of Africa. Diodorus tells us that the country about Carthage was covered with gardens and large plantations, everywhere abounding in canals, by means of which they were plentifully watered. A continual succession of fine estates were seen, adorned with elegant buildings, which indicated the opulence of their proprietors. These dwellings, he says, were furnished with every thing requisite for the enjoyment of man, the owners having accumulated immense stores. The land was planted with vines, with palms, and many other fruit-bearing trees. On one side were meadows filled with flocks and herds. In short, the whole prospect displayed the riches of the inhabitants, while the higher ranks had very extensive possessions, and vied with each other in pomp and luxury.

This advanced state of agriculture very obviously implies that much progress had been made in the mechanical arts and in the sciences. The implements of husbandry, and the apparatus for the construction of canals, dikes, and artificial lakes, and for raising water from the Nile, are the productions of a people well skilled in the use of metals and of the mechanical arts —to say nothing of mining, engineering, and an acquaintance with the mechanical powers.

But what a contrast now! Those regions, once so fertile, so beautiful, the dwelling-place of a great and prosperous nation, are now little more than the roaming ground of beggarly tribes. In no other part of the world have the ravages of time been so deplorable and complete, "obliterating nearly all the traces of improvement, and throwing down the noblest works of art." Amid the dreary wastes of the present day, the traveler meets the ruins of ancient towns, where are still to be seen the finest specimens of architectural skill, and of that taste and luxury which distinguished Carthage in her later years. Fields, which once smiled with the most luxuriant harvests, are now either deformed by the encroachments of the deserts, or overgrown with useless weeds and poisonous shrubs; while baths, porticoes, bridges, theatres, triumphal arches, have mouldered into ruins, or sunk under the hands of the barbarous inhabitants.*

Should the day come when Africa's vast resources shall be drawn out and appropriated to the furtherance of her best interests—the resources of her soil, of her forests, her mines, and all the yet undeveloped riches of the industry and thrift of her 150,000,000 of people, what may Africa then be?

The *commerce* and *manufactures* of certain African States supply no doubtful evidence of the progress by those States in civilization and natural greatness. An ignorant and barbarous people can never be a great commercial people. The skill, enterprise, science, and general intelligence necessary to make a nation a commercial people, must have already raised them above a barbarous condition. And, then, commerce has upon any people a civilizing, elevating influence. No sooner do a people begin to exchange commodities with another people than they begin to exchange ideas.

* Russel's "Barbary States."

Commerce implies an acquaintance with the mechanical arts, and all the skill needed to construct and sail a ship; and, what is more, it implies that a people have arrived at a state of civilization and advancement when, in the multiplication of their wants, they require the productions of *other lands;* and, when, too, in their own domestic progress, they have *exports* to give in exchange for what they require from other lands. Such a condition, of consequence, implies that considerable progress has been made in *manufactures and agriculture.*

It is known that Ethiopia carried on an extensive and lucrative trade with the land of Israel in the days of Solomon; and, if with Israel, undoubtedly with other nations. Berenice, a port on the Red Sea, was, at one time, the great depot and thoroughfare of trade between Europe and Asia. Carthage was another great commercial emporium, and the Carthaginians were the most daring seamen and the most enterprising merchants of ancient times. She carried on an extensive trade with Spain, Italy, Sardinia, and Sicily—with the numerous islands of the Mediterranean; with Asia Minor, Egypt, and Arabia; with the western coast of Africa and England—indeed, with the whole known world. This led to the forming of *trading stations,* in modern phrase called *factories,* where these enterprising merchants, or their agents, for a longer or shorter time, made their residence. Such stations seemed to have existed on the coast of England; for it is said, that the Carthaginians exerted much civilizing influence on the rude tribes of the British Isles; an effect scarcely to be looked for merely from the casual visits of a seafaring people.

The foreign traffic of Carthage very naturally led to

the *colonizing* policy which she is said to have extensively pursued. Her colonies carried with them the industry, enterprise, and virtue of the parent stock. They were settled on the western coast of Spain, on the western coast of Africa, and, probably, in most of the countries where Carthage trafficked. "While Hamilco," says the historian, "was employed in surveying the western shores of Portugal and Spain, his brother Hanno conducted an expedition toward the South, with the view of planting colonies on the borders of Africa. His fleet amounted to *sixty* large ships, having on board 30,000 persons, who had consented to occupy new lands at a distance from Carthage. These he distributed into six towns, which, of course, contained on an average 5,000 inhabitants." This one instance of the colonizing policy of Carthage, which undoubtedly is not a solitary case, indicates on what a stupendous scale colonization was conducted by that people. We also learn that these Carthaginian colonies extended, not only to the coast of Africa and of Spain, but southward, into the *interior* of Africa. And wherever these colonies were met, they were found to possess the elements of civilization and of civil and moral improvement.

"The great trade which the *Genoese* maintained with Cyrenica (in Africa), in the early times of their republic, was one of the richest sources of its prosperity."

Carthage prosecuted, too, a very extensive *land trade* far into the east, west, and south of Africa. Wherever there were mines—gold, silver, precious stones, tin, drugs, spices, dates, salt, slaves—valuable products of any kind, there the adventurous merchants of Carthage went, whether in England, Gaul, the Baltic, or over the scorching sands of the great desert.   No difficulties, however great, no dangers, however appalling, could check the progress of these bold traffickers.

In the case of Carthage, we have a fine illustration of what *colonies* were once able to do for Africa.   Carthage was a *colony;* and well did she show what a colony could do, in connection with such natural resources and capabilities as are found in Africa.   Considering the period when she existed, and the limited facilities for national aggrandizement and permanent prosperity, Carthage was one of the most extraordinary nations that ever existed.   In many respects did the Carthaginians resemble the Puritans of New England. They did much for the regeneration of Africa.

Meroe, in Nubia, seems to have been a great commercial depot and thoroughfare, to which an extensive trade was kept up from the Indian Ocean, and thence, down the Nile, to Egypt, and thence again to Carthage. On this route are still to be met a chain of ruins from the Indian Sea to the Mediterranean.   As a rule, Axum and Azab, between Arabia and the Meroe, and Thebes, Memnonium, etc., united the Nile, Egypt, and Carthage.

The history of ancient *wars* in Africa—armies—conquests—renowned soldiers, affords another criterion by which to judge of the greatness of those ancient States.   The first great captain and conqueror that figures in history was an *African.*   The great Sesostris, who sat on the throne of Egypt some 1500 years before the Christian era, was, undoubtedly, one of the greatest military chieftains that ever lived.   He reduced the Abyssinians to the condition of tributaries; subdued the nations on either side of the Red Sea; advanced along the Persian Gulf, and, if we may credit the history of those early times, he marched at the head of an enormous army into India, crossed the Ganges, having first subjected to his all-conquering sway the then powerful and opulent Empire of Hindostan. Turning his victorious sword then to another portion of Asia, he subdued the Assyrians and the Medes. But not content with the conquests of Asia, we find him next driving his furious car of war into Europe, where he ravages the Scythians. He was the conqueror of three continents.

Again : *sacred history* gives us an occasional glimpse of the military strength of certain African kingdoms— and these notices are the more to be valued, because they are merely incidentally introduced. When *Sennacherib* invaded Jerusalem, and thence carried his conquests into Egypt, he is said suddenly to have turned back when he heard that *Tirhakah,* King of Ethiopia, was coming against him. This was the Sennacherib who so proudly defied Israel, and railed on the God of heaven, and said : " *As the gods of the nations of other lands have not delivered their people out of my hands, so shall not the God of Hezekiah deliver his people out of my hand.*" So confident was he in his numbers and in the military strength of his army, that he feared neither God nor man. Yet, when he heard that the *mighty ruler* of *Ethiopia* was coming against him—the great *African*—he fled before him. It must have been a vast army, and, by no means destitute of the munitions of war and of military discipline; all which presupposes a great and powerful nation, and one considerably advanced in science and the arts.

We read, too, of *Zerah,* at the head of a thousand thousand—a million—of Ethiopians, and 300 chariots, coming against Asa, King of Judah. Possibly these were Ethiopians from the east side of the Red Sea, *i. e.*, from Arabia; still the fact is significant of the same general truth, the early and general advancement of the race—their once controlling position among the nations of the earth. These *Ethiopians* and *Lubims*, with their "very many chariots and horsemen," are, in another place, called a "huge host," which the King of Judah overcame only *because he relied on the Lord.*

And another similar fact: "It came to pass again that (in the fifth year of Rehoboam) Shishak, King of Egypt, came up against Jerusalem, with 1,200 charriots, and three score (60) thousand horsemen, and the people were *without number* that came with him out of Egypt: the Lubims, the Shukhims, and the Ethiopians. And he took the fenced cities which pertained to Judah, and came to Jerusalem.

Such *armies* and such *appurtenances* of *war* indicate, at least, a powerful and rich nation, as well as considerable advancement in the arts and sciences.

But Northern Africa, at a later date, furnishes an evidence of this sort yet more satisfactory. Carthage reared one of the greatest generals that ever fought a battle; and for many years carried on a war, well-matched, with great Rome herself. The great and brave *Hannibal* first led an army across the Alps, and then coped for eight long years with Rome on her territory, and when Rome was at the zenith of her strength. And had there been no Hannibal, the mightiest among mighties, the names of Hamilcar, the father, and Asdrubal, the brother, of Hannibal, would have come down to us as two of the greatest generals that ever blessed or cursed a nation.   Carthage had her rival powers in Africa ; and her chieftains had their rival chieftains. Masinissa, King of Numidia, is spoken of as a valiant general and an enlightened prince.   Juba, Jugurtha, Syphax, Micipsa, and scores of men not named, each in his own way, all men of renown, some allied with Carthage against Rome, others wooing the giant conqueror to lay waste their own native Africa, but all, under more favorable auspices and a better destiny, capable of the noblest daring in the defense of freedom.

CHAPTER IV.

AFRICA AS SHE HAS BEEN—Learning, arts, and science—Government and jurisprudence—Mining and engineering—Architectural monuments.

A FEW more topics remain as illustrations of what
Africa *has been*, and as a presage of what she may be.
Among the many that might be adduced, we select the
following :

The progress made in ancient African States, in
literature, science, and the *arts*, is equally significant of
the advanced condition of those States. In Africa, we
find the nursery of science and the arts. Greece received the first elements of learning from the south side
of the Mediterranean, so did Rome, and so has modern Europe. When all Europe and Western Asia lay
sunk in deep darkness, there was light in Africa. And
when again, in the dark ages, the light of Greece and
Rome had suffered an eclipse, and darkness once more
settled down over Europe, there was light in Africa.
The Saracens and Moors introduced learning into Europe, and did more to draw aside the vail of the dark
ages than any other people. Arabia and Africa seem
joined in sympathy and destiny. They are alike the
land of Ham. We shall, therefore, speak of them in-
discriminately.

The first permanent advance made by the world in
literature, and for the perpetuation of science, was the
invention of an alphabet. This we owe to Egypt. The
alphabet was a result of Egyptian hieroglyphics.

The first step toward writing was to form a *picture* of the object; the second, to put a sign for a *word;* the third, and most important step, was to put a sign for a *sound.* From this modified form of hieroglyphics the transition was comparatively easy to alphabetical writing. Precisely at what time the alphabet began to be used by the Egyptians, we do not, know. Cadmus is said to have brought into Greece sixteen letters of the alphabet (all then in use) 1,519 years before Christ. Learning, like the alphabet, traveled from Africa into Europe, through the Phœnicians, another branch of the family of Ham. We are also indebted for the working of *metals* and the *invention* of *glass* to the *Tyridns.* Again: we owe the *mariner's compass* to these same Phœnicians; and *numerical figures* to the Arabs, all the descendants of Ham.

Or we might speak of *authors and learned men.* Here we might enumerate a no contemptible list. We have spoken of church dignitaries, bishops, and presbyters, men of renown, who did honor both to religion and literature. To the names of Cyprian, Athanasius, Clement, Origen, Tertullian, Lactantius, and Augustin, we may add *Terrence,* the theologian, and Juba the royal scholar and historian. Tertullian was highly esteemed as a man of great genius and a complete master of the Latin tongue. Cyprian, the renowned Bishop of Carthage, and afterward the martyr, was a man of such genius and learning as would have made him an honor to any country. Augustin, Bishop of Hippo, was, too, a man of rare learning and intellectual industry. The author of 230 separate treatises on theological subjects, an exposition of the Psalms, and a great number of homilies; his fame filled the whole Christian world. Few men have ever united such a variety of great and shining qualities.

The devastation of time, in the destruction of libraries especially, have deprived us of much of the direct evidence of the existence of learned men in Egypt and Abyssinia; yet, we have no lack of an inferential evidence. Egypt and Abyssinia could never have become what they were, *without* learned men. In the days of Moses, the term "learning of Egypt" was proverbial. The Greeks were wont to travel into Egypt, that they might sit at the feet of the African Gamaliels and get wisdom. No one might, in those times, make pretensions to learning who had not been taught in the Egyptian schools.

In confirmation, it would be quite sufficient to refer, for a moment, to the period in science and literature called the *Alexandrian*, or the age of the Ptolomies. But we may go back many centuries anterior to this, even to the time of Osymandyas, one of the Pharaohs, who, according to some, flourished 1,500 years before Christ, others say 2,300. To this ancient king is ascribed the honor of originating the first great library of Egypt, and probably the first among the nations of antiquity. And to him was, also, attributed the gigantic work of Thebes, and the Mesononium in the city of an hundred gates. And if this be but another name, as some suppose, for Ozirin Menes, we find him described as the "inventor of arts, and the civilizer of a great part of the world." And, not only was he the renowned patron of books, of learning, and of the arts and sciences, but he was not the less renowned as a statesman and a warrior. He raised, we are told, a "prodigious army, and overran Ethiopia, Arabia, and a great part of India ; appeared in all the nations of Asia, and, crossing the Hellespont, continued his progress through a great part of Europe." This extraordinary man disseminated the arts, built cities, and was universally revered as a god. These things indicate a condition of science, of the arts, of martial skill, and of human progress in general, which are not to be found among a barbarous people.

But if we descend through centuries to the age of the Ptolomies, centuries during all of which Egypt remained a magnificent kingdom, we shall meet a monument of human progress in the existence of the "Alexandrian Library" which puts beyond a doubt the advancement of that period, and advancement, too, in a race since repudiated as not susceptible of any high improvement. This famous library, in the two magnificent edifices which contained it, consisted of 700,000 volumes. In the most beautiful portion of the city of Alexandria, known as the *Bruction*, where stood the royal palaces, and in the vicinity of the harbor, the ancient traveler might have seen the "large and splendid edifice belonging to the Academy and Museum." In this building was deposited the larger portion (400,000 vols.) of this celebrated library. The remainder (300,000) were kept in the Sarapion, the Temple of Jupiter Serapis. The larger portion was burned during the siege of Alexandria by Julius Cæsar. The smaller portion, in the Serapion, was preserved to the time of Theodosius the Great, when the Temple of Jupiter Serapis was destroyed, and the last of that famous library perished. And with these libraries; and several others of African origin that we shall scarcely more than name, perished the annals, at least, the written records, of the high state of civilization, and social and civil progress once reached by the children of Ham. And, with shame be it confessed, the destroyers of these magnificent monuments of African scholarship and philanthropy were Christian barbarians, and not the Arabs under Omar, as usually asserted. The archbishop, Theodosius, headed a crowd of Christian fanatics, stormed and destroyed the splendid temple and its precious contents.

And in this connection we should not overlook the renowned Museum of Alexandria, a sort of university, or college of learned men, where scholars lived and were supported, ate together, pursued their studies and instructed others. This was the first academy of the sciences and arts of which we have a knowledge— not unlike the Royal Academy of Science at Paris, or the Royal Society of London. And if to the Museum and Library we add the no less famous " Alexandrian School," in which poëtry, philosophy, and all the higher branches of learning were pursued to an extent never known before, and in some respects scarcely reached since, we shall not fail to see how it was that this African depot of literature and science became the favorite resort of scholars from every other quarter of the world, and the rallying point whither all who aspired to scholarship should betake themselves, to perfect what, in their own several localities, they had but begun. After the lapse of more than twelve centuries, the term " the learning of Egypt" had a significance unknown in the days of Moses.

But libraries, as indicative of learning, and philosophy, and mental cultivation, were not confined to the Egyptians. Other branches of the great African family were, at different periods, scarcely behind their kindred on the Nile. The Tyrians, a no insignificant branch of the main family, had their literature, their archives of history, their libraries, all of which are believed to have perished with the fleets and fortresses of Phœnicia, in their overthrow by Alexander. In like manner, Marius is said to have destroyed the Punic chronicles at Carthage. A people so powerful and civilized as were the Carthaginians, we may not suppose for a moment, were without libraries, rich in the varied learning of a great people. In Spain, the Moors are said to have had, in the twelfth century, seventy public libraries, of which that in Cordova contained 250,000 volumes. And the Arabians had, in Alexandria, a considerable library of Arabian books.

It is readily conceded that, of all civilized nations, the Egyptians were the first to observe the course of the stars. The zodiac of Dendera, now in Paris, shows the progress which this people had made in as- tronomy. Nor did they make less advances in philosophy, poetry, mathematics, and belles-letters. And not for a few centuries, like Babylon, Greece, or Rome, did this branch of the Hamic family flourish as a great nation and a highly civilized people, but she outlived all the nations of antiquity. "The monuments of Egypt witnessed the rise and fall of Tyre, Carthage, Athens, and Rome," and yet they exist. When Plato lived, they were venerable for their antiquity, and will command the admiration of future generations, when, perhaps, every trace of our cities shall have vanished.

The progress made by certain African States in *the science of civil government* indicates again the advanced condition of those States. Systems of government imply the existence of wise statesmen, and institutions of learning, and civil polity, which are never found, except in an advanced stage of civilization. Carthage was a republic, and enjoyed, perhaps, the most perfect system of civil polity, which has fallen to the lot of any nation before Great Britain. It was not such a republic as we have in North America; yet, in the freedom of its institutions, in the vigor and elasticity of its machinery, and its results on the masses of the people, it was a government far in advance of any other ancient government, save the Jewish. Carthage was once the formidable rival of Rome for universal dominion. "She took the lead," as the historian says, "in all which exalts human nature, and confers the highest blessing on society. Her provinces were opulent and enlightened, including nearly the whole of North and West Africa, the islands of the Mediterranean, and the west of Spain. She could boast of renowned sages and learned fathers of the Church;" her towns did not suffer in comparison with the most celebrated of antiquity, and her commerce swept every sea.

There was undoubtedly a time when learning, commerce, the arts, good and wise government, manufactures, and whatever goes to elevate man, and aggrandize a nation, flourished in connection with a race, which is now regarded as the evidence only of degradation and barbarous ignorance. Civilization, with all that comes in its train, descended the Nile. Ethiopia, Nubia, and Meroe, were great kingdoms before Egypt was, and they contributed largely to make her what she was.

Hippo, Utica, and Leptis were other colonies and

States formed on the northern coast of Africa by the Phœnicians, and, in connection with Carthage, enjoyed, each, its long period of good government and prosperity.

The architectural monuments of Eastern and Northern Africa stand as an enduring history of the former greatness of those kingdoms. These monuments, to some of which I shall refer, afford no doubtful proof of the progress which had then been made in mining and engineering, and to what perfection the useful and ornamental arts had been carried. Did we need any further evidence on this point than that which is furnished by the monuments themselves, a recent very singular discovery would supply the lack. The *Overland Chronicle* (an English paper) speaks of the recent opening of an emerald mine on Mount Zabarak, near (or, as the *Chronicle* says, on an island in) the Red Sea. This ancient mine had been worked in modern times, by the Pacha of Egypt, but its operations had been arrested in the latter years of the reign of Mohammed Ali. A short time since, an English company obtained permission to carry on the digging, which promised to yield them much profit. Recently, R. Allen, their engineer, discovered at a great depth, traces of a great gallery, evidently of extreme antiquity. Here he found ancient instruments and utensils, and a stone with hieroglyphic inscriptions upon it. Belzoni, to whom the world is so much indebted for its knowledge of the wonders of Egypt, visited this mine, and gave it as his opinion, that it had been worked by the ancient Egyptians, an opinion confirmed by the late discovery. The configuration of the gallery, and the nature and shape of the tools found in it, it is said, exhibit great skill in the art of engineering. From the inscriptions on the stone, it would seem that this mine of Zabarak began to be worked in the reign of the great Sesostris (more than 1,500 B. C.), whom history describes as combining the character of a great conqueror, with that of a prince of vast enterprise in the arts of peace.

Indeed, were all written history silent respecting the greatness and grandeur of the ancient kingdoms of Africa, we should still have, in the monuments which remain to this day, unmistakable traces of their greatness. There is probably in the minds of those most conversant with the history of ancient Thebes, Memphis, and Meroe, a very inadequate conception of what those cities actually were. It is quite impossible we should know. Yet, notwithstanding the ravages of 3,000 years, and the yet more fearful ravages of barbarism and ignorance which they have encountered, splendid remnants of those cities still exist. They stand forth, in defiance of time and vandalism, the proud and undemolished monuments of a highly civilized and intelligent people.

Allow me to refresh your minds respecting these extraordinary relics of a by-gone age. In no other way, perhaps, can we get so adequate an idea of what Africa has once produced, and of what she may again produce. I shall refer you but to a few specimens—a pyramid, two or three temples, a sphynx, the labyrinth, a tomb, and colossal statues.

The Pyramids are believed to be the work of the Shepherd Kings, who reigned some 2,000 years before Christ; and, consequently, those colossal piles are nearly 4,000 years old. Had we no other intimation of the perfection to which the mechanical arts had been carried, and the extent of the knowledge o the mechanical powers, we should have it in the existence of these stupendous works. Only conceive of a huge pile of masonry (as the great Pyramid of Cheops) which employed one hundred thousand men twenty years in building—800 feet in height, and the same in the length of the base, with various passages and chambers—one at least 66 feet by 27. The material of which this enormous structure is composed—the huge stones of which it is built—the road constructed, over which to convey the stones from the quarry, a work which, of itself, consumed ten years' labor—all indicate a skill and enterprise, and acquaintance with mining, engineering, the tempering of metals, and the construction of tools and machinery, which belong only to a highly civilized people.

Or take, as another specimen, the Temple of Dendera. We can not, perhaps, select a happier example of the taste and skill of those ancient people in the fine arts. Its columns, statues, sculptures, hieroglyphics, are the admiration of the world. All unite, the most fastidious and refined, in extolling the temple and portico of Dendera. It will quite suffice here to quote the enthusiastic language of Denon (of the French scientific corps under Napoleon), by which he gave expression to his admiration when he first saw this wonderful temple:

"I felt that I was in the sanctuary of the arts and sciences. This monument seemed to me to have the primitive character of a temple in its highest perfection. How many periods presented themselves to my imagination at the sight of such an edifice! How many ages of creative ingenuity were requisite to bring a nation to such a degree of perfection and sublimity in the arts! And how many more of oblivion to cause these mighty productions to be forgotten, and to bring back the human race to the state of nature in which I found them on this very spot? Never was there a place which concentrated in a narrower compass the well-marked memorial of the progressive lapse of ages. What unceasing power, what riches, what abundance, what superfluity of means, must a government possess which could erect such an edifice, and find within itself citizens capable of conceiving and executing the design of decorating and enriching it with every thing that speaks to the eye and the understanding. Never did the labor of man show me the human race in so splendid a point of view. In the ruins of Dendera the Egyptians appear to me giants."

But let us go to Thebes, the hundred-gated Thebes —the city of four thousand years ago—which was twenty-seven miles in circumference, and still bears indubitable marks of having been one of the most magnificent cities that ever graced the face of the earth. It could once send out from its one hundred gates twenty thousand fighting men and two hundred chariots. Babylon excepted, it was the earliest capital in the world. Its destruction dates back beyond the first foundation of any existing city. The glory of Thebes belongs to a period prior to the commencement of authentic history. The extent of its present ruins, which reach about seventeen and a half miles in circumference, and the "immensity of its colossal fragments offer to the eye so many astonishing objects, that one is riveted.to the spot, unable to decide whither to direct his step or fix his attention."

The chief objects of interest at Thebes are the four celebrated Temples of Karnac and Luxor, Medinet Abu and Memnonium ; the famous Tomb of Osymandyas, the Temple of Iris, the Labyrinth, and the Catacombs.   Indeed, the whole extent of eight miles along the Nile, on either side, is described as covered with magnificent portals, obelisks, decorated with .the most beautiful sculpture, forests of columns, and long avenues of colossal statues.   The position and magnificence of the four temples just named give us some idea of the ancient grandeur of Thebes.   Two of the temples, viz., Karnac and Luxor, were on the east side of the river Nile, distant about a mile and a half from each other ; and two on the west side, exactly fronting them—the temple at Medinet Abu being opposite Luxor, and Memnonium opposite to Karnac ; and the four were joined by avenues which are lined all the way by statues, pillars, and magnificent gateways, and guarded by sphynxes.

Conceive for a moment the vast dimensions. of the temple at Karnac.   The length of the principal temple was 1,200 feet, and its breadth 420.   But this superb edifice, which, from the scattered ruins around, seems to have been the principal fane of magnificent piles, all devoted to its use, is surrounded by subordinate temples, huge gateways, and colossal statues, for miles in extent, through which lead avenues in every direction, guarded by rows of sphynxes of vast size, cut out of single blocks of syenite.   Probably all these are but the ruins of buildings, which, in the prouder days of Thebes, were consecrated entirely to the temple.

This edifice has twelve principal entrances, each of which is composed of colossal gateways, besides other buildings larger than ordinary temples.

The grand hall in the temple at Karnac casts into the shade any other room ever yet constructed. This apartment, believed to be the work of Osirei, the father of the great Sesostris, and built near 3,500 years ago, is 329 feet long, and 170 feet wide, supported by 134 columns, twelve of which are 66 feet high, and 21 feet in diameter, and the others 42 feet high, and 9 feet in diameter.

Or fancy yourself approaching the temple at Luxor. The first object that arrests your attention is a magnificent gateway 200 feet in length, and still 57 feet above the present level of the sand. In front of the entrance stand two of the most perfect obelisks in the world, each formed of a single block of red granite, 7 or 8 feet square, and 80 feet high. Entering through such a gateway, on the wings of which are sculptured the most extraordinary pictures of some famous battle and victory, you pass into a portico of great dimensions, from which a double row of columns, with lotus capitals 22 feet in circumference, conduct you into a court 160 feet long, and 140 wide, beyond which is another portico of thirty-two columns, and then you find yourself in the interior of the edifice.

Or cross the Nile, and visit the two corresponding temples on the west bank, and, though the dimensions are not quite so great, the architecture is yet more beautiful. One of these temples is 500, and the other 600 feet in length—one contains six courts, and chambers passing from side to side, with 160 columns, 30 feet high.

Or we might here turn aside among the neighboring ruins, to take a look at some colossal statues, which here sit in gloomy solitude amid the present desolations of the Valley of the Nile; and we shall find no end to our attempts to survey these objects of interest. There stands the Labyrinth, with its 3,000 chambers, 1,500 above the surface of the ground, and 1,500 beneath; with its almost infinite winding passages from court to court, and from chamber to chamber; the ceiling and walls of marble richly ornamented with sculpture, and around the courts, pillars of the most exquisite white marble. In another direction you would meet the colossal Sphinx, which is to be seen near the group of pyramids at Gizeh. This enormous figure, with the head of a man and body of a lion, one of the wonders even in that wonderful country, is 150 feet in length, 63 feet high, though in a recumbent posture, its paws thrown out 53 feet in front. But before you had half contemplated this wonder of architecture, your attention would be arrested by a monument of antiquity no less wonderful, the Tomb of Osymandyas; or you would be tempted to visit those wonderful regions of the dead, those extraordinary excavations which served as the last resting place of generation after generation of the vast multitudes that peopled Thebes.

We are amazed at the magnitude of these ruins— and more amazed when we think to inquire how such massy piles were erected—how were such ponderous stones ever conveyed from the quarry; and, then, how were they ever raised to their places? We meet there shafts, columns, obelisks, 60 and 80 feet in height and 12 feet in diameter, of a single stone. The colossus of Ramases II. is computed to weigh 887 tons. How was such a mass of rock conveyed to the spot—and, then, how erected?

Thus I have taken occasion to refer to the architectural monuments in the land of Ham, not so much for the purpose of describing them—which in so limited space I could not, as for the purpose of showing *what has been done* in that benighted land; and, for the sake of the inference, viz., that *what has been done*, by any particular race of men, or on any given soil, *may be done again*. The most cursory glance over the countries to which I have referred, evinces, at once, that those lands were formerly peopled by a race or races of men far advanced in science and the arts, in civilization, and in all the useful and ornamental arts of life. The number, magnitude, and elegance of these monuments distinctly indicate the state of advancement to which this ancient race had arrived. The Pyramids, alone, in the Valley of the Nile, amount to 172. And, besides these, there are temples, tombs, obelisks, columns, magnificent gateways, sphynxes, and architectural monuments of every description and almost without number.

We, therefore, look for the regeneration of Africa, for her emancipation from the thraldom and ignorance into which she has now sunk. She has abundantly shown her capabilities to rise, assert and maintain honorable position among the nations, and to fulfill her destined mission. When the day of her redemption shall come—when the fiat of Heaven shall pronounce her long and dreary night passed, and the dawning of her day come—we need have no fears that Africa—poor, despised, degraded, forsaken, as she now is—shall rise in her strength, and, in the face of benignant Heaven, take her place among the nations, set free from her bondage, and exonerated from the curse. And the sons of Ham shall, in their turn, be honored and blessed. When Ethiopia shall stretch out her hands unto God, God shall receive her sons into his favor, and in Heaven's blessing they shall be blessed indeed.

CHAPTER V.

African races—Pioneers and first cultivators of the arts and sciences—The negro a primitive race—The pure negro superior to the mixed races—No race ever so advanced under so unfavorable circumstances—A blessing yet for Ham.

It may be asked, were the memorials of human greatness referred to in our last chapter monuments of the skill and general advance of African races? Were not the Carthaginians, Phœnicians, i. e., Canaanites from the eastern shore of the Mediterranean —and the Egyptians, perchance, of an Arabian stock. Still, all we claim is true. They were the sons of Ham. Africa is more especially the land of Ham; yet it detracts nothing from our position, that other branches of the family of Ham should migrate thither, and there display the capabilities of their race.

In a temporal point of view, the race of Ham was the first favored race. In Asia and Africa, and perhaps in America, and possibly in Europe, they took the lead. Early after the Deluge we find them on the plains of Shinar, a highly civilized and an advanced race. The ruins of Nineveh, the architectural monuments of Assyria, the magnificent Tower of Babel, are vouchers for such an assumption. From this ancient and great centre of civilization and progress among the descendants of Ham, on the plains of Shinar, where flowed the Tigris and Euphrates, we can distinctly trace the progress of human improvement. One stream flowed eastward to the Indus, and thence over hither and further India and China; and the other, westward into Arabia and Africa. And a third stream, not improbably, passed over the Mediterranean and the Atlantic into central America and Mexico. The latter supposition seems to find confirmation, not only from the monumental evidence abundantly extant, at the present day, in that part of America, and in the existing traditions, but has a recent confirmation in some documents not long since brought to light. In a late notice respecting the early history of the aboriginal inhabitants of America, it is stated, that M. de Bomburg has obtained two manuscripts, of great value, written by Don Ramon de Ordonez, a native and priest of Chiapas. Some fifty years ago, Ordonez devoted himself, for many years, to the study of the antiquities of Mexico, and his opinions were the result of much patient investigation. The grand point brought to light in the manuscripts is, that Chiapas and Mexico were first peopled by Asiatics, who came thither by the way of the Mediterranean, across the Atlantic. Their arrival was in early times, centuries before the Christian era. They are said to have remained some time at St. Domingo, and afterward crossed over to Chiapas, where, M. de Bomburg says, there are evidences of a settlement earlier than in Mexico. The Spaniards, for obvious reasons, conceal the fact of this early discovery and settlement of America. They would rather monopolize all the glory themselves.

The above opinion is abundantly sustained by the Asiatic character of the splendid ruins of Central America and Mexico. Antiquarians, and, indeed, common travelers, discover striking resemblances in

the ancient temples, pyramids, and various architectural relics of Central America, and in those of
Egypt, Ethiopia, and Hindostan—resemblances not
easily to be accounted for, except on the hypothesis
that they are the work of nations having a common
origin. So striking is the resemblance between the
temples and many of the rites and instruments of the
superstition of India and of Egypt, that native Hin-
doos, when brought, as Sepoys, to join the British
army in Egypt, imagined that they had found their
own temples in the ruins of Dendera. So strongly,
indeed, were they impressed with the identity, that
they actually performed their devotions in these temples, according to the rites and ceremonies practiced
in their own country.

Recent investigations on the subject of races have
developed singular traces of the negro race through
all the countries of Southern Asia. And the same
conclusion is arrived at, by these writers, respecting
the ancient Egyptians. "Of their physical character,"
says Pritchard, "the national conformation, prevailing
in the most ancient times, was nearly the negro form,
with woolly hair." In a later age, as the nation advanced in civilization and mingled with other nations,
these characteristics became modified, and, in a great
degree, disappeared. Writers show a very striking
affinity between the ancient Egyptians and the people
of India, and show that both were strongly marked by
the characteristics of the negro race.

Oriental temples and other public edifices, as, also,
the images that are worshiped in these temples, most
clearly indicate to what race the original occupants
of those temples belonged. Among the Siamese, also,

their chief deities, called Buddha and Amida, "are figured nearly like negroes." And so it may be affirmed of the Buddhists of all Southern Asia, comprising more than 300,000,000 of the human family, their principal deity, Buddha, is represented with negro features and hair.

Travelers in India speak of the ancient city of Nagpoor, and of a ruined city, whose name is lost, near the city of Benares, as "adorned with statues of a woolly-haired race." And the writer of these pages has witnessed, in the celebrated caves of Elephanta, near Bombay, the same peculiarity. The sculptures there are believed to display the oldest forms of the Indian religion. The attributes of the three persons of the triad (the Hindoo Trinity) are there exhibited as united in one figure. Modern travelers do not fail to notice the African appearance of those images, particularly of their hair and features.

We feel constrained to admit that these edifices, idols, and statues were the workmanship of a race very like the negro; and we may not suppose that a fairer race would be likely to so honor a caste which was regarded as inferior. They were, undoubtedly, the works of the "Indo-Cushites," the descendants of Ham, "the original type of the black races of men, and the Ethiopians, whose migration extended from the rising to the setting sun." Hamilton Smith fully adopts the opinion that the negro or woolly-haired type of man was the most ancient, and the original character of the inhabitants of Asia, as far north as the lower range of the Himmalaya Mountains; and from the Indus to Indo-China and the Malay Peninsula, and even in the South Sea Islands.

We may here avail ourselves of so high an authority in Oriental lore as Sir William Jones. He observes that "the remains of architecture and sculpture in India, seems to prove an early connection between that country and Africa." He adds : " The Pyramids of Egypt, the colossal statues described by Pausanias, and others, the Sphynx, and the Hermes Canis, which last bears a strong resemblance to the Varaha Avatar (a Hindoo incarnation), indicate the style of the same indefatigable workmen, who formed the vast excavations of Canara (in Western India), the various temples and images of Buddha, and the idols which are continually dug up at Gaya, or in its vicinity. These, and other indisputable facts, may induce no ill-grounded opinion, that Ethiopia and Hindostan were peopled or colonized by the same extraordinary race ; in confirmation of which, it may be added, that the mountaineers of Bengal and Benhar can hardly be distinguished in some of their features, particularly in their lips and noses, from the modern Abyssinians.

We would, therefore, seem to hazard nothing in the conclusion that commerce and the arts, science and learning, civilization and human improvement in general, were first identified with, and developed through, a race that has now for long ages been associated, only with degradation and barbarous ignorance. And we are equally justified in the conclusion which an intelligent writer has drawn, that "the degradation of this race of men must be regarded as the result of external causes, and not of natural, inherent, and original incapacity."

In the preceding paragraphs we have quoted free-

ly from a valuable work on the "Unity of the Human Races," by the Rev. Thomas Smythe, D.D., of Charleston, S. C. And we are the more willing to give all due credit to such authority, as it is testimony from a source which strikes the mind rather singularly at the present moment. We hear nothing of Dr. Smythe's dissent from the current doctrine of the church and clergy of the South, or of the Divine sanction of negro slavery. In 1850, fully indorsing the opinions of Pritchard, Clapperton, Pickering, and the best ethnological writers, he says : "We may, therefore, as philosophical inquirers seeking after truth, admit the full force of any facts which may encourage the belief that there was a time when the black race of man were the pioneers, or, at least, the equals of any other races, in all the arts and acquirements of man's primitive civilization." Again : he says, "there was a time when learning, commerce, arts, and manufactures were all associated with a form and character of the human race now regarded as the evidence only of degradation, and barbarous ignorance."

But times have changed. In 1861, a new gospel, as touching the negro, obtains at the South. He is no longer a man—has no rights—was born and doomed, by an irreversible curse, to perpetual servitude. The pulpit has been suborned in the interest of the slaveholder. Men like Thornwell and Palmer, whose praise was once in all the churches, have gone at the bidding of the oppressor. They tell us, now, that slavery is a "Bible institution," that it is compatible with the spirit of the Gospel—well pleasing to Heaven—conducive to the greatest good of both oppressed and oppressor—negro slavery the only sure and rightful basis of a Republican Government. Times change; and men change with times.

But to return: the identity between the Indian and Egyptian temples and monuments is not so striking as that between the Indian and the Ethiopian and Nubian. The temples of Nubia, for example, exhibit the same features, whether as to style of architecture or form of worship, as similar buildings do which have been examined in the neighborhood of Bombay; and, especially, this resemblance discovered in those extraordinary excavations hewn out in the solid body of a hill or mountain, and formed into complete and vast temples. The excavated temple of Guerfah Hassan is said to remind one at once of the excavated temples at Elephanta, near Bombay, or the more extraordinary ones at Ellora. And the same interesting resemblances are, also, said to be found between the temples of the Chinese and those of East Africa, all-indicating, again, that the skill and workmanship which reared them descended from the same common stock.

When we speak of temples in Hindostan resembling sacred edifices in Eastern Africa, we refer to the old temples in India, which differ considerably from those of more modern date. These old temples were evidently the work of a race who no longer occupy that country. The descendants of Shem have finally supplanted the sons of Ham, who once extended their possessions, and covered with the works of their skill, and enterprise all those fertile countries of Southern Asia. In some of these ancient temples in India, we meet with the unmistakable traces that the race of Ham once flourished in those lands. The thick lips and the crisped hair are met with on the figures found in those temples.

To what extent the race of Ham were likewise the pioneers and the first cultivators of the arts and sciences in Europe, and the first to introduce the improvements of civilization and the blessings of a more highly cultivated life, we may not be able to determine. True it is, that, so long as the names of Cadmus and Cecrops and Danaus are remembered, it will not be forgotten that the art of writing, and the rich treasures of Oriental wisdom, were transported, through Phœnicia, from Africa into Europe. Not only, then, did Europe and all European races, whereever found, receive their learning from the children of Ham, but, as I said, the art of writing, which alone can perpetuate and make learning practical.

We know, too, that, after the lapse of some centuries, the Carthaginians, as they sallied forth from their African home, became the merchantmen of all Europe. Their commerce extended to Gaul, Spain, England, the Baltic, and to all the islands and ports of the Mediterranean. And commerce is the great civilizer. The Carthaginians could never exchange commodities with those European nations without an exchange of ideas. The sons of Japheth, therefore, were greatly indebted to the children of Ham for their civilization and early advancement.

Nor need we stop here. What Cadmus begun, and the Carthaginians greatly favored, the Saracens, some centuries later, advanced still further. They kept alive, as before said, the flickering lamp of learning during the dark ages, and, through the magnificent empire which, for some centuries, they maintained in Spain, they revived learning in Europe, dissipated the darkness of the dark ages, and did much to prepare the way for the glorious Reformation.

We are, therefore, brought to the conclusion, that the first great developments of the arts, science, general knowledge, and human improvement, commenced after the flood, on the plains of Shinar and in the race of Ham—that by migrations or missions, we know not how, streams flowed forth, both eastward and westward; the westward stream flowing through Arabia, Ethiopia, Nubia, and Egypt, and thence, by the way of Phœnicia, into Greece, Rome, and into Western Europe; and the eastern stream, through Persia and Hindostan, into China, and some collateral branches across the Atlantic into Central America—and that these developments were confined to the descendants of Ham. For whatever reason, wasting and degradation have since been, for a melancholy series of years, entailed on this ill-fated race, they were the first, after the repeopling of the earth, to make progress in empire and the arts of civilized life, in intellectual advancement and great temporal prosperity.

Whether we are to regard the long-protracted depression and degradation of the whole family of Ham as a fruit of the curse pronounced on Canaan, standing a federal head in that family, has already been considered. It would seem more probable that the Canaanites would be the sole, as they are the particular, inheritors of the Divine malediction: "A servant of servants shalt thou be;" yet, in the history of African races (the descendants of Ham, through other branches than Canaan), we seem, as many affirm, to have a general verification of the same curse, or something very much like it. However accounted for, true it is, that Africa has been a carcass preyed upon by every unclean bird. A "servant of servants" has she been—subjected, now for more than 3,000 years, to the most remarkable series of rapine, plunder, cruelty, carnage, and protracted deaths. There is no other such example in all the history of our world. Extensive races—a whole continent—subjected, for more than thirty centuries, to the most appalling miseries, until races, once noble and capable, as we have seen, of a high state of improvement, are reduced to so low a condition, that there are not wanting advocates of the theory that expels them from the family of man— at least, denies their common origin with the white races. But more of this when we come to speak of the curse of Africa.

It is sufficient to add, that, except as a mere matter of earnests, or first-fruits, there has been no true religious development among the black races of Ham. All we have yet seen is a temporal elevation, such as wealth, worldly wisdom, extensive empire, gorgeous works of art, superb monuments of human greatness and pride, magnificent cities, and much that elevates the physical man. The true religion was perpetuated in, and descended through, the posterity of Shem till the coming of Christ. Its patriarchs, prophets, and teachers—its victories, and conquests, and blessings —were confined to this branch of the great family of man. After this notable era in the annals of the world, the sceptre of righteousness passed over to Japheth. And Christianity has since been almost exclusively confined to this race. Are we to believe that the third great branch—Ham, the younger son of

Noah—shall never become the favored race in respect to what is, undoubtedly, the chief design in the Divine mind in the creation of man? Shall not they, who have waited long, and been trodden down, and oppressed, and abused, above any other people that existed —shall not they come up in remembrance before God? No aspect of the Divine character is more clearly revealed than that which makes him to take the part of the oppressed and afflicted. He humbles them whom he is about to honor. He binds up them he has torn. He raises up them he has suffered to be cast down.

Were there no other hope for Africa, we should hope on this ground. And if God does, as we believe, observe some proper proportion between his frown and his favor—between the bitter cup which a people have been permitted to drink, and the returning smiles of his face—we may expect Africa shall be rewarded double for all her sufferings.

We shall, therefore, continue to believe Africa to be a great reservation, where shall yet be garnered some of the richest fruits of Divine mercy toward man—a rich field, that shall, in due time, yield a luxuriant harvest and bring a rich revenue into the treasury of the great King. Like their own great deserts, this singular race, so barren, at present, of all common interest, so fruitless of all that goes to aggrandize a people, seem, as I have shown, kept back for some great future purpose—perhaps for the next great moral development in our world—to be the next great medium through which God will carry out his purposes among men.

Late ethnological researches have brought out results, as touching African races, little expected, yet much to our present purpose. Pritchard, Smythe, Morton, and others, have shown, as far as the nature of the case admits, that the negro race is a primitive race of man—that they were the earliest civilized, and the first civilizers of man—"that there was a time when the black race of man were pioneers, or, at least, the equals of any other races, in all the arts, and acquirements of man's primitive civilization"—a time when "learning, commerce, arts, manufactures, and all that characterizes a state of civilization, were associated with the black race ; a race now associated only with degradation and barbarous ignorance." As evidence of this, we can triumphantly point to the magnificent kingdoms of Meroe, Nubia, and Ethiopia, and to the no less stately monuments of art, as they stand this day, the imperishable memorials of time, scattered along, from the pyramids of Egypt, through all Southern Asia, to Japan ; temples, statues, images, cavern palaces, far surpassing any work of modern art. These are the monuments of the skill and workmanship of a crisp-haired and a thick-lipped race. Writers of great learning and research hesitate not to say, that the aborigines of Hindostan were a race of negroes—at least, had the hair and features of the negro.* Such a race is still found on an island in the Bay of Bengal, on the mountains of India, and in the interior of the Malay Peninsula—indeed, in just such portions as we should expect to find them, on the supposition that they were the aborigines of those countries, and driven out and forced to flee before victorious invaders, who afterward became permanent set-

---

* Of these, we may name Pritchard, Hamilton Smith, Morton, Ritter, Trail, T. B. Hamilton, Sir William Jones.

tlers on the soil. It is a singular fact, that the idols and hero gods of all those countries (I mean, the ancient gods as those of the Buddhists and Jains), have the woolly hair and the thick lip. We can here have no suspicion that the present dominant races in those countries, or that other whiter race, would be ambitious to give to their deities the negro features. Dr. Pritchard, therefore, regards it as an "established fact, that a black and woolly haired race is among the original inhabitants of Asia," especially "in countries about India." And the same writers agree that the ancient Egyptians were of the same race—"that the national configuration prevailing in the most ancient times was nearly the negro form, with the woolly hair." So, likewise, in the extreme east are found indubitable traces of the negro race. In Japan are stupendous and magnificent temples of very remote antiquity, in which the idols are represented as negroes with woolly hair.

And another fact, attested by the same class of writers, and confirmed by Clapperton, and other travelers among the negro tribes of the interior of Africa, is, that *the pure negroes are superior to the mixed races.* Among the pure races are found "large and populous kingdoms, with numerous towns, well-cultivated fields, and various manufactures, such as weaving, dyeing, tanning, working in iron and other metals, and in pottery.

But, what is more, the same authorities assure us that, the pure negro tribes are morally superior to the mixed races; that they all believe in the first principles of natural religion; in one universally powerful Being; in prayer and worship; in rites and sacrifices; in priests and ministers; in the immortality of the soul; in a future state of rewards and punishment; in the division of time into weeks; and they have given a more ready reception than any other people to religions, whether true or false, to idolatry, Mohammedanism, and Christianity.

Such facts abundantly indicate the capabilities of the race for a higher civilization. No race ever advanced so far under so unfavorable circumstances. They were, in their day, far in advance of all other races. And no race, without the stronger element of Christianity, ever made a greater progress. Nor are we without an example of what the negro race is capable of doing under the more powerful influences of Christianity. At one period, Christianity mingled largely with other elements for their advancement; and nobly did they improve under the auspices of the Cross, and noble specimens were they of Christian piety. Africa supplied the first " Protestants." "In North Africa," says the historian, " Christianity flourished very much." The African Church more than once protested against the insolence of the Bishop of Rome, before Rome usurped the position she had now assumed."

There is, it seems to me, nothing in the past history of the negro race, nor in their present condition, that militates against our assumption that they may yet exhibit a higher civilization and a better type of Christianity. Their present degradation is obviously but a result of unpropitious circumstances.

But there are other considerations, that seem to throw something into the scale of the same probability. God is not accustomed to use any one people as the medium of his grace, the instruments for carrying out the purposes of his benevolence toward man, for any very long period of time. The best portion of the race which he ever has used can not long bear the honor. They become proud, lightly esteem the honor conferred on them, undervalue their privileges, abuse the Divine forbearance, and finally provoke God to humble them. Having, by their gross ingratitude forfeited the Divine favor, God will no longer work with and by them. He rejects them—at least, for a time— brings them down, and leaves them to wasting and desolation.

— During a long period of time, as I have remarked before, truth, righteousness, and the Church of the living God were confided to the posterity of Shem. The patriarchs, prophets, and ministers of religion—the agents, agencies, means, and appliances for the preservation of religion in the world, and for its diffusion, were, for many ages, confined to this branch of the human family. And more especially was the seed of Abraham selected as the depository and almoner of the grace of God. He used this medium, till, in their blindness and sin, they rejected his Holy One, and crucified the Lord of life. From that hour the race of Shem have, in a great degree, been set aside. The ministers of Christianity, the almoners of the Gospel, the Church of God, have been very much confined to the family of Japheth. And of all the branches of Japheth's numerous seed, no one has been made so prominent an instrument of advancing the best interests of man as the Anglo-Saxon race. At the present time, nearly all the ostensible and active agencies for carrying out the provisions of the Gospel, and diffusing its blessings, are confined to this race. Beyond the limits where the English language is spoken, or the English Missionary is preaching, and English power is exercised and felt, you will find but little evangelical religion, but little active philanthropy, or expansive Christian benevolence, and but little religious or civil liberty.

But are we more sure that the controlling influence of the Anglo-Saxons over the world shall last, than the man of David's or Solomon's day was that the Jewish race should continue to hold their moral pre-eminence in the world? May not the day come when this Anglo-Saxon blood shall, in turn, become as corrupt and unworthy the Divine favor as the stock of Israel ever did? Is there less danger that they shall become proud and heaven-provoking? And if the day shall come when God shall cease to use them as the chosen medium by which to carry forward his work, where shall we look for a substitute? Already has the sceptre passed from Shem to Japheth—and may it not yet pass to Ham? Long and dreary has been the night which has hung over this race. More than 4,000 years has Ham been the "servant of servants." From generation to generation has he dragged out a miserable existence under the "curse." Though the curse seems to have descended primarily and temporally through the lineage of Canaan—"Cursed be Canaan, a servant of servants shall he be," yet a curse would seem entailed on the general race of Ham. To the Canaanites it was death and extermination—punishment, signal and immediate. To the other branches of the family of Ham it was long and lingering—slavery, oppression, degradation. The annals of history furnish no other such example of a people so long and so sorely trodden down and oppressed. Be it that they have, during all this dark and protracted night, been but reaping the reward of their iniquity, where is the people that would receive more mercy if they only received according to their deserts? The descendants of Cush, who peopled Arabia and Ethiopia, in Africa, and the posterity of Phut and Misraim, who principally peopled Africa, have deeply drunk of the bitter cup. With the notable exception of a few kingdoms on the east and north, almost the whole Hamic race have lain very nearly dormant since the downfall of the empire founded by Nimrod.

But is there no blessing for Ham? Must he lie under the curse forever? Is his a doomed race, beyond all reprieve? We think not. Yet we do not profess to have that direct evidence in the matter which we have in regard to some other races. Still we find an indirect and circumstantial evidence, which affords a comfortable conviction that Ham shall yet be blessed, and blessed abundantly—that the day of his redemption shall come. Ethiopia shall stretch out her hands to God; the long-entailed curse shall be removed. A blessing is in reserve for him. God shall kindly visit an oppressed, an outcast people.

There are indications, ever and anon, in the past history of this degenerate son, which indicate a more auspicious future. Already has he inherited a goodly share of temporal blessing. The descendants of Ham occupied the most beautiful and fertile portions of the globe. The Assyrians, Babylonians, Phœnicians, the Arabians, the aborigines of India, as also the Ethiopians, Nubians, Egyptians, and Carthaginians, were all of the race of Ham. The Phœnicians were the ancient Canaanites. Though Africa seems from a very early period to have been peculiarly the portion of this son of Noah, yet they spread themselves abroad, eastward and westward, from their original centre on the plains of Shinar, built the first cities, made the earliest advances in the arts and sciences, in government, learning, navigation, and commerce. They gave to the world the alphabet; and numerical figures. They enjoyed great temporal prosperity, but they were without God, and, therefore, could not endure. In Africa—Ham's own land—the Carthaginians, a branch of the Canaanitish family, for a time flourished; but they were not seasoned with the salt of the true religion, and therefore they were destined to yield to an early decay. The race of Ham, like that of Ishmael, enjoyed great temporal prosperity and political dominion; but, in respect to spiritual blessings, Ham has never, like Shem and Japheth, basked beneath the benignant smiles of Heaven. We have seen the sceptre of righteousness pass from Shem to Japheth; but shall Ham be forever forgotten? Shall not the sceptre in turn pass to him? Shall not the curse be removed from Canaan, and he yet be allowed to drink of the cup of salvation, and drink, too, as freely of the cup of blessings as he has of the cup of woe?

Such inquiries now demand our attention. We hope we may make it appear quite probable that this at present despised race are held in reserve for the next great moral development in our world.

CHAPTER VI.

Reasons why Ham shall yet be blessed—His connection with the promised seed.

Is there not a blessing in reserve for Ham? Will not God kindly visit him in his oppression, in his protracted rejection? We believe it, because,

1. God is not wont, finally, to cast off a people so—certainly not a whole race. It is much more in harmony with God's way of working, that he should make the African race, in the end, eminent instruments in his hands for the furtherance of truth and righteousness in the world. No other nation has been so long and so signally debased. No race drunk so deeply of the vials of Heaven's displeasure. All nations have seemed to combine to mix the cup of her wrath. Africa has, for ages, been made the victim of the worst passions of man. She has suffered a strange series of unmitigated woes. God has permitted it. But is there no limit to her sorrows? Is worse than the mark of Cain upon her? Is hers a doomed race, destined only to suffer? We think not, and if we had no other reason for our opinion, this would suffice, that God does take the part of the oppressed. He allows them to drink the bitter cup to the dregs, and lets others have rule over them, and to vex their souls and grind them into the dust. Yet he does not forget mercy toward them—nor vengeance toward their oppressors. He will lift up their heads,

5

give them rule over them that hated them, and reward them "double" for all the dishonor put upon
them. God will surely take the part of the oppressed,
and put to shame the pride of man.

2. We are able to quote some particular instances,
well authenticated, of the merciful visitation of Heav-
en in behalf of peoples who had, for a long time, suffered under the Divine malediction. We have an instance in the Moabites. They had displeased God—
they came not to the help of Israel against his enemies, and they were, in consequence, excluded from
the mercies and promises of God, through Israel, for
"ten generations." Yet God afterward put a great
honor on Moab. Though he did not use the nation,
as such, as an instrument in his work, yet he identified Moab in the purposes of his mercy, down to the
end of time. He chose that David and the illustrious
line of kings that followed—yea, that the great King
and Messiah—should, in one line of descent, come
from Moab. Ruth, the Moabitess, was the mother of
Obed, the father of Jesse, the father of David. In
the plenitude of his mercy, God remembered the
Moabites, and conferred on them a double honor. In
like manner, God graciously visited his people after
their captivity, and more signally yet will he visit his
people in their present dispersion and dismember-
ment as a church and nation, and make them a great
nation and a glorious church, and the most signal and
honored instruments in the conversion of the world.
"For their shame, they shall have double; and for confusion, they shall rejoice in their portion; therefore, in
their land they shall possess double; everlasting joy
shall be unto them." Prophecy, we believe, fully jus-

tifies the expectation that God will bless and honor Israel more abundantly than he has ever yet done, and make the people of his ancient election yet more conspicuously the instruments of good to the world. Rich and precious promises remain yet to be fulfilled in them.

And a yet more extraordinary instance of this occurs in reference to the Canaanites, the very race on whom the curse primarily and most signally fell. Even the outlawed Canaan, "the servant of servants," on whose posterity was poured the most signal vengeance of Heaven, should have his name associated with the promised seed; or, rather, his blood was allowed, too, to mingle in the favored stream from which David and David's Lord came. And here we have another of those beautiful illustrations, that our Lord will not suffer to go unnoticed and unrewarded the least kind act done to his people. Though the Canaanites were notorious sinners and a doomed people, God would not allow to pass unrewarded a single right act. Rahab, called the "harlot" of Jericho, was a Canaanitish woman. She conferred a signal favor on the Israelites in their conquest of Canaan. Confident that they would take possession of the country, she entertained the messengers sent by Joshua, and thereby very essentially favored the work of the God of Israel. This same Rahab, doubtless, became a worshiper of the true God; is said to have "dwelt in Israel," to have married Salmon, a priest of Judah, and to have become the mother of Boaz, who was the grandfather of Jesse, the father of David.

Thus our Lord did not disdain to admit into the line of his mortal descent one stream from the very race which had become obnoxious to the annihilating curse; as he had another from a source scarcely more hopeful. Abandoned as Canaan was, God would not wholly exclude him from a participation in the promised seed.

3. There has always been a remarkable connection kept up between the promised seed and the race of Ham. In what I shall say on this topic, I shall identify Africa and Arabia as really the habitation of the same race. Arabia is the land of Cush, though many of the Cushites inhabit Ethiopia, in Africa. Whatever might have been the civil connection between Africa and Arabia, in their early history, their religious history, at least, became intimately connected after the time of Ishmael, and more especially yet after the rise of Mahommedanism. And there is, at this moment, a process going on at the bottom of the Red Sea, which intimates that these two portions of land shall have a yet nearer connection. The Red Sea is yearly becoming less and less navigable, in consequence of the growth of its coral rocks. This process has only to go on, as most likely it will, and Africa and Arabia will be joined by one vast plain, and the two portions of the Cushites—Arabia and Ethiopia—will be united.

As we trace down the history of God's covenant people, we shall see that, in all the developments of mercy to man, there has been a singular regard paid to the race of Ham—not so much in the way of actual blessing, as in a singular and perpetual remembrance. They are all along recognized, the finger of mercy is pointed at them, yet they are strangely passed by.

Abraham, soon after the ratifying of the covenant, is hastened down to Egypt, and there dwells for a time—is brought into favor with the king, and is honored and enriched. What truths he there taught, and what acquired—how salutary and extensive the influence of his example—how much knowledge of the true religion he left behind him, we are not told. But most certain it is, that such a man did not long reside in such a place, and hold so commanding a position among the people, without leaving behind him some indelible traces of his footsteps.

We meet an instance of this singular connection in the person of Ishmael, one of the most singular characters that figures in sacred history. The son of Abraham and Hagar, the Egyptian, he unites in his person a lineal union of the promised seed and an African race—the chosen seed, with which God would build his Church, and that dark, mysterious race of which we are speaking. In Ishmael and his seed we meet a sort of counterpart of Isaac and his seed. His posterity, like Isaac's, became exceedingly numerous—had a particular portion of the earth assigned them—were divided into twelve tribes—and through all ages remained a distinct people. We have in this outcast branch of Noah's family a darkly reflected image of the true Church.

Or I might have named, in the outset, that remarkable instance of piety, which was exemplified, some 600 or 800 years before Moses, in the man of Uz. That remarkable man, Job, was an Arabian, and probably a Cushite. Nor do we suppose that Job's was a solitary instance of the power of the true religion in the land of Cush. An instance of such exalted, enlightened piety, in the princely character of Job, was not likely to have existed alone. Job's friends, they that were near, as well as the three from a distance, were, probably, more or less, worshipers of the true God.

Again: by a mysterious chain of providences, Joseph is made Governor of Egypt. A man of rare integrity and moral worth, one of the promised seed, and, perhaps, as good an impersonation of the true religion as the world had ever had, is exalted to stand next the throne of a most powerful African prince. He stood a teacher in high places, and no doubt his voice was heard. Next, we find the same mysterious providence bringing the whole visible church, and settling them in that corner of Africa, and preserving them there for more than two centuries. This was a most extraordinary step, if regarded only in its bearing on Africa. Here the true worshipers of God prayed, served their God, and exemplified the truth in the face of the most enlightened, refined, and powerful kingdom on earth. Nor did they do these things in a corner. They were a city set on a hill—they were beacon-lights to the nations of Africa.

We find this connection further preserved in the person of Moses. Himself African-born, and the adopted son of Pharaoh's daughter, he takes to himself for a wife one of the daughters of Cush. Josephus says, that Moses, before he was called, in Horeb, to be the deliverer of God's people out of Egypt, was made commander of the forces of Pharaoh on an expedition against the Ethiopians—that, in the event of that war, he was married to an Ethiopian princess, daughter of the conquered king; thus, in his early life, he was joined in marriage to a Cushite of the genuine African stock—a daughter of the race of Ham. Of this woman we hear no more. It does not appear he had a wife when he fled from his adopted country, and took refuge in the land of Midian. Here he contracted marriage with Zipporah, daughter of the priest of Midian. This woman is also called an Ethiopian, or Cushite, of the same race, but resident on the east side of the Red Sea. Here Moses lived forty years and reared a family. Again: when Moses was with the children of Israel in the wilderness, we hear of a murmuring and sedition raised against him by his nearest family friends, Aaron, his brother, and Miriam, his sister, because he had married an "Ethiopian woman." Was this a cry against Zipporah, whose marriage had transpired some forty years before? Or was she long since dead, and he had married another Ethiopian?

Zipporah was, probably, a daughter, by descent, of Abraham, by his second wife, Keturah, and as she is called a Cushite—Ethiopian (black), the inquiry is forced upon us, whether Keturah were not of a kindred stock with Hagar, i. e., of the Hamic race? Midian was a son of Keturah, by Abraham. This offspring, the sons and grandsons of Keturah, Josephus says, Abraham "contrived to settle in colonies; and they took possession of the Troglodytes, and the country of Arabia Felix, as far as it reaches the Red Sea." They would now naturally share and mingle with that other great branch of the Abrahamic family, which, in the person of Ishmael, had so singularly united, as we have seen, the promised seed and the lineage of Ham.

According to Josephus, Ophren, the son of Midian and the grandson of Abraham and Keturah, figured greatly in the early history of Africa. It is related, "that he made war against Libya 'and took it, and that his grandchildren, when they inhabited it, called it from his name, Africa."

Thus we have, in Abraham's second marriage, another connecting link between the two races in question, perpetuated in their united history, but renewed more strikingly in the marriage of Moses with the daughter of the priest of Midian.

Nor is the connection of the chosen seed with Ham broken off after the departure of Israel out of Egypt. Solomon, an illustrious type of Christ, takes his favorite wife from Egypt. She was "black, but comely," he says; of a genuine African race. The extraordinary celebration of the nuptials of this marriage—its being made the subject of one or more of the Psalms designed to be used in exciting and guiding the devotion of the Church in all after-time, and the occasion of those extraordinary songs, called Solomon's, in which there is understood to be a deep spiritual meaning, of profound interest to the Christian, gives no mean significancy to this union. And a circumstance, which may here be allowed some significancy in the connection alluded to, is the fact, so particularly recorded, that "Solomon built a palace for the daughter of Pharaoh, after that he had finished the house of the Lord." This has been taken as typical of the calling of the Gentiles and their union with the Jewish Church. But may we not rather regard it as typical, more especially, of the gathering in of a church from among the outcasts of Ham? After the completion of the Temple—which was a symbol of the Church in the line of the promised seed—a house is built for the daughter of Pharaoh—which we venture to take as a symbol of that spiritual house, which shall yet rise among the black tents of Kedar.

The Queen of Sheba, an Ethiopian princess visits Jerusalem, to see the glory of Solomon, and to hear wisdom from his lips. Philip and the Ethiopian Eunuch kept up the connection between the two races in their day. Paul executes his first Christian mission, and performs the first acts of his illustrious ministry in Arabia, preaching to the sons of Ham. A large representation of Peter's assembly, at the time of Pentecost, were from Africa. Some of the most worthy of the Christian fathers, as prophets had done before them, were preachers of righteousness in Africa. And not the least notable coincidence, the infant Saviour was taken down into Egypt, as if, in some strange and mysterious sense, to identify his mission with that strange and mysterious continent. And we have shown elsewhere, that one of the evangelists, and, at least, four of the early disciples and teachers of Christianity, were Africans; that Christianity, in the dew of her youth flourished on an African soil, under the teachings of bishops and presbyters of a singular renown.

Indeed, we may add, that the connection between the descendants of Abraham and of Ishmael was never broken off. The Jews, during their history, were familiar with Egypt. They had never, from Abraham to Paul, lost this connection. "From 301 to 180 B. C., the period of the Ptolemies, it was a place of shelter for them. In 153 B. C., Onias built a tem-

5*

ple at Leontopolis, which was long the rival of that at Jerusalem. At Alexandria they had the most splendid synagogue, with its accompaniments of schools, which existed in the whole world."

But, what is yet more to our purpose, this singular connection appears, not less remarkably, in the genealogy of our blessed Lord and Saviour. We have seen how Moab, through the descendants of Ruth, who was a Moabitess, was allowed a lineal representation in the holy seed. Boaz, her husband, the father of Obed, the father of Jesse, the father of David, was, through the maternal line, of Canaanitish descent. Boaz was a lineal descendant of Pharez, the son of Judah, whose wife was Tamar, a Canaanitish woman. Here, again, we meet the same interesting connection. Canaan, the most hopeless son of Ham, in despite the "curse," is allowed a representation in the genealogy of Christ, the son of David, the son of Jesse. Is there not hope, then, for the prescribed race? Have they not part and lot in Christ? What God hath joined together, let no man put asunder.

Our conviction that the posterity of Ham shall yet be honored and blessed, is further confirmed by the promise made to Ishmael. Isaac was the promised seed. The covenant, the promises, the church, should, in order and form, descend through Isaac and his seed, and, in this succession, should be made the first and the great display of God's grace to man. This was the favored seed by election, yet not to the exclusion of all other races. Did not God appoint the other lineal branch of Abraham, the branch from Ishmael, as the reserved race, on which should come the reserved blessing, or which should receive the residue of the Spirit? While the blessings of the covenant should descend through the line of Isaac, a promise was given to Ishmael, and its blessings should descend through his posterity. And, though primarily, and perhaps chiefly, temporal, yet, is it all temporal? Is there not a spiritual inheritance yet to be realized by Ishmael, and one much richer than the moonlight one which Ishmael has already realized through the crescent? I think so.

When Abraham perceived that the covenant had been confirmed in the line of his son Isaac, in the fullness of a father's heart, he immediately offered up this prayer: "Oh, that Ishmael might live before thee." The prayer was heard. "God said: As for Ishmael, I have heard thee ;-behold, I will bless him, and will make him fruitful, and will multiply him exceedingly : twelve princes shall he beget, and I will make him a great nation." There is a striking similarity between the blessing pronounced on Isaac and that on Ishmael. With the single and important difference, that the covenant should be established with Isaac, and the Messiah come in his line, and "all nations be blessed in him," and thus Isaac should be pre-eminently a blessing to others, the difference is by no means so great as has been generally supposed.

Are the promises to Ishmael only of temporal blessings? So are those made to Isaac. Yet we feel no difficulty in accepting the latter as promises of spiritual blessings, Subsequent history and further revelations warrant this application. Why, then, confine promises made to Ishmael, couched in nearly the same terms, to temporal blessings? Save in the important particular referred to, it is difficult to discover

the world-wide distinction which has been made between these two sons of Abraham.   In other respects,
we can see more parallelism than contrast.   They
have dwelt side by side, been alike kept distinct peoples, alike the subjects of great temporal promises and
of great temporal afflictions, alike divided into twelve
tribes, alike preserved distinct and unannihilated
amid the wreck of empires and the dissolution of great
civil polities.   The great distinction (besides the one
named) seems to be that the promises to Ishmael
are delayed.   In the wise purposes of God, generations, centuries, are allowed to pass without their
fulfillment.

It is readily conceded that Ishmael has played the
prodigal son.   He has taken the "portion" that fell to
him, and has "devoured it with harlots."   But the
Father's love to him is not annihilated, not exhausted.
It is only suspended.   The precious promises made
to him are delayed.   He shall return, shall come up
in remembrance in a Father's love.   His long captivity shall be turned; the promises to him shall be
fulfilled.   God hath said: "Behold, I have blessed him."   The fiat has gone out that "Ishmael is
blessed."   "Ishmael shall live before the Lord."
Ethiopia shall stretch out her hands to God.   Mercy long delayed, blessings long withheld, shall not
fail.   Poor Ishmael shall not be forsaken forever.
The bowels of a Father's love yearn for a lost son.
He waits with open arms to receive the returning
prodigal.   And as the poor, despised, sable son shall
return and be received with joy, and be put among
the children, and have put on him the best robe, and
the ring on his hand, and shoes on his feet, there

shall be joy, because he that was dead is alive again, he that was lost is found. They that were not a people shall become a people.

But what connection has the destiny of Ishmael with Africa? Much, we believe. Ishmael is the patriarch, the prophet, the priest, the Moses, of the race of Ham, and Mohammed is their Messiah. And, religiously at least, Africa, in connection with Arabia, is the land of Ham. Africa and Arabia are, therefore, closely connected in destiny with Ishmael. Though the descendants of Ham, at an early period, were permitted to dwell in the tents of Shem, as Japheth since has, in India, Burmah, and China, yet their home has been Africa.

We look, therefore, that this long-neglected race shall be visited; that the long-deferred blessing shall be realized; the poor prodigal shall return; and though he shall not be a blessing, in the sense in which Isaac has been, yet he shall be abundantly blessed. And we may expect that the spiritual blessing shall bear some proportion to the very liberal temporal blessing which God promised, in answer to Abraham's prayer; and, also, to the long-protracted and severe afflictions to which the race has been subjected. In those occasional developments, civil, intellectual, artistic, and religious, already referred to, we have seen certain first-fruits of this blessing, prognostics of what shall be.

Africa's great desert is but a fit emblem of the past and present Africa herself. Morally, intellectually, and politically, Africa, as a whole, has, from age to age, been one great Sahara; yet, like Sahara, she has had her beautiful oases. As the historian attempts to traverse her burning, barren sands, his eye is ever and anon charmed with these delightful spots. And the analogy may not stop here. Like those great ocean reservations of Providence which are beginning to appear in the South Seas, but which have remained hid beneath the waves till needed, and the fiat should go forth for them to emerge (through the instrumentality of an infinitude of senseless animalculæ), Sahara may be a great land reservation. When, through the "blessing," Ham shall become enlarged, and need more room, oasis shall reach oasis, and the whole shall become a habitable and fruitful land. The special causes which have operated to make those spots fertile, may yet extensively operate to make the whole so. Should the Great Architect extend water-courses beneath the surface of these deserts, as he has through other lands, they would exchange their present barrenness for fertility and beauty.

We indulge high hopes for Africa, hopes founded on the general course of the workings of Divine Providence, hopes in her own resources ; partial developments having already given some just indication of what these resources are. The capabilities of Africa, as already shown, form a ground, too, of much hope, and the promises of God of yet more. The ecstatic vision of the latter-day glory which Isaiah saw, seems quite to confirm the views here advanced. He saw God's ancient Israel restored to the Divine favor, and clothed in more than its former glory. His light had come, and the glory of the Lord had risen upon him. All nations come to his light, and kings to the brightness of his rising. The Gentiles come—they gather themselves together, and form themselves about and mingle with the ancient Zion. And who are these that come? They are called Gentiles, the Kings of Tarshish, they that come from beyond the seas, "the abundance of the sea," the sons of Japheth. But as the prophet becomes clearer and more specific in his vision, there appear in the very foreground, though scarcely discovered before, "multitudes" bringing rich presents, and on whose banners are written the high praises of their God. They come with acceptance on the altar. And as they arrive, a voice is heard to say: "I will glorify the house of my glory." But who are these that meet with such acceptance before the altar? who hold such a position in the coming kingdom? Read the passage, and you will see. "The multitude of camels shall cover thee, the dromedaries of Midian and Ephah; all they from Sheba shall come; they shall bring gold and incense; and they shall show forth the praises of the Lord. All the flocks of Kedar shall be gathered together unto thee; the rams of Nebaioth shall minister unto thee. They shall come up with acceptance upon mine altar, and I will glorify the house of my glory."

We can not mistake who these are, or whence they come. They are from Sheba, Dedan, Midian, Ephah, Kedar, all habitations of the children of Ham. Or we should have known their localities from their camels, their dromedaries, their flocks, their gold and frankincense. Of this numerous division of the grand army which the prophet saw come to pay their honors to the King in Jerusalem, it is said, "they shall show forth the praises of the Lord."

There is hope for Africa. The prodigal shall yet return, clothed, and in his right mind.

CHAPTER VII.

What more Africa has done—Civil governments among African races—
Ethiopia—Nubia—Libya—Egypt—Carthage—Phœnicia—Meroe.

OUR brief sketch of ancient races, and what they have done, would seem incomplete if we did not take a partial survey, at least, of the progress made by this branch of the great family of man in nationality and government. We have seen them pioneers in the different departments of human improvement—in agriculture, commerce, the arts, and in learning; as, also, in war, engineering, and mining. These things all presuppose a corresponding advance in the science of government and jurisprudence. We may, therefore, expect to find well-organized States, laws, and institutions, which protect men in the pursuit of all that goes to honor and bless a nation.

We wish to show, in this chapter, that, in the early periods of the world, different portions of the Hamic race made such advances, in their national capacity, as to afford a very satisfactory evidence of what they are capable of accomplishing in this line of advancement; and a very satisfactory pledge of what we may expect them to accomplish, in the same line, in their future history. What part the negro races acted in the great nationalities, and in the formation and administration of governments which flourished in India, China, Babylonia, and Assyria, and throughout all the countries of Southern Asia, in times reaching back to a period but little subsequent to the Flood, we have not the means to determine. Reliable annals do not reach back to those remote ages ; and we, therefore, must leave the reader of the histories of those ancient nations to form his own judgment of what credit is due to this race for the no mean advancement which they made in the things which go to make great and powerful nations.

The reader must, however, bear in mind that some of the oldest nationalities, of which we have any intimation, existed in India, China, and the southern portions of Asia ; and, also, even up to the present day, we discover, in the old temples of those countries and in the most ancient monuments of art, the unmistakable traces of the race in question. In those ancient temples are still met the images of gods there worshiped, and statues of the men living and acting in those remote ages of the world's history, having the thick lips and crisped hair, indicating that the dominant race was the veritable progeny of Cush— Ethiopians of the genuine stock. And what has remained, unto this day, a perpetual testimony that this same Ethiopian race did once flourish in those countries, in all the glory we have supposed, is, that remnants of the negro race are still found in the mountains, deserts, and islands of India ; in positions and in a condition just such as we should expect the aborigines would be found in centuries after they had been conquered and driven out from their national inheritance. They are, indeed, to this day regarded as the aborigines of that country. This fact, connected with the one alluded to, that the images of their most ancient deities, and the statues of the men who largely figured in that remote age, bore the indubitable marks of the negro physiognomy, more than suggests that nationalities once existed in those countries which were originated and sustained by that race, and which abundantly vindicate their claims to a measure of capability of which we see little or no evidence at the present day, and which goes far to cherish our expectation that that same race shall again display capabilities that shall command the respect of the world.

Or turn we to the Babylonian and the Assyrian empires, and we again meet monuments of the enterprise, and skill, and power of the same Hamic race; and in a form yet more tangible. Nimrod, the founder of Babylon and the great Babylonian empire, was a veritable son of Cush, the father of the great negro family; and Ninus, his son, profane history makes the founder of Nineveh. It was the union of these two kingdoms that formed the great and magnificent empire of Assyria, Babylon still remaining the capital of the united kingdom. It was at this period that Nebuchadnezzar reigned in his great pride and glory; and now it was that the "Assyrian came down, like a wolf, on the fold" of Israel, and laid waste and destroyed kingdoms, not a few. What we claim here is, that whatever of greatness and magnificence there was in proud Babylon—whatever progress was there made in the arts and sciences, in architecture and trade, in the science of war and of government—whatever renowned statesmen and warriors, kings and conquerors, that ancient kingdom produced—we may claim as specimens of men and things which the Hamic race is capable of producing; and we challenge, for the same race, a repetition of all and yet more than they have yet done.

The Assyrian empire was one of the most ancient, as well as the most powerful, in the world. From its foundation, soon after the Deluge, it continued fourteen and a half centuries, or, as some writers have it, more than nineteen centuries. The simple fact of such a prolonged existence is the best voucher we can have that it had, in political wisdom and civil institutions, in men and all needed resources, the elements of a great nation.

But it is quite sufficient that we fix on two or three points as satisfactorily indicating the national progress reached by the Assyrian empire. Capital cities, works of art, armies, conquests, and conquerors afford satisfactory criteria. None but a nation of the vastest resources, of long-practiced skill and wisdom and of well-trained statesmen, of brave soldiers and well-disciplined armies, could build such cities as Babylon and Nineveh, and construct such palaces, temples, aqueducts, dikes, roads, canals, bridges, lakes, and hanging gardens; or make such conquests, or produce such remarkable men. Babylon and Nineveh were two of the most extraordinary cities that ever existed. Nimrod, who was the same as Belus, founded Babylon more than twenty-two centuries (2,204) before Christ, and made it the capital of the first great empire of which we have any record. It stood in the midst of an extensive plain, covered a surface of 225 square miles—was an exact square of 15 miles on each side, or 60 miles in circumference, and was inclosed with a wall 87 feet in thickness, 350 feet high, and was in compass 480 furlongs, or 60 miles—built of large bricks, and cemented with bitumen, which becomes harder than the bricks or stones which it cements. On either side were twenty-five "gates of brass," which were outlets to as many streets which cut each other at right angles, and divided the city into 676 squares, each of which exceeded half a mile on every side, and was surrounded by houses, "all built three or four stories high, and beautified with all manner of ornaments." But we should find no end to speaking of the palaces, temples, hanging gardens, and the public works of every kind, which made this metropolis the "Great Babylon," the glory of kingdoms, the beauty of the Chaldee's excellency.

The Hanging Gardens and the Temple of Belus stand out, even among the wonders of Babylon, as the admiration of the world. We shall speak only of the latter. It stood near the old palace, and was known from all antiquity, and celebrated in every age as the most wonderful structure ever built. A tower of vast dimensions stood in the centre of it. Its foundation was a square of a furlong on each side, or half a mile in compass, and 660 feet, or the eighth of a mile in height, exceeding that of the largest of the Pyramids, which is but 480 feet high. It consisted of eight towers, built one above another, gradually decreasing to the top, and was constructed of bricks and bitumen. The ascent was on the outside, by means of stairs, winding, in a spiral line, eight times round the tower, from the bottom to the top. In the different stories there were arched rooms, supported by pillars ; and on the top was an observatory, supposed to have been used for astronomical purposes. Yet its design and chief use would seem to have been for a

temple. Its riches were immense, consisting of statues, tables, cups, censers, and other sacred vessels, all
of massive gold. Among these was a statue weighing
a thousand Babylonish talents, and 40 feet high. So
immensely rich, indeed, was this temple, that Diodorus, the historian, estimates the whole at 6,300 talents
of gold, or £21,000,000, or $100,000,000. An incred-
ible amount.*

Babylon owed much to the skill and enterprise of
the great Semiramis. She planned and executed
many of its principal edifices. And having finished
these, she made a tour through the different provinces of her empire, and wherever she went she left
monuments of her munificence, in many noble structures, which she caused to be erected either for the
convenience or ornament of her cities. "She was the
best political economist of ancient times, and may
truly be styled the first utilitarian, for she applied
herself to the formation of causeways, the improvement of roads, the cutting through of mountains,
and the filling up of valleys." She constructed aqueducts, quays, and bridges. The one which spanned
the Euphrates, in the heart of the city, was a most
extraordinary structure.

Nor was Nineveh a less remarkable monument of
human skill and power. The design of its founder
was to make Nineveh the "largest and noblest city in
the world, and to put it out of the power of those who
came after him, ever to build, or hope to build such
another." Nor was he deceived, says the historian,
"for never did any city come up to the greatness and

---

* Rollin's "Ancient History," vol. i., p. 137, Cincinnati edition.

magnificence of this." It was 150 furlongs (18¾ miles) in length, and 90 furlongs (11¼ miles) in breadth; an oblong square, with a circumference of 60 miles. It is said in the Prophet Jonah, "Nineveh was an exceeding great city, of three days' journey," that is, its entire circuit. Its walls were 100 feet high, and of sufficient thickness that three chariots might go abreast upon· them. The whole was fortified and adorned with 1,500 towers, 200 feet high. "This was the rejoicing city that dwelt carelessly, that said in her heart: 'I am, and there is none beside me.'"

This same Ninus was as famous in the achievements of war as in the arts of peace. He not only built the greatest cities, and originated the most extraordinary works of art, of all antiquity, and, perhaps, of any age, but he made some of the most remarkable conquests. In seventeen years he conquered all the nations from Egypt to India and Bactria. His army is said to have "consisted of 1,700,000 foot, 200,000 horse, and 16,000 chariots armed with scythes." After he had made the conquests alluded to, he returned to Babylon, and with the famous Semiramis, now his newly married queen, he gave himself anew to every thing which could strengthen and adorn his empire. A single allusion of Alexander the Great, in a speech to his army, shows the estimate in which the prowess, enterprise, and skill of that remarkable woman were held, at that remote period. In alluding to her he exclaims: "How many nations did she conquer! How many cities were built by her! What magnificent and stupendous works did she finish! How shameful is it that I should not yet have attained to so high a pitch of glory!"

But we have more direct and undoubted illustration of what the Hamic race have done; and not the race of Ham in general, but the descendants of Cush, the veritable negro race. The state or empire, which may claim a very early, if not the earliest, existence in Africa, and, perhaps, the earliest after the Deluge, is Ethiopia. And whatever claims the Shemic race may make, in later centuries, to Assyria, whose founders and early rulers and people were of the race now proscribed, no such claims were ever set up in respect to the Ethiopians. They were negroes, the genuine Cushites. In what we say here, we shall not be careful to distinguish between the different portions of Eastern Africa, known as Ethiopia, Abyssinia, Nubia, Meroe, or Sennaar. They were occupied by essentially the same people, known as Ethiopians, Cushites, or negroes. We must not here ignore the fact, that the ancients were accustomed to apply the term Ethiopian to the black inhabitants of India, and to the natives of interior Africa. The Ethiopians proper —the black woolly-haired race; whose home was to the south of Egypt—figure in ancient history as a nation great and powerful in arts, in commerce, and in arms.

It has been but too common to make Egypt the "cradle of civilization," of the arts and sciences, and whatever goes to make a nation great and powerful. But more modern researches tend to award the palm to Ethiopia. So reliable a historian as Niebuhr gives it as his opinion, that the hieroglyphic writing, and "all we afterward find as Egyptian civilization," originated with the Ethiopians. Be that as it may, the fact remains, "that, within the tropics, south of Egypt, and stretching from the Red Sea westward, toward the Desert, in what is now the region of Nubia, Sennaar, Kordofan, there was, for centuries, a civilized state of native Ethiopians, Cushites, the direct descendants of Ham."

We admire, without exhaustion, the ruins of cities, temples, obelisks, pyramids, and all the various monuments of arts and science, and military skill, which we meet in Egypt, and do not hesitate to award a very high state of civilization to the descendants of Mizraim, the Egyptian branch of the family of Ham; and we do not feel, when on the historic ground of Egypt, that we need any stronger vouchers of the capabilities of that race to reach and maintain themselves in as high a level of human elevation as any other race. Nor do we hesitate to accord to Egypt all the honor claimed for her, of being the " cradle " of learning, of civilization, and of progress in general, to Europe, as she had been to Carthage and Phœnicia. She gave them the alphabet, the numerical figures, a knowledge of the arts and sciences. No one might pass for a philosopher, or a man of learning or letters, who ha not " gone down to Egypt," and conversed with he learned men, and consulted her libraries, and studied in her academies. There was no other nation existing, where the plastic hand of Providence could moul into an instrument for his use a Joseph, or fit for th most extraordinary work ever committed to a singl man his leader, Moses, or educate his chosen Israe for the glorious career which awaited them.

But Egypt had her cradle. Her architecture ha its types in the buildings of Nubia and Abyssinia. " The land of the Pharaohs was indebted to the Ethiopians for the rudiments, and, perhaps, even for the finished patterns, of architectural skill." Karnac, Luxor, and Medinet Abu are modern structures compared with those discovered above the Cataracts. Like the current of the Nile, which, in its overflow, enriches the whole valley below, the descending civilization of Ethiopia built Memphis, and the hundred-gated Thebes, and laid broad the foundation of Egypt's greatness.

Nor would our estimate of Ethiopia's early advancement be lessened, if we consider her military prowess. It is said, she, at one period, extended her conquests even to the Pillars of Hercules, which supposed the subjection of all Western Asia, the south of Europe, and the north of Africa. We meet in the sacred records two notices, in particular, of Ethiopian armies, which give an idea of the military condition of that people. Zerah, the Ethiopian, comes out against Asa, King of Judah, with an army of a "thousand thousand" (a million) of men. Again: Sennacherib was coming up against Israel in great pride and confidence of victory, but no sooner does he hear that Tirhakah, King of Ethiopia, was coming up to meet him, than he precipitately retreated.

But we should quite overlook a main feature of Ethiopia's early greatness, if we did not allude to the moral character of that people. We shall in this feature discover that the singular religious instinct, or peculiar readiness and aptitude, of the negro race to contract and cultivate a religious character, is not a feature peculiar to the present generation of that people. It was a characteristic of the same people 4,000 years ago. They are called in the ancient records,

6

"the blameless Ethiopians," whom Jupiter and all the gods went to visit. Others term them the "most just of men"—"were distinguished among mankind for their "equity, sagacity, and general probity."

It will suffice to transcribe here a single paragraph from Heeren's "Historical Researches:" "Except the Egyptians," he says, "there is no aboriginal people of Africa with so many claims upon our attention as the Ethiopians; from the remotest times to the present, one of the most celebrated, and yet the most mysterious, of nations. In the earliest traditions of nearly all the most civilized nations of antiquity the name of this distant people is found. The annals of the Egyptian priests were full of them; the nations of inner Asia, on the Euphrates and the Tigris, have interwoven the fictions of Ethiopia with their own traditions of the conquests and wars of their heroes, and, at a period equally remote, they glimmer in Greek mythology. When the Ethiopians scarcely knew Italy and Sicily by name, they were themselves celebrated as the remotest nation, the most just of men, the favorites of the gods. The lofty inhabitants of Olympus journey to them, and take part in their feasts; their sacrifices are the most agreeable of all that mortals can offer. And when the faint gleam of tradition and fable give way to the clear light of history, the lustre of the Ethiopians is not diminished. They still continue the object of curiosity and admiration, and the pen of the cautious, clear-sighted historian often places them in the highest rank of knowledge and civilization."

The ancient and celebrated city and State of Meroe, Herodotus says, was a community of negroes, who made a most laudable progress in social, civil, and intellectual cultivation. "They had a fixed constitution, a government, laws, and religion." They sent out their colonies, one of which was none other than that of the celebrated Thebes in Egypt. Meroe was the centre of the great caravan trade between Ethiopia, Egypt, Arabia, Northern Africa, and India.

And with this ancient State is associated one of the most remarkable events of the reign of the wise son of David. The famous Queen of Sheba (the South) is believed to have been the Queen of Meroe. She was an Ethiopian princess, highly educated, thoughtful, reflecting, as appears from the fact that she came to "prove Solomon with hard questions." She was the ruler of a highly civilized and mighty kingdom, as would seem to be indicated by her large retinue, and the rich and abundant presents which she brought. She came "with a very great company, and camels that bore spices and gold in abundance, and precious stones." She had heard of the wisdom of Solomon, how he was the wisest of mortals; and she had come to put his wisdom to the test. And she had heard, too, of the magnificence of his court and the glory of his throne; yet, conscious of her own regal greatness, she did not shrink from a comparison with "Solomon in all his glory." And Solomon did her the greatest possible honor. "He told her all her questions, and there was nothing which he told her not."

To say nothing of the profuse and rich presents which the queen brought to Solomon—gold and precious stones, spices and olive-trees (" and there were none such seen before in the land of Judah"), Solomon gave to her, "all her desire, whatever she asked," and extended to her the most unrestricted confidence and honor. He received her, as she might claim to be—the representative of the only then existing nation that could compare favorably with the kingdom of Israel, when, under the reign of Solomon, it was at the zenith of its glory.

But it is not less to our purpose, and a matter of vastly higher interest, to know that Solomon's external greatness, wisdom, and glory, though duly admired and wondered at, as far exceeding all her expectations, for she said the half had not been told her, yet these things did not constitute the chief, the moving, object of her long and tedious journey. She had heard of the "fame of Solomon concerning the name of the Lord." Her visit was rather of a religious character. She had heard of Solomon's knowledge in the truth and precepts of religion; of his piety and zeal in the worship of Jehovah; and she came to seek the light, and to propose questions which had perplexed her mind on those important subjects. Under the influence of those peculiar religious instincts, which I have said characterizes the Ethiopian more than any other race, she sought, by this journey, to be instructed in the way of the Lord more perfectly. And more especially did she realize this end of her undertaking. For she left her native land a pagan; she returned a believer in, if not a hearty worshiper of, the true God. She admired Solomon's wisdom, and was amazed at the "house he had built—at the meat of his table, and the sitting of his servants, and the attendance of his ministers, and their apparel," but it was the good hand of the Lord, in all these things, that she admired more. It was Solomon's God—the truth and worship of the God of Israel—that she came to inquire after. Here she discovered the source of all Solomon's prosperity. The truth taught this African princess, now at Jerusalem, was the same as was recently taught an African prince from the throne of Great Britain. The prince sent to ask Queen Victoria to tell him what was the source of the prosperity of the British Empire—what had made her so great and powerful a nation? She sent him a copy of the Bible, with a message, that he would find it all in that book.

The Queen of the South discovered whence the glory of Solomon. Hence she said: "Blessed be the Lord God that delighteth in thee, to set thee on his throne, to be king for the Lord thy God, because thy God loved Israel, to establish them forever, therefore made he thee king over them to do judgment and justice." And well did she say: "Happy are thy men, and happy are these thy servants who stand continually before thee, and that hear thy wisdom." She rejoiced in that which she had found. She chose the God of Israel to be her God; and henceforth she and her people adopted the religion of Judah. And from this time onward, through all their generations, the God of Israel has been worshiped, with greater or less purity, in the land of this noble queen.

And may we not accept the visit of this illustrious woman as a delightful presage of the final restoration to the favor of God, and of the ingathering into the fold of the Great Shepherd of the long outcast children of Cush. In the person of her renowned queen,

Ethiopia did, at a period when the ancient church was at the achme of her glory, "stretch out her hand unto God." And that truly illustrious prince and son of the ancient church, and type of Christ, "David's wiser son," welcomed the "black but comely" stranger into the bosom of the ancient Zion. May we not accept this as the promise that all "Ethiopia shall soon"—shall readily, shall most gladly—"stretch out her hands unto God," that " all they from Sheba shall come; they shall bring gold and incense; and they shall show forth the praises of the Lord."

Nor are we without a parallel example in the reign of a subsequent queen of that same country. What the Queen of Sheba did in person, Queen Candace did through her lord treasurer, who, already a proselyte to the Jewish religion, went up to Jerusalem, a little after the time of the crucifixion, perhaps at Pentecost, to worship. Perchance, he had heard of Christ, and would go and see him of whom Moses and the prophets did speak. On his homeward journey he gave himself to the study of the prophecies, to see whether these things were so. Philip, at this point, met him, and taught him the way more perfectly. How readily did he receive the truth, yield assent, and accept Christ as his Saviour! He was immediately baptized, and goes on his way rejoicing—returns to his royal mistress, and to the people of his own land and color, and tells them what the Lord hath done for his soul. Ethiopia receives the Christian faith; and, though its light has now for centuries burned but dimly, it has never been extinguished. Thus, while the religion of Judah was yet at its zenith, were the sable sons of Cush made partakers of its healing waters; and while

Christianity was yet in its early dawn, did its healing beams illumine the mountains of distant Ethiopia. And shall we not hail this, as a joyful omen of that approaching day when "princes shall come out of Egypt," and Ethiopia shall be gathered into the fold.

But let us go down into Egypt, and see what we may find there to confirm our convictions of the early and decided progress of the Hamic race. The Egyptians were the descendants of Mizraim, the second son of Ham. In going down to Egypt, we do but follow the tide, if not of emigration of a portion of the race, yet the tide of civilization and human progress.

In awarding to Ethiopia the honor of being the pioneer nation in human advancement, we do not necessarily award to her the honor of having finally made the greatest advancement. She may have been the legitimate mother; yet, the daughter, cherished by such maternal care, favored by such maternal example, sent forth into the world with such a dowry—indeed, with the skill and experience, and equipped with the resources and appliances for social, moral, and national progress, which such a nation as Ethiopia, in the day of her glory, could furnish, such a daughter, we should confidently expect, would outstrip her renowned mother. It is but meet that she should do so. Hence we go to Egypt, expecting to find the still remaining monuments of her glory more gorgeous—the lady of the Nile more richly adorned—more advanced in learning, science, art, and whatever contributes to human progress. We have seen what Thebes was—how human power and skill have never exceeded the mighty strides she took, in the erection of temples, obelisks, pyramids, the Labyrinth, and

catacombs of this very ancient city. It will quite suffice for the present to say, that Ethiopia reproduced
herself in Egypt, in dimensions more gigantic, in
works more grand and imposing, in proportions more
thoroughly developed, and in a national influence
much more extended and lasting. In all important
indications and elements of human progress—in armies, conquests, national grandeur, architecture, learning, and science, the Egyptians reached a point of elevation which abundantly vindicates their claims to a
high order of capacity for social and national advancement, and to a high order, too, of intellectual
and moral culture.

Such claims are the more triumphantly vindicated
from the fact, that Egypt became the resort of the
learned from all other nations. No man in Europe or
Asia, might expect his pretense to scholarship to be
allowed if he had not been down to Egypt, and there
drawn wisdom from the fountain in the land of the
Pharaohs. ·

But we do not forget that Egypt possessed conspicuous advantages over Ethiopia, inasmuch as her
somewhat more recent expansion into life, and her
more intimate connection with the Israelitish nation,
and other historic nations, especially with Phœnicia,
Carthage, Greece, and Rome, gave her notoriety—
made her known in the world, and herself the subject of history, which her elder sister never enjoyed.
We can do no more than to ask the reader to take
Egypt as she was, with all that was realized in her as
a nation, whether in respect to government, social refinement, civilization, or moral, and intellectual advancement—or in any thing or every thing which goes

to aggrandize a nation—take the Egypt that was, as a specimen of what this branch of the family of Ham is capable of doing. And we believe what has been, may, under equally auspicious circumstances, be done by the same race again.

It does not seem needful to enter into any details of Egyptian history, in order to establish our point. It is enough to present that well-known and justly celebrated nation as a whole, and claim it as a standing monument to the enterprise, industry, skill, science, and wealth of its African builders and proprietors. None but men—full-grown men—wise, industrious, energetic, persevering men—men standing in the full consciousness and dignity of a well-developed manhood—none but such men could have raised, maintained, and commanded such armies, achieved such victories, and extended their conquests to the ends of the earth. And the moment we allow the eye to pass over their architectural monuments, we are amazed at these lasting testimonials of that wonderful people. Centuries pass by—empires rise, and flourish, and pass away—a new world emerges into being, as if it rose from the ocean bed, and new states are formed and expand into being, and the " old world," whose nations have been born and attained their manhood, and reached the decrepitude of age, if not passed away—since these monuments of Egyptian greatness were reared, and yet, many of them remain as unscathed by decay as if they were but the work of yesterday. The mouldering hand of time passes them by untouched, as if they, like the everlasting hills, belonged to the things which can not be moved.

6*

And all this permanence and national durability, and grandeur of achievement in all things that go to constitute a great nation, imply the existence of a government, which, for stability, strength, and political wisdom, is itself worthy of the admiration we so readily accord to the wonderful works which were achieved under the auspices of such a government. What, in point of civilization and general advancement, Ethiopia was to Egypt, Egypt, in her turn, became to Western Asia, to Northern Africa, and to Europe. Her government was distinguished for its humane and just laws. Indeed, the ancient historian (Rollin) says: "The Egyptians were the first people who rightly understood the rules of government."

At this late day we can but inadequately estimate the influence on the different nations of the world, which this more enlightened and advanced people must have had. One of their kings (Osiris) is described as the "inventor of the arts, and the civilizer of a great part of the world." He raised a prodigious army, and overran Ethiopia, Arabia, and a great part of India; appeared in all the nations of Asia, and, crossing the Hellespont, continued his progress through the greater part of Europe. This extraordinary man disseminated the arts, built cities, and was universally revered as a god. In a most important sense, Egypt was the mother of us all. God sent his chosen people to be trained for their extraordinary mission in Egypt; and when disciplined and fitted for the great work before them, he called them forth, gave them enlargement, and established them in the high places of the earth, and used them for many generations as the almoners of Heaven's beneficence to man, and his chosen instrumentality for the moral renovation of the world. The genius of human improvement went out from Egypt, laden with rich benefits from the maternal fountain, and tarried not till he had made the circuit of the nations.

And what is in delightful harmony with what we have said, and worthy our serious regard, Christianity, while yet in its germ in the person of the infant Saviour, "came up out of Egypt." The young child and his mother were there until the death of Herod, that it might be fulfilled which was spoken of the Lord by the prophet, saying: "Out of Egypt have I called my Son."

But let us pass on to the other two great prominent branches of the family of Ham, the Phœnicians and Carthaginians. We linger no longer in Egypt, because she has a well-known history—a ready voucher of all her past greatness.

We shall first speak of the Phœnicians, called, in the Scriptures, Canaanites, and other strong nations which Joshua overcame and destroyed, when he took possession of Palestine. There were different branches of the same great family. Ham was their progenitor. There were at one time, and, it would seem, had been for a long period of time, great and powerful nations. They early lost a knowledge of the true God—grew old and strong in their rebellion against Heaven, till the long-suffering of God with them was exhausted, and he gave them over to an accomplished and final destruction. The malediction of Heaven rested on them: "Cursed be Canaan, a servant of servants shall he be unto his brethren." The pos-

terity of Canaan were great and strong, and prosper-
ed for a time. But being, from the first, aliens from
God and his covenant, and strangers to the promises, they waxed worse and worse in their departure
from God, filling up the measure of their iniquity, till
God gave them up to the unconditional destruction of
their enemies. The hosts of Joshua were commissioned to exterminate them from the face of the earth.
And here the "curse" was consummated.

We turn rather to Phœnicia, in her better days,
when she was, in many respects, an illustrious example to sustain our position. We descend, again, with
the current of human improvement, from the Nile to
the eastern shore of the Mediterranean Sea. We do
not know when to date the origin of this ancient nation. It dates to a period beyond which the light of
history reaches. Before Moses penned the first record of sacred history—before Abraham lived, Phœnicia was a great and powerful kingdom. Two thousand years before Christ, they were found among the
great nations of the earth. They made the most stubborn resistance, and were the last to be driven out by
the Israelitish invaders. And centuries after the conquest by Joshua, it is recorded that the "Canaanites
would dwell in the land." When the "children of
Israel had waxen strong they put the Canaanites to
tribute, but did not utterly drive them out."

A single declaration of Moses distinctly indicates
the advanced condition of this people. He informs
the Hebrews, that they should find, "great and
goodly cities, and houses full of all good things, wells,
vineyards, and olive-trees."

It does not appear that the commission to Israel to

exterminate the Canaanites included all its nations. Different branches, as the Hittites, the Hivites, the Jebusites, etc., were doomed, as the unworthy occupants of the land God had given to his chosen seed, and were, by Divine command, to be driven out and exterminated. Tyre, the magnificent capital of that great nation, was not included in the immediate execution of the Divine malediction. We find Tyre flourishing in great glory in the days of Solomon, and thenceonward to its destruction by Nebuchadnezzar. It had already existed more than fifteen centuries. Again it reappeared·under the name of New Tyre, and flourishes for nearly two and a half centuries more.

And here we would not overlook the very significant fact, that, in the most prosperous days of the Hebrew Commonwealth, there existed a most interesting alliance between Solomon and the King of Tyre. By a very liberal contribution of men and materials Hiram, King of Tyre, participated largely in the erection of the Temple on Mount Zion. May we not receive this, again, as another singular instance of connection and co-operation between the chosen seed and the race of which we speak, which betokens the yet returning favor of God upon those whom he has left as outcasts.

As we said of Egypt so we may say of Phœnicia, simply the duration of such a state for nearly 2,000 years indicates that it possessed elements of greatness and durability, which rank it among the most civilized nations of antiquity. Its government, laws, institutions, political wisdom, wealth, and learning could have been of no mean order. And must we not suppose that, at least, in its earlier periods, it must have contained the salt of a much higher order of morality and religion than characterized its later periods? Else, would such a body politic been preserved?

Again: the world is indebted to the Phœnicians for some of the most useful inventions. Among others, we may name the art of writing, the manufacture of glass, and the art of navigation. It is believed that the alphabet was received from Egypt, yet the art of writing is an invention accredited to the Phœnicians. And the most ancient author (if we except Moses) was a Phœnician. Sanchoniathon, a name not to be admired, either for its euphony, or ease of utterance, is believed to have been cotemporary with Joshua, who died 1427 B. C. Historical fragments of. this very early writer, translated from the Phœnician by Eusebius, are said to remain to this day. These go to show that alphabetical writing was in use among the Phœnicians ages before the Greeks had the slightest acquaintance with it.

We are hence left to infer, not so much from the details of existing history, as from certain data in the shape of isolated facts, what was the real points of advancement reached by this branch of the family of Ham? Commerce, colonies, wars and conquests, and the extent, beauty, and grandeur of their capital city, and the great perfection they reached in the working of metals and precious stones afford other data by which to judge of the social and civil advancement of a people.

The invention of the art of navigation was with them something more than an abstract theory. The

Phœnicians were, properly, the first navigators—the first great commercial people of which we have any acquaintance. They not only conducted an extensive and lucrative trade, on both sides of the Mediterranean, in Asia, Africa, and Europe, but they pushed their commerce through the Pillars of Hercules, formed depots of trade in Spain, and along the western coast of Africa. And tradition gives them the credit of having crossed the Atlantic, and formed settlements, and conducted commerce among the "Isles" of the west, long before Columbus rediscovered this western world. But the trade which this people carried on, at this early day, with distant India, gives us a yet higher idea of their thrift and enterprise. They were, probably, the first who imported to the Mediterranean, and thence to Europe, the commodities of India. Having secured commodious ports on the eastern side of the Arabian Gulf, from which they had regular intercourse with India, from thence their India merchandise was conveyed to the nearest port on the Mediterranean, and thence reshipped to Tyre.

As is usual in the progress of a great and enterprising people, colonies followed close in the wake of commerce. Among their first settlements were those of Cyprus and Rhodes. They then passed into Greece, Sicily, and Sardinia, and thence into the southern parts of Spain and Portugal. Cadiz remains as a monument of the commercial enterprise of this people. The colonies which did them the greatest honor, and which claim our more particular attention, were those on the northern coast of Africa. Carthage was the most prominent of them. We shall speak of this, again, as the next great development of the Hamic family.

Cadmus, also, led a colony of Phœnicians into Greece, and built Thebes in Bœotia, one of the most celebrated cities of Greece; the birthplace of Pindar, Epaminondas, and Pelopidas. He took with him the alphabet, and a knowledge of those things which had made his own nation great and powerful.

But Tyre, for so long the capital of this great Canaanitish nation, the "Queen of Cities, the Queen of the Sea," affords a yet more direct proof of her national greatness. We have in the "sure word of prophecy" (Ezekiel xxvii.), a most glowing description of this remarkable city. In her pride, she said: "I am of perfect beauty." She is called the "crowning city," "whose merchants are princes, whose traffickers are the honorable of the earth." Every thing for use, or ornament, or luxury, were found in her market. And every known nation on the earth is mentioned as her merchants or "traffickers." From the extreme parts of India, Persia, and Arabia, from Ethiopia and Egypt, on the south, to Scythia on the north, all nations contributed to the increase of her power, splendor, and wealth. She sat as queen, "adorned with a diadem; whose correspondents were illustrious princes; whose rich traders dispute for superiority with kings; who sees every maritime power either as her ally or her dependent; and who made herself necessary or formidable to all nations."

"The ships of Tarshish did sing of thee in thy market, and thou wast replenished and made very glorious in the midst of the seas. Thy riches and thy fairs, thy merchandise, thy mariners, and thy pilots, thy caulkers, and the occupiers of thy merchandise, and all thy men of war that are in thee, and in all thy company which is in the midst of thee"—such riches, such resources, should all "fall into the midst of the seas in the day of her ruin." And great should be her fall. All the kings of the earth should mourn because of her. "Her favored situation; the extent and convenience of her ports; the character of her inhabitants, who were, not only industrious, laborious, and patient, but extremely courteous to strangers, invited thither merchants from all parts of the known world; so that it might be considered, not so much a city belonging to any particular nation, as the common city of all nations, and the centre of their commerce."

But we must advance yet another step. Westward the sceptre of empire now moves. Ethiopia had reproduced herself in Egypt; Egypt, in Phœnicia; and now the latter reappears, in a new edition, amended and enlarged, in Carthage.

Carthage was a Tyrian colony, founded on the northern coast of Africa, by Elisa, a Tyrian princess, better known by the name of Dido. Other Phœnician colonies had been planted at Utica, Leptis, Hippo, and Adramentum. Carthage was the chief. The others, though independent States, were in alliance with Carthage as one confederacy. Carthage, the daughter of Tyre, succeeded to a large portion of the trade originally possessed by the mother State. Nor did this long satisfy her increasing power and unbounded ambition. Not satisfied with her trade with India, Ethiopia, and Egypt, on the east, and with the countries which border on the Mediterranean Sea on the north, she pushed her trade into the interior of Africa, civilizing the barbarous tribes wherever she went; occupied Spain and Gaul; thence northward to the Isle of Great Britain, on whose southern coast she formed settlements; and, as some say, advanced to the Baltic, and, perhaps, to Scandinavia, and formed colonies along the western coasts of Spain and Portugal. While, southward, by the Atlantic, she carried her commerce along the western coast of Africa, at least, as far as the Gambia. And yet others maintain that she crossed the Atlantic to America, and visited the shores of the new world.

But we do not forget that war is the entering wedge of commerce. To say that a nation is mighty in commerce, is to say she is, or has been, mighty in war. The sword had prepared the way before her. So it was with Carthage. Her commerce did but follow her conquests. Yet, we need not rehearse the annals of her wars. Her prowess in arms, her naval and military resources, her generals, as they are seen in the conduct of a single war, quite serve to establish our position, as to the power and greatness of that African kingdom. We refer to her wars with Rome. In wealth, power, learning, and science—in commerce and arms—she was for a long time the superior of Rome. And when, for another period, perhaps as long, she stood as the formidable rival of Rome. A braver general than Hannibal never led an army. And Rome, in the glory of her power, never met so formidable a foe as Carthage.

But, what is more to our purpose still, Carthage was a republic. The highest office in the Commonwealth was that of the *suffetes,* called kings, but corresponding to the consuls of Rome, or the judges of the Hebrews. These were elected by the people; and they presided in the Senate. Carthage had her laws, her institutions, her judicatories and judges, all framed in accordance with her character as a republic.

Did we need further illustrations of what the descendants of Ham have done, in maintaining, for a long series of years, great national power and grandeur, as a pledge of what they might do again, we might find it among the Philistines, and other once prominent nations, which play for a long time no insignificant part in the great drama of human affairs. But we would rather adduce, though we can no more than name, the Moors and Saracens as yet more illustrious examples. The Saracenic empire, which extended from the Atlantic to India, and embraced a broad belt half round the globe, was, in its origin and animus, Arabian, the original inhabitants were the descendants of Ham; the more recent race were half-blood, the descendants of Ishmael. It was one of the most magnificent empires that ever existed. In a single century it extended its sceptre over Tartary, India, Persia, and over all the countries thence to the Atlantic. Damascus, Alexandria, and Constantinople fell before it. It quite overran Africa, and established a strong nationality in Spain.

While the western world was buried in the darkest ignorance, the Moors of Spain, "lived in the enjoyment of all those arts which beautify and polish society. Amid a constant succession of wars, they cast a new lustre on Spanish history," through the arts of peace. Schools were founded and numerous public libraries invited the curiosity of the studious. Letters were patronized—geometry, astronomy, and physics were studied—" Cordova became the centre of politeness, taste, and genius." During two centuries their court continued to be the resort "of the professors of all polite arts, and such as valued themselves upon their military and knightly accomplishments." The Mosque of Cordova vied, in size, beauty, and grandeur, with those of Damascus and Jerusalem. And the world-renowned Palace of Alhambra stands, in the grandeur of its ruins, a lasting memorial to the wealth, taste, and general advancement of its African authors.

N. ORR—CO. Sc.

CHAPTER VIII.

Africa as she is—Natural advantages and commercial facilities—Cotton—
Another index of hope.

WE have spoken of the negro as a primitive race of man, widely extending its vast population, and being the representative of learning, civilization, the arts, and government over all the southern countries of Asia, and the eastern and northern parts of Africa. And we are able to trace the footprints of the offspring of Ham along the southern coasts of Europe, and in Central America. They were evidently a highly civilized people at a very early period after the Deluge. The oldest specimens of architecture, the excavated temples of India, paintings, temples, ornaments of various sorts, the workmanship of that ancient race, exhibit a surprisingly high state of civilization. Looking into Egypt, we meet, in her earliest monuments of art, the same indications of advancement, and, what is more, we discover evident traces of the same people.

And it is an interesting fact (if, as stated, it be a fact), that there is no evidence in all these relics that idolatry and polytheism were known till the age of the Pharaohs. This seems to indicate that the primitive condition of man was, not only civilized, but that men, in those remote ages, had not yet forsaken the true God. The patriarchal religion then prevailed, and men, according to the light that shone in those early ages, worshiped God in spirit and in truth. Should further revelations in the undeveloped history of those ancient races confirm our half-formed conviction, that negro races were in the early ages of the world not without the knowledge and practice of the true religion, it would but well accord with what we know to be still the peculiar religious susceptibilities of those races at the present day; and, at the same time, encourage our hopes of their future moral improvement. Morally, as well as physically, Africa and her races may be again what she once was, and much more.

Having spoken of Africa as she was, I come now to speak of her as she is.

It is, however, scarcely more than a single aspect of Africa as she is that I shall touch upon in the present chapter. I mean the natural capabilities and resources of that continent, and its commercial advantages. I think I shall be able to make it appear that Africa, even in her present neglected condition, gives indications of possessing resources which are both fitted and destined to answer purposes vastly more noble than have yet been realized there.

Researches in Africa have made us but partially acquainted with her vast interior. Our acquaintance is very much confined to the sea coast, and we are by no means sure that we are able, from such an acquaintance, to form any thing like a just appreciation of the natural resources of that great continent. Our acquaintance with the interior, so far as it goes, is extremely favorable. The climate, soil, productions, mineral and animal wealth, are spoken of in the most glowing terms. We are encouraged to look into the interior of Africa for some of the finest countries in the world. We can not believe that such countries will be allowed always to lie desolate; but rather that the great Ruler of nations has purposes yet to answer in Africa, quite commensurate with the gigantic resources of the land.

A recent missionary traveler (and these are the best travelers in the world from whom to get correct and useful information), who penetrated some 250 miles into the interior, from Liberia, passing through some thirty villages of the Goulahs, Deys, Queahs, and Condoes, speaks of the country in the following terms:

"Such a country as we passed through, in that missionary tour, I have not seen surpassed in either of the West India Islands, which I have visited from Trinidad to Tortola, and the Virgin Islands. It is an elevated, mountainous country. Ranges of mountains, running most generally parallel with the line of coast, from northwest to southeast, rise up before the delighted eye of the traveler, convincing him that he is no longer in the land of burning sands and deleterious swamps, such as are encountered in proximity with the shores, but in quite another region. And such are the gradual undulations of its surface as would greatly facilitate the objects of agriculture. There are few, if any, very steep acclivities; nothing like the bold, precipitous mountains of our Eastern States. Beautiful and extensive valleys lie at the base of these mountains, which gently slope down to the level country lying between them.

"It is a well-watered country. During the eight

hours' travel which we were frequently obliged to perform in a day, we never walked more than two hours, or two and a half at a time, without coming to some beautiful streams of cool and very pure water, either as tributary of the St. Paul, or some other of the many smaller rivers which intersect that African Canaan. And here it may be proper to add, that my attention was directed to an examination of the adaptation of these streams to the purposes of machinery, sites for mills, etc., and I hesitate not to affirm, that, within the Goulah Country especially, any number of the most eligible situations may be found, where, at any time during the year, good water-power may be obtained for any of the purposes which an enterprising community, agriculturists and mechanics, may require. My journey was performed in the very middle of the dry season, and yet we found plenty of water in the different streams.

"It is well timbered. Through an extensive forest of miles in extent which lay on our return route, I was so struck with the gigantic trees, of immense height, which reared their towering heads, and united their luxuriant foliage in forming above us one dense and rich canopy, that I called the attention of the colored ministers of the Liberia Annual Methodist Conference, who accompanied me, to this evidence of the richness of the country, which God had given to the Africans, and to which their exiled brethren were invited by so many powerful considerations. I measured several trees, and my journal, kept at the time with scrupulous exactness, records 23, 24, 25 feet as the circumference of many of them within 6 feet of the ground. And the variety and superior quality of the wood found in these forests, and, indeed, all along the borders and around the settlement of Liberia, from Grand Cape Mount to Cape Palmas, can not be excelled anywhere within the torrid zone. From a species of poplar, soft, and adapted to all purposes for which the white pine is used in America, up to the teak, a variety of mahogany, a beautiful species of hickory, very abundant at Cape Palmas, the iron wood, the brimstone, susceptible of polish for furniture, of surpasing beauty, and many others, an almost endless supply may be found.

"It is an exceedingly fertile soil. The immense undergrowth of shrub and vine, interwoven around the giants of the forest, so thick, so impenetrable, is the best proof of this. The grains, roots, fruits, and vines of the tropics all concentrate here, and may be raised with an ease, rapidity of growth, and abundance, almost incredible. I have stood erect under the branches of a cotton-tree, in a Goulah village, as they spread forth from the main trunk, laden with bolls, and supported by forked sticks to prevent their being broken down by their own weight, and found, on measuring, that the tree covered a space of 10-feet in diameter. On examining the staple, as the ripened bolls burst into maturity, it was found as good, and equal, in the fineness of its fibre, to the cotton of any country."

Such is the testimony which has always been given of the natural resources of the interior of Africa. All ancient accounts of this continent abundantly confirm this assertion.

Bating her great deserts, no country in the world is capable of sustaining so great a population to the

square mile. The strength of her soil is amazing.
No soil is capable of such gigantic productions. We
can scarcely credit the account of travelers when they
come to speak of the luxuriant growths of an African
soil. They seem to be romancing. Yet, the accounts
are from such men, and so harmonize, that we are
compelled to give them credit. The Rev. Mr. Thompson, of the Mendi Mission, says: "A general feature
of the soil is its great fertility. In the wild state, the
land is covered, either with an almost impenetrable
'bush,' or grass, which speaks defiance to the traveler.
No one who has not seen an African bush, or forest,
can form an idea of its weight, size, density, and impenetrableness. Besides a forest of trees, timber,
from 1 foot up to 30 feet in diameter, a complete jungle of underbrush, vines and thorns, and grass, fill up
beneath, so that to walk or press your way through it
is impossible, till a road is cut. The prairies are covered with grass, as thick as it can stand, from one
fourth to an inch in diameter, and from 12 to 20 feet
high. You may think I exaggerate, but I have seen
and walked through, or rather on, such grass; for a
path is made by breaking it down. I myself measured a tree 108 feet in circumference." Mr. Thompson
speaks, too, of the great strength of the soil, the
amazing rapidity of vegetation, and the astonishing
luxuriance of vegetable productions, and the great variety of the soil, clayey, sandy, mixture of clay and
sand, loamy, rocky, alluvial.

Africa has, of course, a great variety of climate,
and productions as varied as soil and climate. The
northern portions are temperate, the centre lies in the
torrid zone, and, consequently, produces the tropical

fruits, vegetables, grains, gums, minerals, metals, and animals in great abundance. Corn, wheat, sweet potatoes, oranges, pine-apples, plantain, bananas, and many other kinds of fruit and berries; peanuts, ginger, arrow-root, tobacco, castor-oil bean, opium, indigo, bread-fruit, monkey apple, etc., grow abundantly, and without much culture, except to keep down the grass. Then there are the cassada, three kinds of yam, three kinds of cocoa (one hill of which sometimes fills a half bushel), tomatoes, ground cherry, lima beans, which live and bear from year to year, egg-plant, varieties of pepper, okra, kola, limes, etc., with many others.

It has been proved, says another writer, that two crops of corn, sweet potatoes, and several other vegitables, can be and are raised in a year. They yield a larger crop than the best soils in America. One acre of rich land, well tilled, says Gov. Ashman, will produce $300 worth of indigo; half an acre may be made to grow half a ton of arrow-root; four acres laid out in coffee plants, will, after the third year, produce a clear income of two or three hundred dollars; half an acre of cotton-trees, yielding cotton of an equal, if not of superior, length and strength of staple and fineness and color to fair "Orleans," will clothe a whole family; and one acre of canes will make the same number independent of all the world for sugar. The dyes, in particular, are found to resist both acids and light, properties which no other dyes we know of possess.

Yet another writer says: "Africa possesses, almost universally, a soil which knows no exhaustion." Mungo Park speaks of the country as "abundantly gifted and favored by nature." Evidently nothing is needed but skill and industry, to enable Africa to support a larger population, on the same territory, than any other country. With but a small portion of her soil under cultivation, Africa supports some 150,000,000 of people. "Millions of acres lie uncultivated." When these boundless wastes shall be brought under cultivation (all fertile as the richest garden) what a vast population may be sustained! "Four acres of land will maintain a family of six persons." But the productions of the soil are but a part of the means of sustenance in that land. "Their rivers," says a traveler, "abound in·fish. Their sheep and goats are fine and fat. They have plenty of fowl, also wild hogs, wild ducks, and geese. In the Sherbro Country there is plenty of fish and oysters." "The Gold Coast," says another, "and all tropical Africa, is capable of affording incalculable advantages, if the inhabitants can be incited to industry. It is enriched beyond the credibility of those unacquainted with it. Its hills are stored with various metals and minerals, and its valleys are blessed with a fertility scarcely to be exceeded by any country under the same latitude." "It is very remarkable, that tropical Africa will be found, on examination, to possess the richest soil of the whole continent."

We must bear in mind, that these are the productions and gigantic growths of Africa in her almost waste and wild state. Cultivation is doing as little for an African soil as it is for her people. Their crooked stick for a plough, drawn by cows, by means of ropes attached to their horns, may be taken as a befitting emblem both of the state of agriculture and the social advancement of Africa. If Africa, with her thousands of miles of deserts, and her vast extent of almost impenetrable jungle, overtopped with the most gigantic forests, can, with the present extreme indolence of her people, support 150,000,000 (probably 200,000,000) of inhabitants, what might she not, under a high state of cultivation, and by means of an intelligent and industrious people, and under the smiles of propitious Heaven?

A French traveler, of the last century (Poncet, a Jesuit missionary), who spent much time in Abyssinia, speaks in the most glowing terms of the fertility of that part of Africa, when subjected to good cultivation. "There is," says he, "scarcely a country on the globe so thickly peopled, or the soil so rich and productive as the territory of Ethiopia. All the valleys and sides of the mountains nearly to their tops, are, for the most part, subdued and moulded by the hand of cultivation, and the plains are mantled by aromatic plants, which shed around them a delightful fragrance, and which generally grow to a size nearly four times as large as the same species in the soils of India. Streams flow through this country in every direction. They profusely water every plain and valley of Abyssinia; and their banks are garnished with an exuberant covering of the most beautiful flowers. The forests abound with the orange, the lemon, and pomegranate, which load the air with their enlivening perfumes. There are, also, roses, diffusing an odor far more delicious and aromatic than any of the most delightful that are found among us."

Africa was once called "the granary of the Roman Empire."

Napoleon Bonaparte, and the no less shrewd Talleyrand, were not unmindful of the extraordinary capabilities of this singular continent. They thought to make Africa to France what she had once been to the Roman Empire. Napoleon is said to have had his eye fixed on Africa, at one time, not only to make it the granary of France—a no insignificant object, when he was draining France of her sturdiest sons for his armies, but he looked thither for a supply of France with tropical productions, when, in those revolutionary times, she was excluded from the West Indies, and made dependent on England for the products of either the East or West Indies.

Talleyrand is said to have digested a plan for raising, on the northern coast of Africa, and through the labor of the natives, cotton, coffee, sugar, and all the commodities which were usually brought to Europe from the tropical regions of either hemisphere. This, like many other plans of the far-reaching mind of Napoleon, and of his yet shrewder minister, failed only because the toils and hazards of the wars into which his ambition or necessity drew him left no opportunity for their execution. "The thoughts of the Emperor were withdrawn from the colonization of Africa, until it was too late to make the attempt."

The African trade has always been an object of desire by every commercial nation; partly for the actual products of her soil, her mines, and her forests, but the rather because of the prospective benefits of a traffic with her. Keen-eyed commerce has not failed to discover undeveloped resources in Africa, which can not fail to enrich and aggrandize the people that shall secure this trade, and in proportion as these resources have been drawn out, the trade has been lucrative. It is interesting to observe, that, whenever a commercial nation has directed her attention to a trade with Africa, the demand thus created for African products has most readily and abundantly created the supply; and the quantity of exports which have in these instances been carried from that land, enable us to form some just judgment, as to the extent to which commerce might be carried, were cultivation encouraged, and governments such as to invite a safe and open traffic.

When Genoa was enjoying her commercial supremacy, her people carried on an extensive and lucrative trade with Africa. The trade which they carried on with Cyrenaica was, in the early times, one of the richest sources of her prosperity. So important had this trade, at one time, become (1267), and so great was the intercourse between Genoa and Cyrenaica, that the Senate of Genoa deemed it important to institute a college at Genoa, for the study of the Saracenic language.

Again: we may arrive at some just estimate of the productions of Africa, from the importance which Great Britain evidently attaches to the African trade. Not only are companies organized with large capital to carry on that trade, but the Government is expending large sums, and sparing no pains, to secure to herself the rapidly increasing commerce of that continent. She liberally patronizes enterprising travelers into Africa, spends enormous sums in keeping up a large and efficient squadron on the coast— £100,000,000 within the last few years; then, again, we see her pouring forth an immense sum on the celebrated "Niger Expedition," and determines to lose no advantage to gain to herself a trade, prospectively, at least, so lucrative. These efforts and expenditures are, no doubt, based on intelligent and safe calculations of the real importance of an anticipated commerce, and we may receive them, no doubt, as affording some safe intimation of what the resources of Africa shall be when developed.

The great staples of Africa, which are chiefly to form her future commerce, and which afford, at present, a no inconsiderable trade, are cotton, rice, coffee, and sugar; to which may be added, grains, hides, drugs, palm oil, indigo, gums, ivory, gold, and iron. In some of these articles foreign nations are already carrying on a considerable trade, especially Great Britain. But, for the most part, no more is done than just to indicate what are the hidden treasures of the land, and what shall be the importance of that continent, when her resources shall be revealed. Perhaps, I hazard nothing in the assertion, that Africa, under a proper cultivation and a development of her resources, is quite capable of supplying the whole world with those tropical products which are now brought from the East and West Indies, and at a much cheaper rate.

The prospect already is, that Africa will soon become the greatest cotton-growing country in the world. Its climate and soil seem to be peculiarly adapted to the cotton crop. The cotton-tree, which in our Southern States must be planted every spring, lives, in Africa, nine or ten years, and bears as many crops of the finest quality. There is, perhaps, not a more sure prognostic of the approaching dawn of Africa's civilization and speedy regeneration than appears in the late successful attempts to cultivate this one article of commerce. Its bearing on the general interests of Africa must be influential and truly happy. The most important desideratum in order to the amelioration of the condition of Africa has been the want of a legitimate commerce. England, the great commercial nation, and, at present, the great renovating nation, is the most deeply interested in the commerce of Africa, and, more especially, in the article of cotton. Companies have already been formed, in England, with large capital, and agencies established on the coast of Africa, for the cultivation of this article. And well may the friends of Africa, watch with the intensest interest, the success of these agencies.

I shall be the more particular on this topic, inasmuch as it is likely to exert an influence on the destinies of the world, which all do not yet foresee. It will, to a considerable degree, change the course of commerce. At least, it will open a new channel between Europe and the continent of Africa. It will do much to bring Africa within the pale of civilization. It will, more effectually than any thing else, call forth the rich, though latent, resources of Africa in the production of other articles of commerce, besides the one in question. It will do more to suppress the nefarious traffic in flesh and blood than all the armed squadrons of all Christendom; and it will do more than all the emancipation schemes on the face of the earth to annihilate, root and branch, American Slavery. If England can procure her supply of cotton from Africa, instead of from India and America, and procure it much cheaper, it will strike a deadly blow to the whole system of slavery. Slave labor, in many parts of the South, already unprofitable, would soon be made so profitless, that the planters would be compelled to give up the system in self-defense. When omnipotent interest shall thus interpose, the days of slavery are numbered, and especially when we take into the account, that what is said in respect to cotton, is measurably true of coffee, sugar, and other products of our Southern States.

We shall, therefore, inquire, with some interest, what prospects there are that African cotton will, ere long, become a great staple in the commerce of England? What is doing, on the part of England, to warrant any such expectation?

The movement of last year, on the part of the British Government, through the Board of Trade, is worthy of some special attention. During the last year, Capt. Shaw was sent to Western Africa to superintend an expedition, fitted out by several eminent mercantile and manufacturing firms in England, for the purpose of testing, by actual experiment, the possibility of procuring a supply of cotton from the west coast of Africa. He was the bearer of a letter from Lord Palmerston to President Roberts. President Roberts' reply, with certain samples of cotton, the produce of districts of the Gold Coast, which were submitted by the Board of Trade to the Chamber of Commerce at Manchester, with a request that they should report as to the qualities and market value of the same, is worthy of some special notice. President Roberts very justly remarks: "This expedition, my Lord, is destined to produce important and salutary results, especially with respect to the future welfare of Africa, not only by increasing her commercial importance, but, also, as a means of introducing more rapidly the habits of civilization, and the blessings of Christianity among the barbarous tribes of this country. There can be no question as to the success of the enterprise, particularly in Liberia, if properly managed. Cotton, of as good quality as in the United States, can be raised here, and in large quantities, indeed to almost any extent."

The report of the Manchester Chamber of Commerce on these specimens of cotton, was exceedingly favorable. They speak, especially, of the quality of the African cotton. As to fibre, it supplies, at the present time, a very important desideratum. They say: "As it respects the usefulness of this cotton, nothing could be more desirable than the quality which these samples represent. We do not need any large increase of the finest qualities of cotton; our most pressing want is of such qualities as enter into the manufacture of the coarsest and heaviest of our fabrics, and this want the cottons now under review are admirably adapted to supply. Our trade could not receive any greater boon than a large import of them, if sent to us free from seeds, leaf-stems, and other extraneous matters; while a correlative result would arise in Africa, if such an intercourse with this country could, by any means, be established."

CHAPTER IX.

Africa as she is—More about cotton, and its bearing on Africa and on the world—Palm oil, rice, coffee, sugar, and other articles of commerce—Geographical position of Africa.

THE reports of Capt. Shaw, and other agents sent to Africa to make actual experiment of the cotton-growing qualities of an African soil, are exceedingly encouraging. Capt. Shaw, who was sent out from Liverpool, reports, after a single year, that he is about to send home a cargo of cotton. It is found that the cotton plant is indigenous to the soil—that a luxuriant crop will mature in less than five months, and the same plants continue to bear year after year.

A letter, dated Freetown, Sierra Leone, published in the *Manchester Guardian,* says : "You will, I am sure, be glad to learn that a large number of natives are now preparing their lands for planting cotton this year, and I have twenty men at work preparing forty acres of land, about a mile distant from Freetown, for cotton plantation. Every week applications are made to us for cotton seeds to plant during the approaching rains. Some of that which you gave me has been supplied to a few American missionaries in Sherbro Country. They have planted it, and intend to ship the products to England. There is little doubt that a very large quantity of cotton will be raised this year, both in the colony of Sierra Leone, and in the adjoining country."

Thirty varieties of cotton have been found growing

spontaneously in West Africa, some equal to the finest quality of American growth.

An English writer very justly remarks : "That the extension of a legitimate commerce, on the coast of Africa, will do more to suppress the slave-trade than all that our squadron has effected; that the cultiva- . tion of cotton, as an article of barter, might be extensively carried on under becoming arrangements, and that the samples of cotton received from Dahomey have been of the most encouraging kind."

Attempts are now making, in the kingdom of Dahomey, for the growing of cotton, which promise great success. The Danish settlements there have been ceded to the English, who are consummating their plans, through the British Chamber of Commerce, for the raising of cotton in Africa. For this purpose John Duncan has been appointed British Consul at Whydah, the principal port of Dahomey. He is charged to encourage the culture of cotton, to engage the natives in the same enterprise, furnish them with seeds, and in all possible ways to promote the object of his mission to Africa. And it is not a little interesting that he has been able to report, not only success in his own personal efforts, but no sooner was his intention known, that he would purchase cotton of the natives, than it was brought to him from all quarters. The natives need but a market, and they will bring out the resources of the soil without stint.

I have already referred to the importance which the people of Great Britain attach to their commerce with Africa. This shows the thorough conviction which they have of the value and abundance of the products of an African soil. The following remarks of Lord Palmerston go far to sustain the same opinion. They are, undoubtedly, based on safe·data. His lordship says, in a recent speech in Parliament :

"No part of the globe offers more scope for the commercial enterprise of this country than the interior and the coast of Africa.

"We have a demand for the things she produces, and she stands in want of the goods that we can supply. In many other parts of the world, where there is a larger population to consume what we can export, there is a want of commodities to offer in return.

"Our trade with China has been limited, to a certain degree, by want of the commodities to exchange for our products. But, in Africa, commodities for barter abound. There is hardly any thing of value which can not be procured there, to offer in exchange for the goods that we can supply. Cotton might be grown on the western coast in infinite quantity, and of the best quality. And, recollecting how precarious is the source of supply which we now derive from the United States of America—recollecting how the growing manufactures of America, herself, are now annually absorbing more and more of the cotton which she produces—and recollecting what a vast amount of our own population depend upon the manufactures from that raw material for daily bread, it becomes matter of the most extreme importance that we should seek out other sources of supply. Palm oil, an article also of great value, and much used, is found in abundance in that country ; there are also coffee, ivory, gold—in fact, hardly any thing of value and utility that might not be produced, or found, in Africa, and that might not be received in return for our exports.

"I say, therefore, it is an object of great national importance, that, by an end being put to the slave-trade, we should be enabled to enter into commercial intercourse with the vast population of that region."

These sentiments are encouraging, whether considered in reference to the annihilation of the slave-trade, or the attention which the commerce of this country is attracting in England.

Truly, Africa presents an inviting field for commercial enterprise; and no people better understands its importance than the English.

As would also appear from Lord Palmerston's remarks elsewhere, England then carried on a commerce with Africa, to the amount of £5,000,000 annually—now, more than double that amount.

The connection between cotton and slavery is well established and very intimate. With many persons, the first objection to the abolition of slavery, is the supposed increase in the price of cotton cloth which would result from it. What if Africa, by furnishing an abundant supply of cotton, should remove this objection, and pave the way to emancipation! Such a thing is among the possibilities, perhaps among the probabilities. In relation to the matter, Dr. Irving, a missionary to Africa, has written to Dr. Shaw the annexed remarks. The letter is published in the proceedings of the Royal Geographical Society:

"In December, 1853, I was ordered on service to Abbeokoota, with Commander Foote, then senior officer. There I was much struck with the superior appearance of the people, and their great capabilities, the productiveness of the soil, the variety of objects which might lead to an extensive and lucrative commerce with

England, more especially that of cotton, which is indigenous, and carefully cultivated by the Yarubas.
These comprise a population of nearly three million
souls, clothed entirely in cloths manufactured by
themselves.   On my return to England, I represented
these things to the Church Missionary Society, and
many of the samples of African productions I brought
home, excited great attention among manufacturers
and others.   The cotton proved to be of the very
quality required for the purposes of manufacture.
Among them was, also, an entirely new kind of silk,
respecting which, several eminent merchants in London are very anxious for further information.   I volunteered to go out and examine the country between the
Niger, Bight of Benin, and Lander's route, between
Badagry and Boussa, a country, excepting at one or
two points where our missionaries had been the
pioneers, never yet visited by white men.   My offer
has been accepted, and I start as agent for Yaruba,
with the sanction of Sir James Graham and Lord
Clarendon.   The necessary instruments for making
observations have been forwarded to me."

We have referred to an expedition fitted out from
Manchester, for the purpose of testing the cotton-
growing capabilities of Africa.   We are now able to
present the report of this Association :

"The Manchester Commercial Association has received intelligence of the successful result of some experiments in cotton cultivation, at Cape Coast Castle,
in Africa.   A year and a half ago, some of the members
of this Association subscribed upward of £1,500, toward an experiment of this kind.   The money was
sent to agents (generally merchants) at Cape Coast

Castle. A site was selected, about five miles inland, on the banks of a small stream, and the process of planting the indigenous cotton shrub was commenced. The plant is perennial, and grows to a considerable size, the stalk being, in many cases, several inches in diameter. The seeds are kidney-shaped, and they lie matted together in the pod, very much like the Brazilian species. From time to time, the most favorable accounts have come to hand. So long since as October last, it was announced that thirty acres of ground had been cleared, and then bore 19,600 'trees,' all of which were 'fresh and healthy, and seemed to be growing fast. They are almost covered with unripe pods, blossoms, or buds, and, in two or three weeks after having had the benefit of the October rains, they will look better than they do now. In two or three months, many of those first planted will realize a good crop.' So wrote the agent; and as an earnest of the truth of his expectations, there were received in Manchester last week, five bags or bales of cotton, each weighing 150 pounds, and a sample parcel weighing thirty or forty pounds, all the produce of one farm mentioned. The cotton has been examined, and found very closely to resemble Brazilian, or rather Egyptian. It is of extremely good color, and fair, short staple; has been well cleaned (without injury) by saw-gin, and is worth fully sixpence per pound. The cost of its production and transit to Manchester, is said not to have exceeded three pence per pound, a result strongly confirmatory of the assertion that cotton cultivation in Africa may be rendered remunerative. As to the disposition of the native Africans, they have been found, in this instance, to accept work on the farm with abso-

lute avidity, not only on account of the readiness with
which the wages asked were paid, but, apparently, with
an intense desire to imitate or assist Europeans;
and they evinced pride in being brought into connection with the whites. Men, as many as were required in the clearing and preparatory operations,
worked diligently and regularly for two dollars a
month; women, for a dollar and a half, and stout lads
for half a dollar, without rations in any case. According to the last accounts respecting the farm, men
have rarely been employed since the 'trees' have been
planted, the labor of women and children being found
quite sufficient for all ordinary purposes. The hands
worked eight hours a day, and seemed thoroughly contented with themselves and their masters. The example became contagious soon after the experimental
farm was cleared; for, so long since as October last,
several European residents had started plantations
on their own account, and on one lot alone there were
20,000 flourishing trees. The average yield has been
found to be most satisfactory. Now, those who have
hitherto conducted the experiment so nobly originated by a few gentlemen in Manchester, are desirous that regularly trained persons should be sent
out to superintend the several plantations which must
ere this be in existence. The originators are most desirous to see the resources of the Cape Coast Castle
district more fully developed; and, we think, we have
stated enough to show that, while extended operations
could not fail to be highly advantageous to the trade
of this district, they would certainly return remunerative profit for any investments."

We dwelt longer on the capability of Africa to supply cotton—even to supply, if need be, the whole world—because of the immediate and very important bearing it has on the coming destiny of America, and of the States of Europe. Most undoubtedly, the life and soul of American slavery is to be found in the cultivation of the cotton plant. The demand for slaves, the price of slaves, the extent and duration of slavery, keep pace with the demand for cotton. The measure in which France and England have been co-partners with us in the use of slave labor, show how deeply they have been partakers of the great American sin; and should they be made to drink yet more deeply of the cup of Heaven's displeasure, we need not think any strange thing has happened. Such are the common, as they are the righteous, retributions of God.

We have spoken of the capability there is in the soil and climate of Africa to supply cotton to any conceivable amount, and we know there is, in successful operation, a commerce between England and the western coast of Africa, quite sufficient to transport a full supply to Europe; and we have just seen, in a report of one of the African Companies, that every desirable facility is afforded in the form of cheap and ready labor of native Africans. "They have always been found to accept work with absolute avidity—men for two dollars a month, women for one dollar and a half, and stout lads for half a dollar, without rations in either case."

The bearing which all this must have upon American slavery, upon the African slave-trade, and upon the general amelioration of the condition of Africa, can not be mistaken. Whether American slavery shall die a death of violence, through this dreadful war, may still remain, in the minds of many, a matter of doubt. Yet fewer will doubt that its days are numbered—that its final demise is only a question of time. Africa's soil is growing, and fast bringing to maturity, the remedy which shall eradicate the disease, root and branch. The question of a cure is solved in the number of bales of cotton raised and transported to Europe. That number completed, and slavery has its death-blow; and with slavery goes that most barbarous and inhuman of all traffics, which makes " merchandise of the bodies and souls of men." And what, as an entering wedge to prepare the way for all civilizing and Christian agencies, will not a legitimate commerce do for Africa? The awfully demoralizing influences of the slave-trade ceasing to be, industry will be encouraged, enterprise will spring up, and commercial relations with nations more enlightened and civilized will do much to disinthrall her people from their ignorance and superstition, and raise them from their degradation.

Be it that cotton is king. We acknowledge his majesty. And, as we see him about to remove the place of his throne, from his adopted land to his native soil in Africa, we follow him with a hearty " God save the king." May he reign there, not to trample under foot, and to forge manacles for, a helpless race; but reign in mercy and in might, till he shall proclaim liberty to the captives, undo the heavy burdens, break every yoke, and let the oppressed go free.

But will the removal of the cotton market to Africa or to India so surely strike the death-blow to the great system of involuntary servitude in America? Some fear it, more hope it; all expect it. Says the *Westminster Review*: "There is no doubt that the loss of a greater part of our cotton market will be the ruin of the slave system of the United States, and the very efforts which have been made by the South to save that hateful institution from destruction, by forcing our manufacturers to seek other sources of supply, will operate more powerfully in extinguishing it than any measure which could have been taken, for its suppression, by the Federal Government, under the inspiration of a hostile President. It was mainly by our cotton-trade that the slave-trade was supported; and when this support is weakened, as it inevitably must be, the slave-trade will become proportionably insecure;" and the whole system of American slavery be among the things that were.

Though Africa presents the most hopeful source of a future supply of cotton, yet she is but one of the sources toward which England is looking for such supply. "India embodies all the constituent qualities necessary to become the first cotton-producing country in the world." Already means are being vigorously employed to develop her resources, with the "hope," as an English writer says, "that she may, ere long, rival America, both in the quantity and quality of her produce, in the English market." India has under cotton cultivation, nearly four times the area cultivated in the United States; yet, on account of an inefficient cultivation, its resources are but miserably developed. The Bombay Presidency alone (the smallest of the four divisions) is said to contain 43,000,000 acres of land, admirably adapted to the growth of cotton, greater by one-tenth than the whole extent of cotton lands in the United States. If one-fourth of this area were so cultivated that it should produce even a moderate crop per acre (say 100 lbs. of clean cotton), it would give 1,075,000,000 lbs., equal to the whole quantity consumed at present by Great Britain.

We shall speak, in its place, of the determined efforts which England is making in other countries than Africa (India is but one of half a score) to supply her demands for cotton, and thus forever free herself from a dependence on the fields of slaveholders. It is sufficient here simply to quote the opinion of a late traveler in England. He can state, he says, from personal knowledge, that it is the "unanimous, hearty, and earnest determination of England to depend no longer on the South for the chief supply of cotton."

"The entire people are thoroughly in earnest on this subject. Parliamentary and philanthropic Societies are now earnestly engaged in providing for the anticipated crisis. Commercial men are now actively engaged in stimulating the supply of cotton from other countries. The Southern monopoly of the cotton-trade is broken up forever. Among the agencies now at work, lately formed to promote the import of cotton from other countries into England, the following will show that secession has defeated its own object—i. e., the supremacy of Southern commerce:

The British Cotton Company, Manchester.

The Manchester Cotton Company, Manchester; capital, $5,000,000; Chairman, Thomas Barzley, Esq., M. P. for Manchester. Sphere of operations, India, Australia, etc.

The East India Cotton Company, London; capital, $1,250,000.

The Jamaica Cotton Company, London; capital, $100,000; Chairman, Samuel Gurney, Esq., M. P.

The Coventry Cotton Company, Coventry; capital, $250,000.

These are among the first results of the alarm now felt as to the cotton supply in England. There are, in addition to these, two Societies, with wide reach, which will soon tell powerfully upon the question. One is the Cotton Supply Association, of Manchester, which is now actually stimulating cotton production in India, Australia, Africa, the West Indies, and other tropical regions. The other is the African Aid Society, of London, formed to aid American free blacks to emigrate to Africa and the West Indies, where they may engage in cotton culture. Its object is nearly identical with that of the Colonization Societies, superadding the idea of cotton culture as an immediate work for the free blacks.

" The determination is to deliver England from dependence upon the South. African cotton can be delivered at Liverpool for four and a half pence, which is much cheaper than American, and of an average quality. Let the merchants connected with the Southern trade not forget these facts. In any event of this war, secession has opened the eyes of the British, and the South has lost the monopoly of the cotton-trade. Among the numerous mistakes which Southern politicians have made in forcing the South into an attitude of rebellion against the Government, none will tell more directly against their future interests than that in relation to cotton. They supposed that " Cotton was king," and that all nations would bow down before it.   This is a fatal mistake.   Various attempts have been made to turn the attention of the British consumers to other fields of cotton supply, with little success, however, until within a year or two.

" The contest now is virtually against the attempts of the British to obtain cotton from Africa, India, and the West Indies.   When in England, the writer had full opportunity to inform himself upon this question. from the British point of view.   He can state, from personal knowledge, that it is the unanimous, hearty, and earnest determination of the British nation to depend no longer on the South for the chief supply of cotton.

"Lord John Russell has officially requested the British Consuls to stimulate cotton culture throughout the British tropical dominions."

But we pass on to other articles of African production, and next :

Palm oil is mentioned by his lordship as an article of export of great value, and, doubtless, it is destined soon to be an article of vastly more importance than it is at present.   As other resources for the obtaining of oil fail, as fail they are beginning to, the civilized world will be obliged to look to Africa for their supply.   And there is good reason to believe that Africa will be able to supply this great and increasing demand for an indefinite time to come.

Palm oil is produced by the nut of the palm-tree which grows in the greatest abundance throughout Western Africa.   The demand for it, both in Europe and America, is daily increasing.   The average import into Liverpool of palm oil, for some years past, has been at least 30,000 tons, valued at £800,000 sterling.

But I introduced this item rather for the purpose of calling attention to the recent discovery and manufacture of a new article of African production, called Herring's Palm Kernel Oil, or African Lard, which promises to be an article of great value.

The common palm oil is obtained from the exterior part of the nut, while the kernel of the nut has hitherto been cast aside as worthless. Recently, a machine has been invented, by which a beautiful oil, quite superior, both in quality and appearance, to the palm oil, has been obtained. When in its liquid state it is transparent as water; and in taste, when used, as it may be, for cooking purposes, it is not excelled by the best lard.

After being made and set by, it assumes a consistence like that of hard butter, and has to be cut out with a knife or spoon; its appearance, in this state, is very beautiful, presenting such richness, clearness, and adaptedness to table purposes, that one would not suppose it to be a product of Africa, or the interior part of the palm nut; nor would it be supposed that this oil is obtained from the same tree from which palm oil is, for there is as much disparity, both in their appearance and taste, as there is between lard and butter.

It is said that the kernel of the nut will produce as much of this superior oil, as the nut itself will of the common oil.

Coffee is another article of commerce, which is produced, perhaps, with as great facility, and as abundantly, as cotton. It is, says a writer, produced so abundantly in some parts, that 200 pounds can be purchased for a dollar. A single tree in Monrovia yielded four and a half bushels in the hull at one time, which, on being shelled and dried, weighed thirty-four pounds. And it must here be borne in mind, that the coffee-tree, in Africa, continues to produce from thirty to forty years, and yields two crops a year.

Rice, with a little cultivation, is said to equal, in some parts of Africa, the fertility of the imperial fields of China, and sugar-cane grows with "unrivaled magnificence." These two very essential articles of commerce may evidently be produced to almost any extent that human skill can be brought to bear on the cultivation. No soil is capable of a greater variety, or of more abundant productions. The following additional list comprises a few of those already made articles of commerce :

Ivory is procurable at all points, and constitutes an important staple of commerce.

Cam-wood, and other dye-woods, are found in great quantities in many parts of the country. About thirty miles east of Bassa Cove is the commencement of a region of unknown extent, where scarcely any tree is seen except the cam-wood.

Gums of different kinds enter largely into commercial transactions.

Dyes of all shades and hues are abundant, and they have been proved to resist both acids and light.

Pepper, ginger, arrow-root, indigo, tamarinds, oranges, lemons, limes, and many other articles which are brought from tropical countries to this, may be added to the list. Indeed, there is nothing in the fertile countries of the East or West Indies which may not be produced in equal excellence in Western Africa.

The soil is amazingly fertile. Two crops of corn, sweet potatoes, and several other vegetables, can be raised in a year. It yields a larger crop than the best soil in the United States. One acre of rich land, well tilled, says Governor Ashman, will produce three hundred dollars' worth of indigo. Half an acre may be made to grow half a ton of arrow-root.

Or, we may pass from the productions of her soil to the richness of her mines. Gold dust has been an article of commerce from Africa since the days of Herodotus. The source of most of this gold is the Kong chain of mountains, from whence it is washed down by the mountain streams. When these mountains shall be explored, and their mines worked by modern skill and science, another source of unlimited wealth will be opened in the heart of Africa. Rich and extensive beds of iron ore have also been discovered in the interior, and the natives are beginning to learn the art of working it. Iron is found in an uncommonly pure state. It can be beaten out into malleable iron without the process of smelting. Africa is exceedingly rich in minerals, precious stones, and metals. It seems quite probable that Africa, which once produced that profusion of gems and the precious metals which, in the days of Solomon, so beautified and enriched Jerusalem, shall again bring her " gold and incense," when, numbered among the renovated nations, she shall " show forth the praises of the Lord."

Gold is found at various points of the coast. It is obtained by the natives by washing the sand which is brought down by the rivers from the mountains.

An exploration of the mountains will, probably, re-. sult in the discovery of large quantities of the metal. It is calculated that England has received, altogether, $200,000,000 of gold from Africa. Liberia is adjacent to the " Gold Coast."

Or, turn we to the forests of Africa, and we meet the same exhaustless stores of wealth. Dye-woods, timber for ship-building, cabinet work, and for every purpose needed, everywhere abounds in her immense forests, and will, ere long, form a most lucrative commerce.

And, not only are these forests themselves an exhaustless source of wealth, but those huge trees and thick jungles shelter vast herds of animals; which offer to commerce scarcely a less profitable traffic. The wealth derived annually from a single animal, the elephant, is immense. Droves of 700 or 800 are sometimes seen at the same time. The number scattered over the continent, says a traveler, is countless. As they all have tusks, and some of these weigh 120, 130, and 140 pounds each, the quantity of ivory which Africa may produce is almost without limit.

We know little of the real resources of Africa till we penetrate into her interior. Accounts of late travelers have confirmed the suspicion, that the great unknown interior would open up a new history for Africa. The interior is no longer looked upon as a " desert waste." Some years ago Becroft, the bold and intelligent English traveler, showed that it is accessible to navigation and trade, that the climate is as healthy as that of the tropics generally; that there are regions of beautiful and fertile country, affording opportunities for legitimate commerce of indefinite extension. This adventurous traveler explored the river Niger within forty miles of Timbucto. He has thrown light on thousands of miles of richly fertile and wooded country, watered by that great stream; and upon the ivory, vegetable tallow, peppers, indigo, cotton, wool, palm oil, dye-woods, timber-woods, · skins, and a great variety of produce, which invite the trade.

Writers on Africa quite agree that the coast is the least interesting and inviting, and the least healthy portion. As far as European and American travelers have penetrated, which is, from the west only to the extent of some 200 or 300 miles, and from the south some 500 miles, they give the most glowing picture of its fertility and beauty, and the salubrity of its atmosphere. "Most happily," says one, "for a tropical region, the mountains or hills approach to within a short distance from the sea-shore, but have not the lofty and rugged character of those of South America. They abound with limpid streams, furnishing every facility for manufacturing, and are covered with stately forests. It is not improbable that this may be the character of the country for many hundred miles back of the republic of Liberia; and if such should be found to be the case, it will form one of the most magnificent abodes of man on earth. Even the portion already known is of sufficient extent to form an empire as large as France; and there is no reason why it may not, in two or three centuries, become as enlightened and populous, as it will unquestionably be better governed."

And not only is the soil of the interior represented as excellent and the country beautiful, but, what we scarcely expected, the climate is described as delightful and salubrious. Rev. Mr. Thompson, in his account of a late tour into the interior, speaks of the climate as delightful: "No such oppressive heats as you have in July and August; nights cool and bracing —the rainy season cool and something like October in America. At this distance from the low lands, and with such a high rolling country, with no stagnant lakes or swamps, no wide river bottoms, no sluggish streams, or overflowing of country, I see no reason why it would not be as healthy a country as any, when once cleared up, settled, and cultivated, as are the Eastern States. I firmly believe it. I see no natural cause of sickness here any more than in any new uncultivated country. Could land be bought in this country, I should try hard to buy a good tract for an earthly home for me and mine as long as God shall continue us here, and for others who might wish to enjoy it, and for a nucleus or radiating point for spreading the Gospel through all this country.

"A thorough Christian colony in this interior, with their horses, oxen, ploughs and harrows, axes, scythes, houses, barns, and mills, wagons, roads, fences, farms, and waving fields, joined with the rich blessings of education, the influence of a holy example, a pure life, a just government, and apostolical zeal to save the souls of the heathen, would, I believe, be just the means in the hands of God to put in operation influences that would, in a century, transform Africa, and make it naturally and morally a 'new world.'"

"The country in the interior," says Mr. Thompson, "is not flat and low, like that nearer the coast, but high, hilly, beautifully rolling, and very fertile. Under white men's cultivation it would be as the 'garden of the Lord.' But African agriculture is very meagre, being done only with a large knife, or a tool something like a light cleaver."

But we must not overlook, in this survey, the geographical position of Africa. Africa occupies, upon the globe, a central position. Embedded in the ocean between Europe, Asia, South America, and the Antarctic continent, she is more favorably situated for an extensive commerce than any other portion of the globe. Not only has she the material for the support of a vast population, and an immense commerce with every part of the globe, but her maritime facilities give her every possible advantage. On the north, through the Mediterranean, she is within a few hours'—at most, within a few days'—sail of all the principal marts and emporiums of Europe. With Asia she may enjoy nearly the same facilities of communication; and a few days' sail brings her merchantmen into every principal port of America.

Nor is Africa wanting in the facilities for an *internal trade* and *navigation*. A great portion of Eastern Africa is drained by the Nile and its branches; and large portions of the interior and the eastern slope of the Kong Mountains are drained by the Niger and its branches, while all that fine and fertile country between the Kong mountains and the Atlantic is intersected by the Senegal, 1,000 miles in length; the Gambia, 700; the Rio Grande, Rio Numez, Rokelle, Camaranca, Mesurado, Cavally, Rio Volta, etc., from 300 to 400 miles in length. Eleven degrees further south, we meet the Congo, an immense river, which has been navigated 400 miles. "Besides the larger rivers, the whole coast is thickly indented with inlets, or arms of the sea, extending into the country, and almost invariably receiving at their terminations small rivers, which may be navigated for some distance by flat-bottomed steamboats, and which will float down the timber of the forests, and afford sites for mills and manufactories.   The riches of the whole Atlantic slope can, therefore, be poured, with perfect facility, into the lap of commerce."

Such being the natural advantages and resources possessed by Africa, and such the facilities for making these real and permanent advantages, we may well pause here and ask, what shall be the future destiny of Africa?   Shall she always remain as she has been, scarcely more than a blank and a blot on the map of the world? or, has she yet a destiny to work out which shall abundantly vindicate the wisdom and benevolence of God, in endowing her soil with such fertility, and her forests and her mines with such riches? We fully believe that Africa is reserved for a great and a good destiny, which is yet scarcely begun to be developed.   We believe it, because a wise Providence does nothing in vain—does nothing without a wise and benevolent plan.   He does not make preparations, except in view of an end.   He does not provide resources—prepare a great system of means, except in reference to a result.   But no great civil, moral, or religious end, has yet been answered in reference to Africa.   With just exception enough, as I have shown, to indicate her capabilities, she has been a "desert waste."   And her people, though they have, at times, shown themselves capable of reaching the higher grades of civilization and human aggrandizement, and as statesmen, soldiers, scholars, and Christians, realizing the great ends of human life in a way inferior to no other race, yet, as a race, they have done nothing adequate to their capabilities.

We think, therefore, that we are warranted in the conclusion that a great and good destiny yet awaits Africa—a destiny commensurate with her capabilities.

8*

CHAPTER X.

Can Africa produce men?—Specimens of statesmen—Soldiers—Scholars--
Men of science—Writers, novelists, poets—Men of wealth, position.

No one will, perhaps, question that Africa does really possess all the natural advantages needful to raise her to an equality with either of the other continents. The wonderful fertility of her soil, the richness of her mines, and the superabundance of the natural resources which, if but developed, fail not to enrich a nation, have been shown to be quite equal to a high degree of national aggrandizement. And testimonials have been produced that African races have attained to honorable eminence among the nations of the earth. But can these do the same again? While such names as Sesostris, who drew kings at his chariot wheels, and left monumental inscriptions of his greatness from Ethiopia to India—while such names as Euclid, Homer, Plato, Terrence, the refined and accomplished scholar, Honno, Hamilcar, his son, and Hannibal, are found in the annals of the Hamic race, we do not lack vouchers for the past or precedents for the future.

But, have these races the social, intellectual, and moral capabilities of reproducing their former greatness? Our appeal, here, must be to facts, and we will here confine our inquiry principally to the negro race—the repudiated, down-trodden, despised negro. Are negroes capable of rising to any such level as we have supposed? Do we meet with individual instances among the present generation of Cushites which encourage such an expectation?

Common candor here demands that, in the specimens we shall adduce of the progress and achievements of the black man of the present day, we do not exact of him an absolute equality. If, after so many ages of uniform, systematic, unremitting degradation, and the almost entire lack of the means and opportunities of improvement, we meet with a few who have, in spite of mountain obstacles thrown in their way—obstacles which very few of our own race ever surmounted—if, in the absence of all encouragement—yea, if in the face of every conceivable discouragement—if, in the absence of the means and opportunities of raising themselves from the low and depressing depths of degradation to which the system of American slavery has reduced them, a few are found to rise, to assert their manhood, to make themselves men—not to the high level of the Anglo-Saxon standard, but to an ordinary level of mediocrity, we should be obliged to concede to them capabilities of improvement, which, it is doubtful, we may find in any other race.

Our Anglo-Saxon race, once quite as low and helpless as the poor Ethiopians, whose cause we plead, showed no such elasticity, flexibility, or improvability till after the heavy yoke had been broken from their necks for some centuries. But, we may claim for Young Africa something more than that meagre, mediocre advancement which, in the circumstances, is all we have any right to expect, viz., a superiority above the great mass of their own depressed and down-trodden brethren. We mean to claim for them capabilities of competing with white races. We shall, for this purpose, produce a few specimens from the multitude that lie before us, to show that there are lying almost dormant, beneath the superincumbent rubbish of centuries, elements which, though long suppressed, ever and anon loom up, and vindicate their claims to stamina of character and intellectual resources not inferior to other races. Africa still produces *men*.

A colored writer and ex-slave has greatly facilitated my purpose, by collecting some scores of instances of the "black man's" genius, achievements, and capabilities of raising himself to positions altogether creditable to him, as a member of the great fraternity of man. I shall select from this collection, and greatly abridge, as few as will suffice to illustrate my point— enough to show that, notwithstanding the crushing pressure of ages, men of the crisped hair and thick lips have become statesmen, scholars, soldiers; brave, accomplished, successful ; men of science ; writers, poets, novelists, dramatists ; men of business and wealth ; men of good social position ; and Christians, illustrating, in an eminent degree, the religion pure and undefiled—the spirit of the meek and lowly One.

1. Let us see what occasional examples of statesmanship we may discover in her modern sons, as illustrations of what they can do, and as a prognostic of the rising star of Africa. But, here our expectations should be very limited. No field has now for centuries been afforded for their development in this direction. They have enjoyed no nationality of their own, if we except Hayti and Liberia. Liberia has already reared statesmen that do honor to the name. Ex-

President Roberts rose from the condition of a slave in the Old Dominion, self-educated, and passed through every stage of political life, till he reached, and filled with all honor, the highest office in the Republic. His state papers—the whole course of his administration—presents to the world a man who would have done himself credit in the senate of his native land. In saying this, we do but confirm an opinion entertained of the ex-President by his numerous friends in England and America. Nor does Liberia lack men in her senate, in her courts of justice, or in the presidential chair, abundantly competent to fill every civil office. But,

2. Does the present generation of this proscribed race produce soldiers adequate to defend their rights and enlarge their borders, as their future progress may require? Braver, more successful generals never led an army than the men who arose, some of them from the ranks of slavery, in the revolutionary struggles of St. Domingo. The armies of Napoleon were forced to yield before them. We need only repeat the names of Toussaint L'Ouverture, Rigaud, Dessalines, Christopher, and Petion. It will be quite sufficient that we speak of the first as scarcely more than a representative man.

Aroused from the ominous dream of ages, the slaves of St. Domingo demanded their freedom. At first, they were as an enraged mob without a leader. All seemed waiting with hope that some black chief would arise adequate to the emergency. Nor did they hope in vain. A chief arose in the person of a slave, by the name of Toussaint. He was the grandson of the King of Adra, one of the most powerful and wealthy monarchs of the west of Africa. By his own energy and perseverance he had learned to read and write, and was held in high consideration by both planters and slaves. Of his character as a general, we may quote the testimony of his enemy, who said: "Toussaint, at the head of his army, is the most active and indefatigable man of whom we can form an idea; we may say, with truth, that he is found wherever instructions or danger render his presence necessary."

"Veneration for Toussaint," says his historian, "was not confined to the boundaries of St. Domingo. It ran through Europe. In France, his name was frequently pronounced in the senate with eulogy. No one can look back on his career without feeling that Toussaint was a remarkable man. Without being bred to the science of arms, he became a valiant soldier, and baffled the skill of the most experienced generals that had followed Napoleon. Without military knowledge, he fought like one bred in the camp. Without means, he carried on a war. He beat his enemies in battle, and turned their own weapons against them. He laid the foundation for the emancipation of his race and the independence of the island. From a slave he rose to be a soldier, a general, and a governor, and might have been King of St. Domingo. His very name became a tower of strength to his friends, and a terror to his foes. Toussaint's career, as a Christian, a statesman, and a general, will lose nothing by a comparison with that of Washington. Each was the leader of an oppressed and outraged people—each had a powerful enemy to contend with, and each succeeded in founding a government in the New World.

"When impartial history shall do justice to the St. Domingo revolution, the name of Toussaint L'Overture will be placed high up on the roll of fame."

3. "Ethiopia is stretching out her hands" to contribute a no contemptible share to the science, the literature, and the intellectual advancement of our country. Though, for the most part shut out from our schools, academies, and higher seminaries of learning, and subjected to a most unreasonable and damaging prejudice, which would seem enough to cast an "impassable gulf" between them and all intellectual improvement, yet, in spite of these most formidable disabilities, we meet, among this class of our citizens, writers, men of science, orators, philosophers, professional men, men even of superior talents and acquisitions, who have been able to extort the but too reluctantly conceded commendation of their white countrymen ; but who have enjoyed the more cheerfully extended meed of praise from the British Isles.

As a writer, I should, in justice, first cite William Wells Brown, author of the "Black Man," which has so liberally supplied me with specimens from which to select. William was a slave in Kentucky—made his escape to Canada—was without education, which he supplied by the most praiseworthy industry and perseverance — traveled, as a lecturer, extensively through the United States ; and traveled and lectured yet more extensively in Europe. "During which time," he says, "I wrote and published three books, and lectured in every town, of any note, in England." Among his works we notice " Clotelle," " Three Years in Europe," "Sketches of Places and Persons Abroad," and "Miraldo, the Beautiful Quadroon." And, we may add, the real service done to his kin in the publication of the "Black Man: his Antecedents, Genius, and Achievements." Of Mr. Brown's character, as a writer, we need only quote two or three opinions of English papers.

Speaking of his "Three Years in Europe," the Rev. Dr. Campbell, in the *British Banner*, says: "We have read this book with an unusual measure of interest. Seldom have we met with any thing more captivating. There is in the book a vast amount of quotable matter. A book more worthy the money has not, for a considerable time, come into our hands." The *London Times* says: "He writes with ease and ability, and his intelligent observations upon the great question to which he has devoted and is devoting his life, will be read with interest, and will command influence and respect." The *Eclectic Review* says: "Though he never had a day's schooling in his life, he has produced a literary work not unworthy of a highly educated gentleman." The *Literary Gazette* responds: "The appearance of this book is too remarkable a literary event to pass without a notice. Altogether, Mr. Brown has written a pleasing and amusing volume, and we are glad to bear this testimony to the literary merit of a work by a negro author." Speaking of Mr. Brown as "charming" his British audiences "with his eloquent addresses," the *Scotch Independent* says: "We have just received his "Three Years in Europe," and it is as a writer that he creates the most profound sensation. He is no ordinary man, or he could not have so remarkably surmounted the many difficulties and impediments of his training as a slave."

In this connection we should mention such writers as Alexander Crummell, Frederick Douglass, and William J. Wilson. "Such men," says a British journal, "will lose nothing by a comparison with the best educated and most highly cultivated of the Anglo-Saxons." A full-blooded negro, of tall and manly figure, a graduate of Cambridge University, England, a mind stored with the richness of English literature, and well versed in classic lore, Mr. Crummell may be presented as one of the best and most favorable representatives of his race. He is an Episcopal clergyman and Professor in the Liberia College, and author of a valuable work on Africa. Frederick Douglass is too well known as a strong man, a vigorous writer, an effective speaker, an earnest reformer, and an uncompromising advocate of universal freedom, to need comment here. We shall, however, for the double purpose of giving a true portraiture of the man, and, at the same time, of returning a very sensible answer to a very senseless "hocus-pocus, hypocritical canting of a certain class of blatant politicians;" who triumphantly ask: "What shall be done with the slaves, if emancipated?" give his reply to the question. His answer is characteristic of the man, and of the writer:

"What shall be done with four millions of slaves, if emancipated? Our answer is: Do nothing with them; mind your business, and let them mind theirs. Your doing with them is their greatest misfortune. They have been undone by your doings; and all they now ask, and really have need of at your hands, is just to be let alone. They suffer by every interference, and succeed best by being let alone. The negro should have been let alone in Africa—let alone when the pirates and robbers offered him for sale in our Christian slave markets—let alone by courts, judges, politicians, legislators, and slave-drivers—let alone altogether, and assured that they are to be thus let alone forever; and that they must make their own way in the world, just the same as any and every other variety of the human family. We only ask to be allowed to do for ourselves. Let us stand upon our own legs, work with our hands, and eat bread in the sweat of our brows. If you see him plowing in the open field, leveling the forest, at work with a spade, a rake, a hoe, a pickaxe, or a bill—let him alone; he has a right to work. If you see him on his way to school, to the ballot-box, or to church, don't meddle with him, nor trouble yourselves with any questions as to what shall be done with him. Don't pass laws to degrade him; nor shut the door in his face, nor bolt your gates against him.

"What shall we do with the negro, if emancipated? Deal justly with him. He is a human being, capable of judging between good and evil, right and wrong, liberty and slavery. He is, like other men, sensible of the motives of rewards and punishments. Give him wages for his work, and let hunger pinch him if he don't work. He knows the difference between fullness and famine, plenty and scarcity. But will he work? Why should he not? He is used to it, and is not afraid of it. His hands are already hardened by toil, and he has no dreams of ever getting a living by any other means. 'But would you turn them loose?' Certainly! Our Creator turned them loose, and why should not we. 'But would you let them all stay here?' Why not? What better is here than there?

Will they occupy more room as freemen than as slaves? Is the presence of a black freeman less agreeable than that of a black slave? You have borne the one more than 200 years—can't you bear the other long enough to try the experiment?"

Yet we must not forget that this letting alone—this throwing them upon their own self-reliance—does not excuse our kind and timely interposition in their transition from bondage to freedom. They have long been defrauded of their very manhood, of all the means and appliances by which to sustain that manhood. When we shall have restored them, not only to the possession of themselves, but to a self-sustaining position, we may then "let them alone." Restore what we have taken away, and leave them to take care of themselves.

But we are to speak of poets, male and female; philosophers and orators; novelists and dramatists, and all of the ebon hue. And who should we place at the head of the sable worthies but the celebrated novelist, dramatist, and accomplished scholar and gentleman, Alexander Dumas. In the maternal line, he was removed only in the second degree from an unadulterated negro of Congo. His grandmother was a negress from Congo. His father (and this adds one to our military list) was the well-known "negro general" in the army of the first Napoleon. "Dumas is now sixty-three years of age, and has been a writer for the press thirty-eight years. During this time he has published more novels, plays, travels, and historical sketches, than any other man that ever lived." A man of great genius, and fertility of imagination, and masterly power of expression, no writer fills a more prominent place in the literature of his country, and none has exercised a more potent influence upon its recent development than this son of this negro general, Alexander Dumas, of Paris.

But we must pass by such names as Charles L. Reason, and George B. Voshon, professors in the New York Central College; and Placido, who, while yet a slave, had a volume of poems published in England, which were much praised for talent and scholarly attainment; and James M. Whitefield, the Buffalo barber, "noted for his scholarly attainments, gentlemanly deportment," and poetical genius; and many others, whom we can not so much as name, but who have done themselves honor, and literature good service, both in poetry and prose, and given the most indubitable vouchers that literary taste, linguistic attainments, and historical researches, have no prejudice against color, but rather that they who seek them as silver, and search for them as for hid treasures, shall not search in vain. Passing by these, we select our examples where the reader may least expect to find them. We pass by the poets that we may introduce the poetesses. And here we call up the names of Phillis Wheatley, Francis Ellen Watkins, and Charlotte L. Forten.

Phillis, when a child of seven or eight years, was torn from her African home, and imported (1761) to Boston, and became the slave of Mrs. Wheatley. She early showed a singular genius; and, encouraged by her mistress, learned to read, and acquired the ordinary branches of education with astonishing rapidity: became a good Latin scholar, and "translated one of Ovid's tales, which was no sooner in print in America, than it was republished in England, with eloquent commendations from the Reviews." In January, 1773, she published a volume of thirty-nine poems, dedicated to the Countess of Huntington. Emancipated at the age of twenty-one, she sailed for England, where "she was received, and admired, in the first circles of London society." Her poems were now collected and published in a volume, with a portrait and memoir of the authoress.

A writer, of her own color, in a beautiful sketch of this extraordinary girl, says : " A sold thing, a bought chattel, at seven years, she mastered the English language in sixteen months, carried on an extensive epistolary correspondence at twelve years ; composed her first poem at fourteen ; became a proficient Latin scholar at seventeen ; and published, in England, her book of poems, dedicated to the Countess of Huntington, at nineteen ; and sailed for England, where she received the meed due to her learning, her talents, and her virtues, at twenty-two."

"Francis Ellen Watkins is a native of Baltimore, where she received her education. She has been before the public some years as an author and public lecturer. Her "Poems on Miscellaneous Subjects," "show a reflective mind, and no ordinary culture; her essay on 'Christianity,' is a beautiful composition. Many of her poems are soul-stirring, and all are characterized by chaste language and much thought."

Charlotte L. Forten, "unable, on account of her color, to obtain admission into the schools of her native city" Philadelphia), was educated at the Higginson German School, in Salem, Massachusetts. "Here she soon received the respect and esteem of her fel-

low-pupils." Near the close of her term the principal of the school invited the pupils, each, to write a
poem, to be sung on the last day of their examination.
Among fifty or more competitors, Charlotte bore
away the palm. A most respectable and intelligent
audience very generously accorded honor to whom
honor was due. We give a single stanza of her fare-
well address:

> " Fórth to a noble woik they go:
>   Oh, may their hearts be pure,
> And hopeful zeal and strength be theirs
>   To labor and endure,
> That they an earnest faith may prove
> By words of truth and deeds of love."

"Aside from having a finished education, Miss Forten possesses genius of a high order. An excellent
student, and a lover of books, she has a finely cultivated mind, well stored with incidents drawn from the
classics. She evinces talent, as a writer, for both
poetry and prose." In the one, her " Glimpses of
New England," and in the other, "The Angel's Visit,"
do her honor, showing that the gifts of nature are of
no rank or color.

4. Or go we to the rostrum, the stage, or the studio
and we still meet the " labor of Egypt, and the merchandise of Ethiopia and of the Sabeans." If in research of a portrait painter, go to Boston and inquire
for Edwin M. Bannister, or William H. Simpson. Both
these individuals have raised themselves from very
obscure beginnings, and gained a very praiseworthy
eminence in their profession, in spite of the most formidable obstacles in the way of their early education.
Mr. Bannister's barber's shop was his studio, till the
force of his genius compelled an acknowledgment of

his merits. "He is a lover of poetry and the classics, and is always hunting up some new model for his gifted pencil and brush." He has a picture representing "Cleopatra waiting to receive Marc Antony," which is said to be beautifully executed.

Mr. Simpson is, too, a colored artist in Boston—still young, of unmixed blood—who has already gained a reputation in his profession, which many have labored a lifetime in vain to secure. "His portraits are admired for their lifelike appearance, as well as for the fine delineation which characterises them." The patronage he is receiving in Boston is very flattering. His portrait of John T. Hilton, which was recently presented to the Masonic Lodge, "is a splendid piece of art." Indeed, no higher praise is needed than to say that a gentleman in Boston, distinguished for his good judgment in the picture gallery, wishing to secure a likeness of the Hon. Charles Sumner, induced the senator to sit to Mr. Simpson for the portrait. The artist is said to have been signally successful.

In Drury Lane and Covent Garden, London, you may see upon the stage the "African Roscius," alias Ira Aldridge. He was born in Senegal, Africa, but, when quite young, brought to America and educated as best he could be, in the face of an inveterate prejudice. His father, an African prince, who had escaped to this country in consequence of a rebellion, having himself received an education, designed to educate his son for the ministry. For this purpose he removed him to Scotland, where he entered the Glasgow University, and graduated with honor. On leaving college, he chose the stage, and "shortly appeared in a number of Shakspearian characters in Edinburgh, Glasgow, Manchester, and other provincial cities," and soon after appeared in London, where he was dubbed the "African Roscius."

5. But let us knock at the door of the learned professions and see if the sons of Ethiopia will give us a response here. Is she represented in the ranks of the ministry, of the law, and of medicine? The sacred office, we are quite sure, is in no danger of being dishonored by such men as Dr. James W. C. Pennington, late pastor of the Shiloh Church, in New York City; Wm. Douglass, of Philadelphia; Rogers, of Newark; not to overlook the young, eloquent, and promising John Stella Martin, and Bishop D. A. Payne. We select these without pretending to know that, either in ability or fidelity, piety or usefulness, we should concede to them any pre-eminence over scores of others of their colored brethren. We find their names convenient for reference. Could we recall their names we could mention not a few, who, though yet bound in the flesh, are free in the spirit; who have been taught of the Spirit, and whose lips are touched with a coal from the upper altar. Some of these preachers at the South, who own not their bodies, but God owns and blesses their souls, are represented as truly eloquent and successful preachers.

But we will not pass over the names mentioned so hastily. Dr. Pennington was born a slave, of unmixed blood, on a farm in the State of Maryland. By trade a blacksmith, with no opportunities for learning, and ignorant of letters till he made his escape to the North. Through intense application and industry, he repaired the deficiency—at length turned his attention to Theology, and became a useful and efficient preacher of the Gospel. He was several years pastor of a church in Hartford—visited Europe three times, preaching and lecturing extensively and with great acceptance—received the degree of Doctor of Divinity, at the University of Heidelberg, Germany, and on his return, was settled as pastor over the Shiloh Church, in New York. "The doctor has been a good student, is a ripe scholar; is considered a good Latin, Greek—and German scholar, and is deeply versed in Theology." Few men, of any nation or color, have reached his present status in the face of so formidable difficulties.

The successor of Dr. Pennington, in the Shiloh Church, Rev. Henry H. Garnett, was, in like manner, born a slave. He has gained the reputation of a "courteous and accomplished man, an able an eloquent debater, a good writer, an evangelical and acceptable preacher—and, in every sense of the term, a progressive man." "One of the most noted addresses ever given by a colored man in this country, was delivered by Mr. Garnett, at the National Convention of colored Americans, at Buffalo, in 1843. None but those who heard that, can have an idea of the tremendous influence which he exercised over the assembly."

William Douglass was a clergyman of the Episcopal Church, and for a number of years rector of St. Thomas Church, Philadelphia. "He had a finished education—was well versed in Latin, Greek, and Hebrew—possessed large and philanthropic views, but was extremely diffident. Mr. Douglass was a general favorite with the people of his own city, and especially the members of his own society. He was a talent-

9

ed writer, and published, a few years ago, a volume of sermons, which were filled with gems of thought and original ideas."

Elymas Payson Rogers was a Presbyterian clergyman, and pastor of a church in Newark, N. J. "He was a man of education, research, and literary ability —not a fluent and easy speaker, but logical, and spoke with a degree of refinement seldom met with. He possessed poetic genius of no mean order. His poem on the 'Mission Compromise,' contains brilliant thoughts and amusing suggestions." Mr. Rogers was of unmixed race. With a most praiseworthy zeal and self-denial, in 1861, he volunteered to visit Africa, as a pioneer to the settlement of a colony in the interior. He was attacked with a fever, and died in a few days. No man was more respected by all classes that knew him.

John Stella Martin was born, a slave, in Charlotte, North Carolina, in 1832—was both slave and son·to his owner. At the tender age of six years, the boy and his mother and sister were taken from the old homestead, at midnight, carried to Columbus, Ga., and exposed for sale. The boy was separated from his mother and sister, and became the property of a stranger. At the age of eighteen, on the death of his master, he was sold; at twenty, resold; and, at twenty-five, made his escape and fled to Chicago. Next we hear of him as a popular lecturer, and next as a preacher. Of a lecture he gave in Coldwater, Michigan, the following notice appeared in the weekly paper :

"Our citizens filled the court-house to hear J. S. Martin speak for his own race, and in behalf of the oppressed. The citizens admired, and even were astonished at his success as a public speaker. He is a natural orator, and, considering his opportunities, is one of the most interesting and forcible speakers of his age, and of the age. Indeed, he is a prodigy. It would seem impossible that one képt in 'chains and slavery,' and in total ignorance, till within a few months, could so soon attain so vast a knowledge of the English language, and so clear and comprehensive a view of general subjects. Nature has made him a great man. His propositions and his arguments, his deductions and illustrations, are new and original; his voice and manner are at his command, and pre-possessing; his efforts are unstudied and effectual. The spirit which manifests itself is one broken loose from bondage, and stimulated with freedom."

Next we hear of Mr. Martin as the popular and successful pastor of a church in Buffalo; and next, as the pastor of Joy Street Church, Boston, where he has been preaching "with marked success," for three years. And, last of all, we read in a New York paper of a late date:

"ARRIVED IN ENGLAND.—Rev. J. Stella Martin, the celebrated young colored minister, of Boston, U. S., well known for his eloquent orations on the American crisis, delivered in England some eighteen months ago, arrived at Liverpool by the Asia, on the 29th. We understand he has been invited to take the pastorate of a church in the suburbs of London."—Star.

We have spoken of Frederick Douglass as a writer. This "fugitive slave" is still better known as a lecturer and preacher. "His advent as a lecturer," says one, "was a remarkable one. White men and black men had talked against slavery, but none had ever spoke like Frederick Douglass. Throughout the North, the newspapers were filled with the sayings of the 'eloquent fugitive.' He often traveled with others, but they were all lost sight of in the eagerness to hear Douglass. He is polished in language and gentlemanly in his manners. His voice is full and sonorous. His attitude is dignified, and his gesticulation is full of noble simplicity—always master of himself. Few persons can handle a subject with which they are familiar better than he." Professor W. J. Wilson says of him: "In his every look, his gesture, his whole manner, there is so much of genuine, earnest eloquence, that they leave no time for reflection."

We would next call up Bishop D. A. Payne. Not quite satisfied with the tender mercies of the "patriarchal institution" in Charleston, S. C., he betook himself to the North—at length completed a regular course of theological study, at Gettysburg, Pa.—soon he became distinguished as a preacher in the Methodist Church, in Baltimore, and was, some years since, elected Bishop, and is now located in the State of Ohio.

"Bishop Payne is a scholar and a poet; having published a volume, in 1850, which was well received, and gave him a place among literary men. His writings are characterized by sound reasonings and logical conclusions, and show that he is well read." Devotedly attached to his down-trodden race, the bishop recently put forth a very noteworthy address to " The Colored People of the United States." If we may take this as the voice of their leaders to the captive hosts, when on the eve of their deliverance, we have no reason to fear their exodus from the house of bondage shall be otherwise than peaceful toward us, and profitable to themselves. I shall quote a few paragraphs to show, first, what is the word of command—what the fatherly advice of the bishop at this impending crisis of their destiny; and, secondly, to show something of the character of the prayers that are, at this moment, going up into the ears of the Lord God of Sabbaoth:

"A crisis is upon us which no one can enable us to meet, conquer, and convert into blessings for all concerned, but that God who builds up one nation and breaks down another."

And in view of this crisis—in the face of the hopes and fears that alternately elevate or depress his suffering people, the bishop exclaims: "Let every heart be humbled, and every knee bent in prayer before God. Throughout all this land of our captivity, in all this house of our bondage, let our cries ascend perpetually to heaven for aid and direction.

"To your knees, I say, O ye oppressed and enslaved ones of this Christian republic, to your knees, and be there. Before the throne of God, if nowhere else, the black man can meet his white brother as an equal, and be heard.

"Haste ye, then, oh, hasten to your God; pour the sorrows of your crushed and bleeding hearts into his sympathizing bosom. It is true, that on the side of the oppressor there is power—the power of the purse, and the power of the sword. That is terrible. But listen to what is still more terrible: on the side of the oppressed there is the strong arm of the Lord, the Almighty God of Abraham, Isaac, and Jacob—before his redeeming power the two contending armies, hostile to each other and hostile to you, are like chaff before the whirlwind.

" Fear not, but believe. He that is for you is more than they who are against you. Trust in him—hang upon his arm—go, hide beneath the shadow of his wings."

The address concludes with a very characteristic prayer. We shall take this as a beautiful epitome of the sighs and groans, the prayers and supplications, with strong crying and tears, which are continually ascending to the God of the oppressed throughout the length and breadth of the land of their bondage. Like the bondmen in Egypt, and the more earnestly as the day of their redemption draws near, "they sigh by reason of their bondage, and they cry." And is not their cry to come up unto God " by reason of their bondage?" And does not "God hear their groaning?" But the prayer :

"O God! Jehovah-jireh! wilt thou not hear us? We are poor, helpless, unarmed, despised. Is it not time for thee to hear the cry of the needy—to judge the poor of the people—to break in pieces the oppressor.

"Be, oh, be unto us what thou wast unto Israel in the land of Egypt, our counselor and guide—our shield and buckler—our Great Deliverer—our pillar of cloud by day—our pillar of fire by night!

"Stand between us and our enemies, O thou angel of the Lord! Be unto us a shining light—to our enemies confusion and impenetrable darkness. Stand between us till the Red Sea be crossed, and thy redeemed, now sighing, bleeding, weeping, shall shout, and sing, for joy, the bold anthem of the free."

But we have given too much space to the cloth. The other learned professions have had their honored representatives. Here we can no more than name Langston, the eloquent "black lawyer" of Oberlin, Ohio, and Robert Morris and John S. Rock, successful lawyers in Boston.

And among them who are an honor to the medical profession we may name James McCune Smith, of New York City, and James Derham, of New Orleans. Dr. Smith, an able writer and general scholar, has, for the last twenty-five years, been a practitioner in New York, where he has stood eminent in his profession. Dr. Derham, an imported negro, by his own genius and energy raised himself to be one of the ablest physicians in New Orleans. Dr. Rush says of him: "I found him very learned. I thought I could give him information concerning the treatment of diseases; but I learned more from him than he could expect from me."

We had intended to devote a paragraph, at least, to Benjamin Banneker, the "negro philosopher," and another to Sir Edward Jordon, who, a colored man, passed from the condition of a clerk to that of the able editor of a journal, a member of the Assembly, and to the honor of knighthood. Nor did we intend to pass, with so brief a notice at least, representatives of the class who have raised themselves, by their industry and perseverance, to position and wealth. Such is Robert Purvis, a wealthy and highly intelligent gentleman, who resides near Philadelphia. But there remains one personage to whom we must not give the go-by so easy. It is Joseph Jenkins, of London, who, for genius, versatility of talent, and indomitable perseverance, has, in this or any generation, few of his like, either white or black.

Our author introduces Joseph as he met him for the first time in Cheapside, London. He was then the earnest distributor of hand-bills in the service of a barber. A few days after he saw the same individual in Chelsea, sweeping a crossing. Here, too, he was equally as energetic as when met in Cheapside. Some days later, Mr. Brown, while going through Kensington, heard "rather a sweet, musical voice singing a familiar psalm, and, on looking round, was not a little surprised to find that it was the Cheapside bill-distributor and the Chelsea crossing-sweeper." He was now singing hymns and selling religious tracts. Next he appears at the Eagle Saloon, acting the part of Othello, in Shakspeare's tragedy, the observed of all observers. As he entered, he was greeted with "thunders of applause, which he very gracefully acknowledged." Tall, with a good figure and an easy carriage, a fine, full, and musical voice, he was well adapted to the character of Othello. He soon showed that he possessed great dramatic power and skill. The effect upon the audience was indeed grand. The Othello of the evening was known to them as Selim, an African prince. When the curtain fell, the prince was called out, when he was received with deafening shouts of approbation, and a number of bouquets thrown at his feet, which he picked up, bowed, and retired.

Next, our Othello—our African prince—is met in the pulpit of a mission chapel in the suburbs of London—the earnest, eloquent, and disinterested preacher; disinterested, because he will receive no compensation for his services. Here he showed himself the eloquent and accomplished preacher. Imagine the astonishment of our narrator, when, of a Sabbath evening, incidentally entering the aforesaid chapel, he discovered in the preacher the identical bill-distributor of Cheapside, the crossing-sweeper of Chelsea, the tract-seller and psalm-singer of Kensington, and the Othello of the Eagle Saloon.

But who is this man of so singular versatility of genius? Whence came he, and by what combination of auspicious or fortuitous circumstances did he become such a man? He shall tell his own story.

The service ended, the narrator and the preacher are introduced. They had several times met before, and under circumstances widely different. As they walked together on their way to their respective lodgings, Mr. Jenkins gratified the excited curiosity of his companion by a brief narrative of his previous history. "You think me rather an odd fish, I presume," said he. "Yes," I replied. "You are not the only one who thinks so," he continued. "Although I am not as black as some of my countrymen, I am a native of Africa. Surrounded by beautiful mountain scenery, and situated between Darfour and Abyssinia, two thousand miles in the interior of Africa, is a small valley going by the name of Tegla. To that valley I stretch forth my affections, giving it the endearing appellation of my native home and fatherland. There I was born, and there received the fond looks of a loving mother. My father being a farmer, I used to be sent out to take care of the goats. As I was the eldest of the boys, my pride was raised in no small degree when I beheld my father preparing a farm for me. In the mean time, I had the constant charge of the goats, and, being accompanied by two other boys,

9*

202 . THE GREAT NEGRO PROBLEM SOLVED.

who resided near my father's house, we wandered miles from home, by which means we acquired a knowledge of the different districts of our country.

"It was while in these rambles with my companions that I became the victim of the slave-trade. We were tied with cords and taken to Tegla, and thence to Kordofan, which is under the jurisdiction of the Pacha, of Egypt. From Kordofan I was brought down to Dongola and Korti, and thence down the Nile to Cairo, and, after being sold nine times, I was taken by an English gentleman, who brought me to this country and put me into school. But he died before I finished my education, and his family, feeling no interest in me, I had to seek a living as best I could. I have been employed to distribute hand-bills for a barber in Cheapside in the morning, go to Chelsea and sweep a crossing in the afternoon, and sing psalms and sell tracts in the evening. Sometimes I have an engagement to perform at some of the small theatres, as I had when you saw me at the Eagle. I preach for this little congregation over here, and charge them nothing, for I want that the poor should have the Gospel without money and without price. I have now given up distributing bills; I have settled my son in that office. My eldest daughter was married about three months ago, and I have presented her husband with the Chelsea crossing, as my daughter's wedding portion." "Can he make a living at it?" I eagerly inquired. "Oh yes; that crossing at Chelsea is worth thirty shillings a week, if it is well swept," said he. "But what do you do for a living for yourself?" I asked. "I am the leader of a band," he continued, "and we play for balls and parties, and three

times a week at the Holborn Casino." "You are
determined to rise," said I. "Yes," he replied;

> "Upward, onward, is my watchword.
> Though the winds blow good or ill,
> Though the sky be fair or stormy,
> This shall be my watchword still."

Here is a man, of unmixed blood, a negro of the
primitive stock—brought from the interior of Africa—
having received neither good nor bad from the civilized world—left to struggle with all the disadvantages
of poverty—a stranger in a strange land; and yet he
not only acted well his part in some position or avocation, which is a sufficient commendation for any one
individual, but he distinguished himself in half a
dozen positions or avocations, and some of these of a
character to show a high order of talent. We may
justly hold up this case as an irrefragable argument
that Africa—that Ethiopia, the land of the negroes,
and the early cradle of civilization and of Christianity,
has not lost its capability to produce men. As we
have said of the exhaustless physical resources of
Africa which lie unused, waiting for the plastic hand
of civilized man to come and appropriate them to the
purposes of human advancement, so we may say of
the vast mental and moral resources which yet lie dormant, waiting the sounding of that trumpet which shall
proclaim to the millions of Africa a resurrection from
centuries of mental and moral death. The examples
we have cited we may take as pledges of the capabilities of the race—as precursors of what shall follow.

But while we claim such cases as we have adduced,
as illustrations of what African races are capable of
producing, and what we are warranted in expecting

from them, we do not present these as new and
strange developments in the race. What is, is what
has been; and what has been, is what, we expect, shall
be again. We quote Joseph Jenkins as a man who
displayed a most remarkable versatility of genius, and
in one short life made very remarkable attainments;
and we have brought in illustration men who passed
their earlier years in a crushing servitude; yet in middle life we find them scholars, writers, well versed in
literature, history of the classics; lawyers and physicians, well read in the studies of their professions; or
divines, who, in acquisitions in theology, in philosophy
and metaphysics, in Greek, Latin, and Hebrew, compare well with their brethren of a more favored race.
Yet we do not present these as any thing new under
the sun. The fact that Dr. Pennington, ex-President
Roberts, or Professor Crummell have made their
present attainments and reached their present positions, although the morning of their lives was made
bitter in the "Iron Furnace," is not more strange than
that Henry Diaz, the black commander in Brazil,
should "be extolled, in all the histories of that country, as one of the most sagacious and talented men
and experienced officers of whom they could boast;"
or that the modern Hannibal, an African, should have
gained, by his own exertion, a good education, and
rise to be a lieutenant-general and director of artil-
lery under Peter the Great; or that Don Juan Latino,
a negro, should become teacher of the Latin language
at Seville; or that Antony William Arno, a native of
Guinea, should take the degree of Doctor of Philosophy at the University of Wittemberg; or that James
J. Capetein, fresh from the coast of Africa, should be-

come master of the Latin, Greek, Hebrew, and Chaldaic languages; or that James Derham, as already mentioned, an imported negro, should be considered one of the ablest physicians in New Orleans. We might extend the catalogue—there is no lack of materials. Blumenbach boldly affirms of the negro: "there is no savage people who have distinguished themselves by such examples of perfectibility and capacity for scientific cultivation." Edward Everett, in a public address before the Colonization Society, at Washington, 1853, speaks unhesitatingly of the "aptitude of the colored race for every kind of intellectual culture."

Mr. Everett cites instances which had fallen under his notice, especially during his connection with Cambridge University, and utterly repudiates the idea that there is any general inferiority of the African race. He says: "They have done as well as persons of European or Anglo-American origin would have done after three thousand years of similar depression and hardship. The question has been asked, 'Does not the negro labor under some incurable, natural inferiority?' In this, for myself, I have no belief."

CHAPTER XI.

The curse of Africa—Portuguese adventurers and residents—Desolating piracies—Jesuitism.

THE capabilities and resources of Africa, both to produce men and to realize all the great purposes of civilized life, have, perhaps, been made sufficiently to appear. Yet all the great and good things that have heretofore come of Africa seem rather as exceptions —anomalies—as sweet waters from a bitter fountain, as good fruit from a corrupt tree. Indeed, it must be conceded that these things are but little more than exceptions from the long-established order of degradation and suffering which has been the common inheritance of that mysterious land. And so protracted, and sore, and afflictive have been her sufferings, that we need not marvel that other races have, for centuries, looked upon her as being the doomed subject of some dire malediction of Heaven. Nor is it strange that men should, unthinkingly, for the want of another solution of the great problem, fix on the " curse of Canaan," as the solution sought.

While we can discover no good authority for extending the curse pronounced by Noah on the youngest son of Ham to the entire Hamic race—indeed, not deeming it altogether clear that God cursed even Canaan—yet, we are constrained to concede that the dealings of Providence toward Africa and her race have been exceedingly mysterious. If under no Divine malediction, why then have they been left to be so strangely preyed upon by every unclean bird? The most malign agencies have been permitted to act against them. They have for a very long period, and, no doubt, for reasons which we know not now, but, as her history develops, we shall know hereafter, been given up to rebuke and scourging by some of the most malignant powers of sin. As in the world in general, so in Africa in particular, sin has been allowed its perfect work—to take root, to expand, to mature and bring forth its poisonous fruits. God would first have the universe see what sin can do— what, with all the wealth and resources, and power, and pride, and ambition of the world, the "prince of this world" can achieve—then what Christ and holiness can do.

Not till it has been made to appear how certainly sin, if allowed unrestrained dominion, works desolation and final ruin, does He, that has the power over sin, interpose his almighty arm, and arrest its deadly ravages, and say: Hitherto shalt thou come, and no further. And the reflecting observer can scarcely have overlooked that a people or nation which God designs especially to exalt, he first especially humbles; and more usually does he humble them for a long time, as well as bring them very low. It is in this way that he magnifies his mercy, and exalts his power, and prepares a people to fulfill a great and good mission in the world, and prepares the world to accept their mission as heaven appointed.

We shall try Africa by such criteria, and see what of the hand of God we can discover in all his singular dealings with her. The following chapter shall be devoted to the dark phases of Africa's history—the curse which has so long been the portion of her cup.

How far Africa may have been the subject of the direct malediction of Heaven I do not attempt to determine. I have shown elsewhere that neither the negro race, nor any African race, was the subject of the " curse of Canaan." That curse, whatever it was, extended not beyond the posterity of Canaan; which people ceased to exist long centuries ago, and which, indeed, does not seem ever to have been an African race, either while they enjoyed a nationality, or after their dispersion.

Nor need I stop to inquire what reasons there may be lying far back in the annals of the early progenitors of the African races, why such a sore and protracted series of afflictions have been entailed for forty or fifty centuries on that ill-fated continent. Certain it is that she has been left to suffer the most mysterious succession of calamities. No wonder that, to many, the withering curse pronounced on Canaan (a son of Ham), has seemed to have had a more literal and dreadful fulfillment in the race of Ham generally, than in the race of Canaan in particular. "A servant of servants shalt thou be." Most signally did the different tribes of the Canaanites suffer the righteous judgments of Heaven in the days of Joshua; and the suffering remnant that escaped, no doubt, in their miserable dispersion, suffered the literal fulfillment of the curse. But the other branches of the family of Ham, which, with their great progenitor at their head, peopled Africa, seem to have been the more special and perpetual inheritors of a curse. Yet we would scarcely hazard an opinion here. We know little of the secret reasons of God in his dealings either with nations or individuals. Of Providential dispensations we can but very inadequately distinguish which are disciplinary, or which retributive. Those eighteen on whom the tower of Siloam fell were not sinners above all men that dwelt in Jerusalem. Irrespective of merit or moral character, God often sorely abases those whom he is about signally to honor.

We would, therefore, choose to speak of Africa simply as she stands before us in the annals of her singular history. And here the voice of her wailing salutes our ears, especially from four different channels. The destroying angel, which, in more modern times, has laid her waste, has appeared: 1. In the form of a large and corrupt class of voracious Portuguese adventurers and residents, who prowled on her coasts, as so many ravening beasts, after the discoveries of the latter part of the 15th century. 2. In the shape of the desolating piracies of that same period, and as nearly connected, too, with the same class of reckless and abandoned adventurers. 3. The curse of Jesuitism. 4. The yet more dreadful and protracted curse of the slave-trade. Each of these particulars demand a separate consideration.

All four of these deadly plagues of Africa are of Portuguese origin, and, to a great extent, inflicted afterward by the Portuguese. Of all the nations that have cursed Africa, the Portuguese have been the direst curse.

I. These marauding adventurers committed their merciless depredations on Africa during two centuries —from about the year 1440, when Antonio Gonzales seized and first made slaves of the natives, to 1642, when the Dutch took possession of their principal forts; soon after which their power in Africa was broken by the growing influence of the Dutch, the English, and the French. There is, perhaps, not a blacker page in history than that which records the atrocities of the Portuguese in Africa.

Though it does not apear that the Portuguese ever established an extensive government in Africa, yet they erected forts, strongly fortified themselves there, and quite controlled the western coast. So universally predominant was their influence, that, in the course of the 16th century, says the historian, the Portuguese became the common language of business, and was everywhere generally understood by such natives as had intercourse with foreigners.

Of the character of the Portuguese on the coast, and their influence on the natives, some idea may be formed from what has already been said. Africa became a cage of every unclean bird—corrupt and corrupting each other, each generation seeming to wax worse and worse—"a place of banishment for criminals convicted of various outrages, violence, and robbery; a place where fugitives from justice sought and found a refuge; a place where adventurers, who hated the restraints of law, sought freedom and impunity." "No wonder, therefore," says a writer who had been there, "that the histories of those times give an account of unparalleled violence and inhumanities perpetrated at the place by the Portuguese, while under their subjection, not only against the natives and such Europeans as resorted thither, but even among themselves." Bad as the native character originally was, Portuguese influence rapidly added to its atrocity.

This is abundantly evinced by the series of wars which commenced among them about this time. The Portuguese, says another writer, were men of the "basest behavior," cruel, revengeful, and corrupt above all men he had ever known. And the representatives of other European nations, though not sunk so low in the scale of moral turpitude as the Portuguese, it is affirmed were the most miserable excrescences of civilization and Christianity. The Spaniards, for their shameless atrocities, were detested, even by the natives. "The influence of English, Dutch, and French, on the natives, was, in some respects, different from that of the Portuguese; but, whether it was, on the whole, better, is a question, says one, of some difficulty." The Dutch are accused of gaining the favor of the negroes by teaching them drunkenness and other vices; that they "became absolute pirates, and seized and held several places on the coast, to which they had no right but that of the strongest."

The English had their regular traders and their privateers engaged on the coast of Africa. Of the former it is said: "only a part seemed to have been comparatively decent," while the latter are described as "loose privateering blades, who, if they could not trade fairly with the natives, could rob."

Deeply, indeed, has Africa been left to drink the dregs of human bitterness. Her land is full of ferocious beasts; but harmless are these compared with the giant beasts of prey in human form which she has had to encounter. For centuries she has been made the boiling cauldron into which has been poured the burning streams of iniquity—the scum and offscouring of all the western nations. The only marvel is that

in the native African character there is a single redeeming trait remaining—that her people are not
totally corrupt, totally abandoned and sunk in the
depths of human degradation past all recovery. Perhaps no other people could have outlived the torrents
of iniquity which, wave after wave, have been suffered
to pass over them.

But I have no more than begun to speak of Africa's
wrongs—of the burning curse which she has been left
to suffer. I shall therefore present as the next aspect
of the same appalling subject,

II. The singular concatenation of evils inflicted on
Africa by the numerous hordes of pirates which infested the coast during the last half of the 17th and
the first half of the 18th centuries. Particularly after
the partial breaking up of the buccaneers in the West
Indies, in 1688, and still more after their suppression
in 1697, they spread themselves over the whole extent
of the Atlantic and Indian Oceans, and the coast of
Guinea became a principal haunt, and Sierra Leone a
yet more favorite resort. No part of the coast is said
to have suffered so severely as the part now known as
Liberia, and its vicinity. The river Mesurado was
called Rio Duro, on account of the unheard of cruelties practiced there. These hordes of abandoned men,
"restrained by no moral principle, by no feeling of
humanity, by no sense of shame," perfectly versed in
all the vices of civilization, landed wherever and
almost whenever they pleased upon the whole coast,
with armed forces which the natives had no means of
resisting, and compelled the inhabitants to "become
the partners of their revels, the accomplices or dupes
of their duplicity, or the victims of their violence."

No people, perhaps, were ever, since the world began, subjected to so dreadful a training in moral depravity. The influence of the pirates was for a long time over-powering along nearly the whole coast, and, wherever met, they were the most rapacious, remorselessly fero-cious, and licentious race that ever disgraced sea or land. When not at sea, they committed the most re-morseless depredations on shore.

Thus, again, rolled over the suffering sons of Ham another burning tide of iniquity, with scarcely a re-maining vestige of virtue. For theft, licentiousness, cannibalism, the offering of human sacrifices, and all sorts of abominations connected with the most abject ignorance and sottishness, there was, if historians may be credited, not elsewhere their equal. But their cup was not yet full. Two woes had passed, and two more, not less desolating, were to come. They were now prepared for conversion to Rome's Christianity, and,

III. The Jesuits came to consummate what the Portuguese and pirates had begun. A late writer, an officer on board one of our ships on the African coast, speaks of the "waxing and waning of the fortunes of the Jesuits in proportion to the prosperity or depres-sion of the slave-trade." He speaks particularly of the Portuguese province of Angola, the capital of which was Loanda. Nowhere in Africa has the apostacy of Rome had a ranker development; and nowhere do we find a more nefarious mart of slaves. While the slave-trade was at its zenith, Loanda was a place of great opulence; the Mother Church was in the glory of all her abominations. Her Jesuits had a congenial field, her priests occupied palaces—"grand and mag-

nificent churches, convents, and nunneries" were met
on every side, and wealth, and grandeur, and Church
prosperity kept pace with the awful strides of the nefarious traffic in human flesh.   But with the decay of
the slave-trade, the place has quite fallen into delapi-
dation.   Those "splendid temples," he says, " are now
the habitations for the moles, or workshops for con-
victs guilty of the foulest crimes."   "The fraternity is
now unrepresented by a living man."

We can scarcely gauge the dimensions of a curse
which should identify Christianity with that most
abominable and devastating trade.   Christianity is
emphatically the hope of the world.   But that system,
called Christianity, which was introduced into the
capital of the Portuguese province, in Africa, was
more to be feared than the terrible faith of the Arabian prophet, or the most cruel system of Paganism.
It was a religion of money and of blood.   It was without truth, without a Sabbath, and without mercy.   It
brought with it no truth-telling Bible, no sacred rest
of the Sabbath, no pure moral influences.   We can
scarcely conceive how a people could suffer a greater
moral disaster than the introduction among them of
so bad a counterfeit of Christianity.   Spare the "stay
of bread" and the stay of water, and you may poison
whatever else you please.   The religion of Jesus is
the Bread of life.   Mutilate, corrupt, poison this, and
you have doomed the immortal spirits of a people to
a never-ending perdition.   It was a blighting curse
when this form of false Christianity unfurled in Africa
her blood-stained banners.

Would that the fact might be blotted from the annals of the world's history, that the only Christianity

then known to those benighted tribes was a Christianity that indicated and had a most guilty complicity with the atrocious slave-trade! From the first, the Romish missionaries are declared to have countenanced the traffic. But soon they were justly chargeable with more than a mere toleration. "They participated in the traffic themselves—they gave the full force of their example to countenance all the enormities which were inseparably connected with it." Persons convicted of celebrating the rights of the native religion were, by them, sold to the first slave-ship that appeared. Vessels engaged in the traffic "could always depend on the missionaries to give them material aid in making up their compliment of slaves. Nor were these holy fathers too scrupulous, occasionally, to sell their own domestics to such captains or supercargos as had done them favors. In return for a flask of wine, given him to celebrate the sacrament, Merolla gave the Portuguese captain a negro slave." Indeed, the missionaries seem to have felt that there was no serious harm in consigning any number of the inhabitants of the country to foreign servitude, "provided only that they were baptized, and not permitted to fall into the hands of heretics." Sad and humiliating, indeed, is the picture which Christianity is made to present in that land of darkness and spiritual death. It showed not the soul of an angel, but the soul of a demon—not the spirit of liberty, but of bondage—not the spirit of peace and purity, of love and righteousness, but it breathed the soul of all abominations, of all the cruelties and atrocities concentrated in the odious traffic.

This traffic has now long been the giant curse of

Africa. It has, from century to century, passed as a withering sirocco over that poor land. Three woes are passed, never to return ; but the fourth is yet pouring out the vials of its wrath upon her in almost unmitigated fury. The atrocious slave-trade shall form the subject of our next chapter.

CHAPTER XII.

The curse of Africa—The slave-trade the dreadful consummation of the curse.

IV. The slave-trade is the climax of evil which has befallen the land of Ham. No pen will ever be able to delineate its disgusting details—no human conception fathom the depths of its iniquity. Forty millions of the sons and daughters of Africa have been feloniously extracted from her soil, and reduced to a wretched foreign bondage; while it is said, that nine-tenths of the resident population of Africa are slaves to the other tenth.

It is quite impossible that I should, in so limited a space, give you any thing like a complete delineation of this monster curse; yet I may draw a picture sufficient for our purpose. We are at present chiefly concerned with the influence which this traffic has had on Africa, especially the degrading influence. If no other influences had been at work to debase the children of Ham, this alone is quite sufficient.

Did it fall within the range of our present plan, we might rehearse the harrowing tale of the cruelties of the capture, the detention on the African coast, and the "middle passage." In the whole history of human atrocities, there is not another such chapter. Let us look at a few of these appalling facts.

It is well known that very decisive measures have been taken by some of the Christian governments,

10

especially by Great Britain and the United States, to suppress the slave-trade. Hundreds of millions of pounds have been expended for the support of the preventive squadron on the coast of Africa, and, no doubt, good has been accomplished. Yet it has quite failed of its main end. Keen-eyed avarice has managed so far to elude the sternest vigilance of the squadron, that the trade is said actually to have increased during this same period—and not only to have increased, but to have been carried on with vastly more rigor. Since the traffic has been illegitimate and been branded as piracy, it has been conducted in a manner greatly to increase its cruelties. The comparatively commodious vessels then used in the trade were at once exchanged for the fast-sailing "American clippers," than which vessels of no form afford so miserable accommodations for slaves. Hundreds are packed like so many herrings in a space so cramped as not even to allow of a comfortable sitting posture.

It is estimated that 200,000 human beings are still reduced to bondage annually by this nefarious traffic; and this is but the smaller number of those who are sacrificed to this cruel Moloch. In the seizure of every 1,000 a still greater number are made victims of slaughter. Almost the only cause of war in Africa is for the capture of slaves, and these wars are the most barbarous and exterminating of all wars. A native chief contracts to supply a slave-dealer with 100 or 500 slaves. He makes an incursion into a neighboring tribe—surprises the inhabitants of some peaceful village—burns their houses over their heads, that, in their flight, they may seize on the young and strong for slaves, while all the aged and young children are slaughtered. In the accounts of these "skirmishes," as they are called, we are informed that 20,000, 40,000, and sometimes 60,000, or 100,000, are victims of slaughter. But those who meet death in the common fate of war are the favored victims. A fate a thousand times worse awaits them who escape the slaughter. Those who are not seized at once flee to the mountains and hide themselves in caves, whither the barbarous soldiers pursue them, and fire their muskets in the caverns; and if they can not induce them to quit their places of concealment, they build fires at the entrance of the caverns, and either suffocate the negroes, or compel them to surrender. At other times, the mountain to which the refugees have fled is surrounded and all access to the springs of water cut off, and nothing remains to these wretched beings but death in the most horrid shape, or slavery ten-fold more to be dreaded. In some instances the whole adult population is massacred, and only the children are reserved for sale. One writer says: "I should think, if my information be correct, that, in addition to the 7,000 or 8,000 taken captive, at least 15,000 were killed in defense, or by suffocation, at the time of being taken."

But the waste of human life in the seizure is but one item in the whole account. The mortality during the detention on the coast before sale and shipment is terrific. The bodily wrongs and deprivations to which they are subjected, added to the excruciating agonies of mind which such a condition induces, are the fruitful source of malignant diseases which sweep off multitudes. In many instances not less than fifty

per cent. must again be deducted for this item of
mortality. Not more than two out of three of all
seized are ever put on board the slave vessel. The
maimed, the diseased, the insane, the blind—all who
have become, from any cause, unsalable, are abso-
lutely murdered. At the great slave marts it frequently happens, too, that the market is overstocked,
"in which case the maintenance of these wretched
beings falls on the Government." The king orders an
examination to be made, and the infirm, sickly, and
unsalable are removed to a separate factory (1,000 of
these miserable objects have been seen at one time),
whence they are conveyed, pinioned, to the banks of
a river, where, a weight being appended to their
necks, they are rowed into the middle of the stream,
and thrown into the water and left to perish. The
King of Loango, who has been known to boast that
he could load eight slave ships a week, did not hesitate to cause the prisoners taken in his predatory ex-
cursions to be murdered, if, on their arrival at the
coast, there was no market for them. To save himself
the trouble and expense of their support, "they were
taken to the side of a hill, a little beyond the town,
and coolly knocked on the head."

But all these sufferings are but preliminary to the
horrors of the "middle passage." These sufferings
beggar all description. "Never," says the immortal
Wilberforce, "can so much misery be found condensed
in so small a space as in the slave ship during the
middle passage." The most appalling accounts have
been written, and yet, from the nature of the case, but
little of the horrid reality is known. Those unparalleled deeds of darkness are suffered to come to the

light as little as possible. We blush to own a relationship with these monsters in human form, and would not, if not compelled, believe men capable of acts of unrelenting humanity befitting only apostates of the nether world. But it is no part of our business to rehearse these atrocities, but simply to point to them as marks of the withering, burning curse which has fallen so heavily on poor Africa—an awful drain on her of 500,000 annually.

Our business is rather with the influence which this atrocious trade has exerted on Africa. We shall here see cause to wonder, not why Africa is sunk so low, but why she has not sunk lower. We can not look amiss to discover the baneful influence of this trade. Morally, mentally, socially, in reference to domestic relations and happiness, as well as physically and commercially, Africa has suffered incalculable wrongs. And—

1. The deadliest blow is doubtless the moral devastation which that trade has inflicted. It has not left a single moral principle uninvaded. The whole tendency of the principle and practice is to annihilate, root and branch, the last vestige of moral feeling. The natives have been, by this trade, brought in contact with the most profligate and abandoned class of men on the face of the earth, while the traffic itself is the most demoralizing. Speaking of the moral desolation inflicted on Africa, by this trade, an intelligent writer says: " All moral virtue has been extinguished in the people, and their industry annihilated by this one ruinous cause. Polygamy and domestic slavery, it is well known, are as universal as the scanty means of the people will permit. And a licentiousness which

none, not even the worst part of any civilized community on earth can parallel, gives a hellish consummation to the frightful deformity imparted by sin, to the
moral aspect of these tribes." This is the picture
we have drawn of the moral condition of tribes which
once occupied the country now known as Liberia, and
I may add Sierra Leone.

An intelligent and excellent English minister was
once called to visit a man then on his death-bed, who
had been for many years engaged in the African slave-
trade. He had been commander of a swift and successful ship, but had been often compelled to throw
his poor captives to the sharks and the sea, to save
his vessel from the cruisers, or to lighten it in the
storm; and had passed through the various terrible
scenes incident to the prosecution of that infamous
traffic. And now he was dying; in the full maturity
of his powers, and in the midst, if we remember
rightly, of pecuniary prosperity and social comfort.
The minister spoke to him of repentance. "Repentance," was his reply, "I can not repent! You have
seen many sorts of men, Sir, and, perhaps, you think
you have seen the most wicked and desperate among
them. But I tell you that you don't know any thing
about an African slave-trader. His heart is dead.
Why, Sir, I know perfectly well—I understand it fully
—that I shall die in spite of every thing; and I know
that I shall go to hell. There is no possible salvation
for me. It is perfectly impossible but that I shall be
damned. And yet, it don't move me in the least. I
am just as indifferent to it as ever I was in my life."
And so he died; with despair perfected into insensi-
bility and death; the very fires of Divine wrath, as

they flashed upon his face, not starting a sigh or a pulse of emotion.   His heart was " dead !"

2. The mental degradation inflicted by this trade is awfully disastrous.   To say nothing of the debasing influence which such a traffic must necessarily have on the minds of a people, which must be degrading beyond conception — truly brutalizing, whether we consider the traffickers or those who are preyed upon by those human vultures, education, all mental improvement, schools, institutions of learning, must be almost entirely precluded.   The horrid state of things induced by the slave-trade takes away all incitements to intellectual progress.   It makes the condition of the Africans like that of the brute animals, in which the stronger prey on the weak.   The one cultivates the ferocity of the tiger, and pounces on his prey without feeling or mercy; the other is like the hunted hart on the mountains, who never feels himself safe from a bondage a hundred-fold worse than death.

3. The influence of the slave-trade on the social relations of Africa is likewise disastrous beyond computation.   It destroys all society.   It annihilates, at a blow, all confidence, and, of consequence, sunders the chain which binds society together.   It cherishes the most debasing fear, jealousy, distrust, and hatred on the one side, and the most brutal avarice and unfeeling barbarity on the other.   It engages in its behalf the worst passions humanity is heir to ; and, consequently, it can produce nothing but the bitterest fruits.   Property, happiness, life, are utterly insecure. There is no stimulant to industry, no security for any thing.   A man may by his honest efforts acquire a property, or go on prosperously for a while in rearing

up a family, but no sooner has the one or the other become large enough to tempt the cupidity of some neighboring chief, than a quarrel is instigated, the peaceful dwelling is seen in flames, the father and mother are killed, the salable children are dragged away to be sold to the slave-dealer, and the property seized. "In such a case," as Wilberforce says, "the same longings which are called forth in the wild beast by the exhibition of his prey," instigate the unfeeling avaricious chief to seize on his defenseless neighbor, who, in his turn, lives in a state of continual suspicion and terror. Park, in his journal says: " Slavery has produced the most baneful effects, causing anarchy, injustice, and oppression to reign in Africa, and exciting nation to rise up against nation, and man against man ; it has covered the face of the country with desolation." And all these evils, and a thousand more, have Christian nations inflicted on Africa, in exchange for which she has received ardent spirits, tawdry silks, gewgaws, and beads. What a return for such a sacrifice ! The heart's blood of Africa for trinkets, rum, and tobacco ! The curse of the slave-trade has become doubly dyed in the curse of rum.

4. As already intimated, the slave-trade is a fell destroyer of all domestic relations. It comes as a perfect blight and leaves all in ruins. Not only may the hand of ruthless violence come any moment on a household—their dwelling be consumed over them, and death or slavery annihilate them in an hour— member torn from member in a manner more agonizing than the pangs of death—but jealousy and distrust and fear reign in such terror throughout the land,

that the domestic relations are scarcely more than a name. So callous, so destitute of "natural affection," so perfectly sordid and brutal does this traffic make a people, that a father sells his child, or a child a parent. We are in little danger of exaggerating the demoralizing influences of the slave-trade.

5. But there is one other general respect from which we will, for a moment, look at this form of Africa's curse. It is more especially in a physical point of view—the bearing on commerce, manufactures, education, agriculture, population, and all pecuniary interests. Governor Ashman speaks of large sections of country, once fertile and under a high state of cultivation, but since completely depopulated, and reduced to a desert by the slave-trade. Nothing could so effectually annihilate the agriculture of a country. Her fertile soil is left to yield no more than the least minimum of a supply of the necessities of a barbarous people. Commerce is confined almost entirely to the trade in slaves. Wherever the slave-trade still prevails, or has prevailed, it almost completely annihilates all legitimate commerce, and spreads its blighting influence over every honest calling in life. There are, under such circumstances, no incitements to industry, no motives to accumulate property—to build houses, cultivate farms, and gather the comforts of life about one. There is no security for property. One may sow, but another may reap down the fields of him that sowed while the sower may be toiling, in unrequited labor, in some foreign land, and watering another soil with the burning tears of an unpitied slavery. Africa is just what any land would be, where there is no security for property,

10*

happiness, and life. Man may vegitate and suffer there, but he can not live and thrive.

No other race of people on the whole face of the earth has ever been subjected to such a concatenation of debasing circumstances. We have seen how, for the last four centuries especially, Africa has been a carcass preyed upon by every voracious and unclean bird. What a most abandoned, marauding class of Portuguese begun, the hordes of pirates who next infested the African shores carried forward with a loyalty to the Prince of the power of darkness, perhaps, never surpassed, backed by as loyal a set of Jesuits as ever served the devil in saints' attire. Then followed the climax and consummation of Africa's malediction all concentrated in one. The slave-trade was but the realization and the perfection of all those monstrous iniquities which had heretofore been practiced on poor Africa. It was a land and a sea piracy, concentrating their vengeance, and refining their cruelties, and compounding their inhumanities, for one grand onslaught on the doomed race. And how has this demon of avarice, of cruelty, of all inhumanity, glutted his insatiable maw! He has annually devoured half a million of victims, under circumstances the most shameless and appalling, until a number greater than the present population of that continent, have been feloniously extracted from Africa, or have miserably perished in the seizure, the detention, the "middle passage," and the "seasoning."

An intelligent writer on Africa draws the following woeful picture in these her darkest days—how her condition waxed worse and worse, till the voice of Wilberforce was heard, and the strong arm of the

British lion was reached out to smite the monster trade of the sadly demoralizing influence of slave-traders on the native population. He says :

"For four centuries, or five, if we receive the French account, they have been in the habit of constant intercourse with the most profligate, the most licentious, the most rapacious, and in every respect the vilest and most corrupting classes of men to be found in the civilized world—with slave traders, most of whom were pirates in every thing but courage, and many of whom committed piracy whenever they dared—and with pirates in the fullest sense of the word. Before the year 1600, the influence of these men had been sufficient to displace the native languages in the transaction of business, and substitute the Portuguese, which was generally understood and used in their intercourse with foreigners ; and since that time, the Portuguese has been, in like manner, displaced by the English. By this intercourse, the natives were constantly stimulated to crimes of the deepest dye, and thoroughly trained to all the vices of civilization, which savages are capable of learning. During the most fearful predominance of undisguised piracy, from 1688 to 1730, their demoralization went on, especially upon the windward coast, more rapidly than ever before, and became so intense, that it was impossible to maintain trading houses on shore ; so that, on this account, as we are expressly informed, in 1730 there was not a single European factory on that whole coast. Trade was then carried on by ships passing along the coast, and stopping wherever the natives kindled a fire as a signal for traffic. And this continued to be the usual mode of intercourse on that coast, when the British Parliament, in 1791, began to collect evidence concerning the slave-trade. Nor were factories re-established there, till the slave-trade and its attendant vices had diminished the danger by depopulating the country."

We call these accumulated, long-protracted, unmitigated sufferings of Africa her "curse." Whether this be the realization on the race of Ham of the curse pronounced by Noah on Canaan, as a member of the Hamic family, we do not affirm. It may be retributive, it may be disciplinary, it may be simply preparatory to the manifestations of the Divine mercy and goodness which shall yet be made in favor of this race. The Great King of nations, whose way is in the sea, and his path in the great waters, and whose footsteps are not known, has dealt in a very singular manner with this continent, or rather with this race. We can not fathom his purposes—we would speak with no undue positiveness of the future destiny of Africa. Yet we may form some safe conjecture from the past, of what the future shall be. There is an analogy in God's working. If, in one instance he exalts them he abases, we look that he should do it again. If we find him taking part with the oppressed—lifting up the head that hangs down, magnifying his power by giving strength to the weak, and bringing succor to the helpless, we call this his way of working, and expect its recurrence under similar circumstances.

Here lies our ground of hope for Africa. There is much in the providential history of Africa's past which seems to demand a brighter future. In the drama of her past history, lights and shades have not been proportionately mingled, as is the wont of Providence, in his dispositions of human affairs. Other scenes, brighter, grander than the past, seem needful in order to preserve the harmony of the Divine workmanship. Not only in the Divine arrangements must mercy mingle with judgment, but mercy must in the end triumph over judgment. The pillar of fire and the cloud have not been hid from this great branch of the family of man, but hitherto the dark side has been turned toward them, and they have stumbled and fell. Shall not the light side be yet turned toward them, and they no longer stumble and fall, but lift up the drooping head, and rejoice in the returning smiles of Heaven?

In my next, I shall undertake to prescribe a remedy for the long-continued and multiplied ills of Africa. Deep and deadly as is the wound, there is, we believe, a cure.

CHAPTER XIII.

The cure — Her great desert reclaimed—Commerce—Colonization — Their relations to Liberia—The colonists and the whole country.

WE have spoken of Africa as the mysterious and unknown land—a land held by a wise and all-seeing Providence in reserve for some great future purposes —probably for the exhibition of a higher state of civilization, and a better type of Christianity than the world has yet seen. I have referred you to the past history of Africa, especially to her monumental history, presenting what Africa has been as a pledge of what she shall be. Again : the negro race has been presented as a primitive race of man — the earliest civilized—the race in which learning and the arts first flourished — who first organized civil governments, built cities, and formed great empires. We trace this race as the probable authors of the most ancient works of art in all the south of Asia, in Africa, and Central America. Though, physically, the race of Ham has been thus singularly favored, yet, morally, a strange and mysterious curse has hung over that whole race. We have, therefore, ventured to suggest that, in like manner as the descendants of Shem and Japheth have, each in their turn, been the chosen race, in which the true religion has been preserved and did flourish—in Shem until the coming of Christ, and in Japheth since—so .shall poor, oppressed, long-forgotten Ham come up in remembrance, and last, though not least, share in the rich benedictions of

Heaven. That great continent, so prolific in natural resources—with such untold riches lying dormant in its soil, forests, and mines, and a people so beautifully susceptible, as past history has shown, of the highest grade of civilization and of religion in its highest spiritual type—shall, under some yet future dispensation of Divine grace, play an important part in the great work of human progress and of the world's salvation. Nothing is more sure than that God will espouse the cause of the afflicted—lift up the head that is bowed down—break the bonds of the captives. He will take the part of the oppressed. And if he will, as he promises, make the day of his gracious visitation light and cheering, in proportion to the depth and gloom of the darkness that has preceded—if the light and joy shall be in proportion to the sorrow—what may we not expect for Africa? For more than fifty centuries a dark and impenetrable cloud has settled down upon Africa, ever and anon skirted on its borders by the gleaming up of brilliant lights. It has been most emphatically the land of darkness and groans, the land of oppression and death. Our hope of Africa's exaltation lies in the depth of her present degradation.

Africa's great desert, as before hinted, is a fit emblem of the present and past civil and religious condition of that continent. With the exception of a few smiling oases amid these arid wastes, here lies a vast territory (in its extreme length from east to west 3,000 miles, and 1,000 in breadth), the most perfect desolation that mars the beauty of this earth. Barren wastes, drifting sands, hideous serpents, and ferocious beasts, and every thing but beauty, and loveliness, and fertility, meet and hold revel on this great waste of creation. Here is a territory as large as Europe, and capable, under other auspices, of containing as mighty and opulent kingdoms as Europe now has, which is, at present, as complete a waste as if it were sunk in the bottom of the sea. And such physically is, and such has been, Africa. But shall it always remain so? We think not. We have hope for these great desert wastes, that they shall yet smile in all the luxuriance of Oriental beauty and magnificence—that they shall be covered with a fertile soil, and teem with a numerous population—those immense plains be covered with magnificent cities, smiling villages, and the emporiums of trade—and schools of learning, and all the arts and ornaments of civilized life, shall bless those now hopeless and desolate regions.

In like manner we expect Africa, the great moral desert of the world, shall yet be as the garden of the Lord—her broad surface be covered with civilized nations—liberty there find a new field, and religion a new and interesting development. Like the great Sahara, her type, she has had her oases—kingdoms, cities, institutions of learning, monuments of arts and science, all indicating what may be yet realized on that soil—and may I not say, what shall be.

But you may ask what reason I have to expect that Africa's great natural desert shall ever be reclaimed from the dominion of desolation, and be numbered among the habitable, fertile, populous, portions of the earth? And then, that, in like manner, Africa herself shall be morally renovated? The second question has been in a manner answered. The first admits of an answer which may not be void of interest.

Nothing is wanting in order to reclaim these deserts which would not, in the lapse of time, be realized by a sufficient supply of water. This is manifest,
I think, in the case of the existing oases which are
met in different parts of the great Sahara. These,
doubtless, have their origin in the supply of water in
that portion of the desert. Water, even in sand, produces some vegetation. This decays, and at length
(with other accretions) produces a soil, which continues to spread from the fountain or spring as a centre,
till a fertile spot of miles or leagues is formed. And
so luxuriant does vegetation at length grow there, that
travelers speak of trees, on these islands in the great
waterless ocean, seventeen feet in circumference.

Would not a similar result be gained by the same
means in any part of that great desert?

We then have an obvious intimation here how all
those vast African deserts may yet become fertile
regions, and support as great a population as any
other portion of the earth. Should it please the
Great Architect of our world to perforate these great
deserts with internal water-courses, as he has other
portions of the earth, it would put into operation
causes which would at once begin to transform the
now boundless wastes into fertile and beautiful fields,
and spread over these wide domains busy towns and
flourishing kingdoms. He that sendeth his springs
into the valleys, and maketh them run among the
hills, that they may give drink to every beast of the
field, and habitation among the branches of its sturdy
trees, to the fowls of heaven, can, when it shall please
him, and when, in the fulfillment of his benevolent
purposes, he shall need a larger area of available sur-

face on the earth, and after (and perhaps before) he shall have used other great reservations which have heretofore lain waste, he can, and probably will, convert this great roaming ground of the Bedouin Arabs into pleasant and fertile habitations of man. He will give unto it the glory of Lebanon and the excellency of Carmel and Sharon. He shall water the hills from his chambers; the earth shall be satisfied with the fruit of his works. He shall cause the grass to grow there for the cattle, and herb for the service of man, that he may bring forth fruit out of the earth. And there shall the trees of the Lord be full of sap, and the cedars of Lebanon which he hath planted.

Thus does God make room when and where he pleases for the accomplishment of his great and benevolent purposes, either by changing a desert into a habitable land and a fruitful country, or by reclaiming a new continent from the ocean, or by employing the most insignificant insects to construct a new world in the midst of the Pacific. But to return from our wanderings.

The withering curse of Africa, we have seen, is the slave-trade. In proportion to its prevalence, it blasts every hope of improvement. It annihilates every generous feeling, suppresses all liberty, stifles education, depopulates the land, and spreads a perfect moral desolation over its people. It paralyzes all industry, saps the foundation of all virtue, and shuts out the remotest possibility of a people's prosperity. Such is the CURSE. But is there a CURE? Can Africa be redeemed from the curse? Is there a remedy which can reach her case?

There is but one sovereign cure for all human woes

—but one sure regenerator of corrupt humanity—but one restorer of the ruins of the fall. It is a pure and undefiled religion. No nation with a false religion can be a free, enlightened, prosperous, and permanent nation. There is, therefore, no hope for Africa, except in the introduction and prevalence there of a pure Christianity. But Christianity works through a system of means. We must remove obstacles—we must secure the means. We have seen the slave-trade to be the withering curse. This must first be removed. There is no hope for Africa while she is made the victim of this evil.

We have said that we believe in the regeneration of Africa. But how shall this be? By what means shall the long-depressed and suffering sons of Ham be lifted from their degradation, and take their place among the favored races?

The time draws near, we believe, for the renovation of Africa. As prognostics of this we see the regenerating race—the race which God at present chooses to use as the regenerating race—are turning their faces toward Africa, and cogitating plans for its regeneration. No portion of the world is at present exciting so much interest in England and America, and this interest is evidently yearly increasing. Indeed, the great heart of humanity is beginning to throb for poor Africa. The pulse of the world's pity is quickened—the heart's blood warms at the thought of the unmitigated and protracted wrongs of that suffering continent. There is a feeling daily gathering strength and determination that Africa's wrongs shall be avenged. The voice of humanity forbids the longer continuance of the past series of outrages which have

been practiced on her. This voice is heard in no uncertain accents in the British Parliament and in the
American Congress, and has been echoed from the
high places of nearly all the nations of Christendom.
Some of the greatest minds that represent these nations are employed in behalf of Africa. Benevolence,
too, philanthropy, enterprise, commerce, the researches
of science, are, as never before, engaged to benefit
Africa. This long-forgotten continent has strangely
come up into remembrance, and is largely sharing the
pity and benevolence of the world. There is, too, a
strong expectation abroad in the world—I may call it
a presentiment—that the day of Africa's gracious
visitation is near, and that her future destiny shall be
as singular and mysterious as her past history has
been. Strangely, indeed, has she been permitted to
relapse into a state of the lowest degradation—perhaps to emerge into a higher life. This is the day of
her rebuke—the day of her protracted "captivity."
But the Lord may turn her captivity, and restore her
to his favor.

We do not doubt that Christianity must be the final
and efficient cause of this renovation. We have confidence in nothing else. We present all other agencies as merely instrumental and preparatory to the
great and all-sufficient agency, the Gospel. They are
the messengers that go before and prepare the way.
The Gospel is the mighty arm that shall conquer and
subdue—that shall create all things anew. Yes,
Africa must be evangelized. Her moral deformity,
blacker than the ebon color of her skin, must be washed
in that fountain open for the cleansing of Judah and
Jerusalem. But there are secondary causes conducive

to this one great end. We are, at present, more particularly concerned with these. The slave-trade must be destroyed. The vast natural resources of the continent must be drawn out; the people must be enlightened; social relations must be formed; a productive industry must be created and engaged to ameliorate the condition of the people. These ends must be gained before the children of Ham can be elevated—or rather as the means of their elevation. But how shall these ends be gained? Principally in two ways: 1. By a legitimate and enlightened commerce. And, 2. Especially by Christian colonies.

Three points are here regarded as settled: 1. If Africa is to be regenerated, it should be done through herself—by drawing out and employing her own resources, and through the agency of her own people. 2. That the settling of efficient Christian colonies on her coast is the only effectual and permanent method of suppressing the slave-trade. 3. That colored men only can with safety settle on the coast of Africa. There is much in the nature of the case and more in the providential aspect to indicate that Africa shall, under God, be her own regenerator. But we will direct our attention for a few moments to the two principal instrumentalities through which help is likely to come to Africa.

I. COMMERCE.—The misery of Africa heretofore has been, that she has had no legitimate commerce. A legitimate commerce will do much to suppress the slave-trade, to call out the resources of the country, to excite the industry of the people, to promote the civilization of the natives, and to prepare the way for the introduction of Christianity. Africa has always been

in want of the products of other lands. But unfortu-
nately, the first commercial nation with which she became acquainted (Portugal) taught her that the flesh
and sinews of her sons and daughters were the only
exports that Christian nations wished in return for
the imports brought her. Other Christian nations
followed in the bloody wake of Portugal, making no
demand for legitimate articles of commerce, but only
for slaves. The supply answered to the dreadful demand. And soon the native conscience became sufficiently obtuse, and the native mind sufficiently brutal-
ized, to supply these human chattels in any quantity
demanded. Till quite recently (and not now, except
to a limited extent), the natives of Africa were not
aware that even Great Britain and America wished
to exchange their goods for other commodities than
slaves. The natives, as soon as they learn that other
nations are ready to trade with them in other articles,
are not slow to provide those articles. They show
themselves desirous to conduct a different trade. Is
cotton, ivory, gold-dust, palm oil, coffee, rice, sought
in exchange for what they want, they are eagerly supplied. So extensive has the commerce of Great Britain already become with Africa, that "slave-dealers
complain," says Lord Palmerston, "that the British
are spoiling their trade." And I may safely affirm,
that, in proportion as a lawful commerce is introduced
into any portion of the coast of Africa, the slave-trade
is diminished. The motives to it are very much taken away; and, besides this, commerce brings a barbarous nation out from the darkness in which they
have involved themselves, and introduces them to the
civilized nations, and makes them ashamed of their

inhumanities. They are unconsciously compelled to an amelioration of their condition.

We have alluded to the interesting fact, that commerce provokes the industry of a people, and creates for itself the resources for an enlarged and continued traffic. By creating a demand, it secures a supply. We have seen with what readiness the natives of Africa responded to the demand made by English commerce for cotton, coffee, palm oil, etc., clearly indicating that as soon as sufficient time shall be allowed to elapse to provide a supply of the articles demanded by foreign commerce, and capable of being supplied by that country, there will be no lack of a supply. The necessity which Africa has felt for a traffic in slaves will, of course, be done away; and a few years' intercourse with the improved class of foreigners that will, as the abettors of a lawful traffic, frequent her shores, will quite destroy the disposition to pursue such a trade. We may, therefore, indulge the most sanguine hopes that the days of the slave-trade are numbered—that causes are at work which will most effectually and forever annihilate it.

While I speak with great confidence of the efficacy of a legitimate commerce to blot out the slave-trade, I am not unmindful of, nor do I undervalue, the very laudable efforts of Great Britain, France, and America to suppress the trade by an armed force. Millions of money and many valuable lives have, within a few years, been expended on the African coast for this purpose. And I believe the united naval forces of those nations were never employed in so worthy a cause. Nor have they, as some are fond of asserting, failed of the object. Though they have, no doubt, in some respects, aggravated the cruelties of the trade by making the trade contraband, and for this reason imposing on the wicked traffickers the necessity of greater secrecy, and oftentimes of vastly increased cruelties, yet this is very far from showing that they have rendered no service to the cause. The least they have done (and this is much) is, they have recaptured thousands of those wretched beings, who were being dragged into a bondage worse than death, and restored them to their native land; they have broken up many a slave factory on the coast; and, more than all, they have produced a moral impression on the world at large against this whole traffic, which is worth a thousand times more than all it has cost. The presence of these naval forces are expressions of the will of nations, and help to brand in deeper disgrace the horrid traffic in flesh and blood. As a matter of force, the strong arm of naval power may put down the slave-trade; but needful as this is, the traffic, if suppressed, will not stay suppressed unless other efficient means be employed. The moment the strong arm of military power be withdrawn, all things would return into the same channel. Military force may gain the victory, but commerce and other kindred means will perpetuate it. No naval force on the earth can put down a traffic that pays so good a profit. The cravings of avarice will devise means to elude the utmost vigilance. A profit of 400 or 500 per cent. will brave any blockade ever laid. A member in the British Parliament stated, that a man could be bought on the coast of Africa for twenty pounds, conveyed to Cuba for six pounds ten shillings, and sold on his arrival there for one hundred pounds, thus leaving a clear profit to the slave-dealer of seventy-three pounds ten shillings, or about $365. In vain will be all the attempts permanently to destroy this trade, unless a substitute be introduced. A legitimate commerce is this substitute.

Time is too short ever fully to repay Africa for the wrongs she has suffered on account of the slave-trade. It is an indellible wrong.

It has been abundantly shown that the natural resources of Africa are sufficient to form the basis of an extensive commerce. Already England has a commerce with Africa of $28,000,000 annually; $210,000,000 worth of gold-dust has been brought to England from Africa. And all this, while in not a single article have the exports from Africa but just begun to be cultivated. Nothing is more evident than that, there can not be a shadow of an excuse for the slave-trade in any lack of commodities with which to carry on an exchange with other nations. No more is needed than to draw out the exhaustless riches of that land, and she will need no other exports. We have the declaration of Lord Palmerston, as far-seeing and philanthropic a statesman as England can boast, and one who seems fully awake to the importance of African commerce, and who clearly comprehends the beneficial results which would accrue to England from such a commerce, we have his lordship's declaration, that "No part of the globe offers more scope for the commercial enterprise of England than the coast of Africa." When once the energies of the people shall be engaged in supplying the material for and prosecuting an extensive commerce, an end will be put, most effectually, to the slave-trade.

11

But this is contemplating commerce only in the lower grade of its influences. It has a higher province—a higher sphere of influence—a transforming power on the social, civil, and moral habits and interests of nations, which raises it far above the mere pounds and pence of a barter of commodities. It is commerce that builds cities—that accumulates wealth and provides capital for carrying on great and beneficial enterprises—that furnishes the facilities for a higher order of education—that concentrates the numbers and means needful to carry out great public and philanthropic schemes. The influence of cities on a nation is immense.

Trading stations, factories, trading communities, illustrate what I mean. The Tyrians and Phœnicians, on the eastern shore of the Mediterranean, were such. These trading stations formed the medium between Egypt and Greece, and became the channel through which the arts, the sciences, and the civilizing and elevating influences and institutions of the former found their way into the latter. Through this channel the alphabet, as we have seen, traveled from Africa in Europe, and first, in the rising State of Greece, laid the foundation of her literary and scientific greatness. Commerce is not only the great civilizer of nations, but literature and science are vastly indebted to it—and religion not the less so. Give Africa a commerce such as she is capable of sustaining, and you have done vastly more than to annihilate the slave-trade. You have at once opened the channel for the introduction of all that can bless her.

We have a remarkable illustration of the influence and expansibility of a trading community, in the history of the East India Company. A company of traders go out to India under the broad wing of commerce. They establish themselves on the Ganges, simply as a trading company. But what expansion of their plans—what enlargement of the sphere of their influence and power, till boundless wealth and dominion were included in their wide grasp! And not only has the result been a vast empire, but commerce has here, again, as is her wont, become the medium through which has flowed into India, through many a fertilizing stream, the best riches of Europe. European science, a Christian literature, the principles of Christian governments and jurisprudence, the printing press, the priceless book of Divine truth, translated into the dialects of the country, the merciful and civilizing day of sacred rest, books, free schools, and institutions for the higher branches of learning; and, above all, there has plentifully flowed in through this same channel, the benign influences of Christianity, a boon infinitely richer than all the precious treasures which avarice or honest gain has carried away. But for the influence of commerce and its natural expansion into a great civil power, not a Christian mission could have existed in the country— not a female school had been established till this day —not a translation of the Bible made into a language of the country, but all had remained as for centuries before—one unbroken cloud of darkness, ignorance, superstition, and death.

We do not think the expectation unreasonable, that trading communities (likely to be formed) on the coast of Africa, should exert a similar influence.

Already the growing commerce with Africa is making its influence felt. We are, no doubt, indebted to this for the increased interest and sympathy which is felt for Africa. She is by this means brought into notice—her cry is heard—her groans are pitied—the warm heart of humanity throbs—the bowels of Chris-tendom yearns to bring relief to the suffering.

We are able here to refer to British trading compa-nies, recently established, which are omens of great good to Africa. One which lately came into successful opera-tion, called the "West Africa Company," demands a special notice. Taking this as a representative of the roused energies and the combined efforts of Great Brit-ain to evolve, for her own interest, and evidently to bless Africa, the commercial resources of that continent, we may quote a few paragraphs from a late circular of that company. We shall get, at least, a *hint*, that such well-organized agencies will not exist many years before England will declare herself-independent of slavehold-ers' cotton, and slavery will be left, minus its profits, and King Cotton will be "relieved from-his command."

While our dreadful war lingers, and the South are fighting to desperation, and to their own destruction, for the perpetual enslavement of the black race, and half of us at the North are vacillating between everlasting right, and a great and disgraceful wrong, and sordidly and ignominiously calculating which is the best policy, to do right, or to do wrong—to let the oppressed go free, that we may, as a nation, receive the benediction of heaven, or to forge tighter their chains, and risk the awful retribution threatened against them that oppress the poor and helpless—while thus essaying to dodge the right, and to dare the wrong, cotton seeds are germin-ating in a genial soil—cotton plants are taking root in

Africa, in India, in Turkey, in Brazil, and Australia, and maturing beneath the sunshine of approving heaven, and and will soon set whirling again every spindle in England, with a power and velocity that shall whirl into an ignominious oblivion the last vestige of American slavery. But what of the " West Africa Company?"

" The object of the company is to establish trading stations, factories, and depots on the coast of Western Africa, and by means of organized agencies, to bring down and collect for shipment at such stations the valuable products of the interior ; to import goods, and introduce machinery for cleaning and pressing cotton, and for other purposes ; and generally to enter into commercial relations with the native traders, by means of barter, traffic, or otherwise ; and thereby to open up, in exchange for British manufactures, a practically illimitable market for cotton and other products, and to secure their transmission to the ports of the United Kingdom.

" The capabilities of Africa to meet the commercial requirements of Europe are evidenced in the variety of its productions, and the increasing extent of its trading operations ; and it has long been a matter of surprise that the encouragement of native industry should have been left to associations of a philanthropic character, or to a few merchants intent upon the enormous profit which exclusive dealings with the natives incontestably afford.

" The cultivation of the cotton plant, and the employment of African labor on its native soil, have already been sufficiently tested. There is abundance of labor seeking employment, a fertile soil well adapted for its growth, and a population actively alive to what will benefit themselves. No expensive or uncertain experiments are required to test the ability or the will of the natives to supply this country with cheap and good cotton. The testimony of the officers of the Niger expedition concurs with and confirms the evidence of Dr. Livingston, and other African travelers, that indigenous cotton is growing in abundance throughout vast districts, covering many thousands of miles of territory, and only waits to be gathered. Some tribes of the natives are largely engaged in manufacturing cotton into clothing for their own use. It is calculated that more than 200,000 pieces of these cloths are annually exported from Africa into the Brazils. In fact, only buyers on the spot are wanted to take from the natives what they have to offer, giving in exchange manufactured goods suitable to their requirements.

" In a letter from Dr. Balfour Bakie, in command of the Niger expedition, to the Secretary of State for Foreign Affairs, which Lord Russell caused to be inserted in the London *Gazette* of August 29, 1862, he emphatically urges his lordship 'to call attention, in England, to the peculiar eligibility of this portion of Central Africa (Bida Nusse) as a cotton-field.' Again, speaking of Sudan, and the Yoruba Country, he proceeds to say : 'Here cotton is already in abundance, and cultivated by a people able and willing to work, and accustomed to its habits and rearing ; nothing is required but increased demand, means of purchase, cleaning, and shipment. The rest would speedily follow.'

" Another practical authority, Mr. Clegg, of Manchester, who has an establishment at Abeokuta, states : 'For very many years my instructions have been to cease buying cotton when more than a halfpenny per pound is the seed, and my young Africans have again and again written to say that at that price far more was brought to them than they could buy.'

" Mr. I. Lyons McLeod, Hon. Secretary to the African Aid Society, in a letter to the *Times*, March 28, 1861, writes : 'It is a well-attested fact, that from Western Africa (shipping port Lagos), cotton in abundance may be purchased at 2d. per lb., and, allowing for exorbitant overcharge for cleaning, freight, etc., it may be sold from the same locality in Liverpool at $4\frac{1}{2}$d. per lb. This cotton is equal in quality to New Orleans at $6\frac{1}{2}$d. per lb., proving beyond doubt that from Western Africa, which is nearer to our shores than the cotton districts of America, we may obtain the same amount of cotton for £20,000,000 for which we are paying the slaveholders of the United States £30,000,000. In Western Africa—Yoruba Country, and along the valley of the Niger' (the localities above referred to by Dr. Balfour Bakie), ' the natives are ready to supply any amount of cotton for Manchester and Glasgow manufac· turers.'

"These testimonies appear to demand the most serious attention and consideration at the present crisis.

" There is abundant evidence to show that India can not for many years supply the quantity or quality re· quired. The Egyptian supply is the only one which might be supposed likely to compete with that imported from West Africa ; but the Egyptian cotton imported into England has never hitherto reached 200,000 bales in any one year, and if doubled (which it can not be for two or three years), it will not suffice to make up the deficiency created by the reduced supplies of ordinary Americans. Besides, the average price of Egyptian cotton has been 8d. per lb. for several years. African cotton, equal to middling Orleans, can be delivered in Liverpool at a cost to the importer of fourpence half penny per lb. In the seed, in Africa, it may be procured in unlimited quantities at about one halfpenny per lb. ; cleaned cotton about threepence. Payments being made in barter, the profits on the goods reduce the cost price of the cotton considerably.

" It is not the intention of the West Africa Company to become cultivators of cotton ; the company will simply be purchasers of cotton, which will be brought down to their stations by native traders, and thence shipped to the ports of the United Kingdom.

" Several well-known firms, having used African cotton in their manufactories, are able to report favorably of its qualities for working.

" The company will not, however, depend on cotton alone for realizing a good dividend on the capital employed. The interchange of commodities will be widened to the largest possible extent, so as to include every other product of Africa, which will pay an· enhanced value in this country. These products, which consist chiefly of palm oil, shea butter, gold-dust, ivory, hides, indigo, copper, ground-nuts, pepper, arrow-root, gums, dye woods, ostrich feathers, timber for ship building, and other articles of commerce equally suitable to the requirements of our markets, will also be made the media of trade, so as to suit the industry and keen trading instincts of the various classes of native producers. The fact that the production of palm oil, shea butter, and other valuable articles, is in excess of the local demand, can be shown by the latest and most indubitable authorities. The Rev. Samuel Crowther, writing to the Church Missionary Society lately, states : 'At the Delta of the Niger alone, millions worth, in red oil and black oil from the kernels of the palm nut, rot away annually for want of inducements to collect them.'

"From an official report received through the Board of Trade, it appears that in 1856 upward of 220,000 tons of these kernels, from which oil of the value of £3,789,000 might have been extracted, were actually thrown away on the coast. The amount thus lost represents in actual value a sum of upward of a' million sterling, more than all the tallow exported from Russia in that year; and when it is considered that the tallow was paid for in cash, and that the bulk of the trade with Africa may be carried on by barter of the manufactures of Manchester, Glasgow, Birmingham, the Potteries, and Sheffield, it is impossible to overrate the benefits which will accrue to this country by developing the resources of Western Africa.

"As there is no currency in the country, trade is conducted by means of barter, so that a market for English productions will be opened at every point from which the company draws its supplies of raw materials; a profit both ways will thus be obtained by the company, viz., upon the goods sold in Africa, and *vice versa* upon the cotton, palm oil, etc., imported and sold in the English markets.

" The West Africa Company will commence operations under peculiarly favorable circumstances, owing to the fact that their agencies on the west coast of Africa are already organized; and competent acclimatized persons, native merchants and others, at Abeokuta, Elmina, Lagos, Cape Palmas, and in the Niger River, are ready to act in behalf of the company the moment it commences business.

11*

"From the foregoing statements, aken together with the fact that this company will possess unusual facilities for successful mercantile operations, owing to its large capital and connections, it is confidently expected that its transactions will produce very handsome dividends. Persons having a knowledge of the African trade will readily understand that to name what would be a probable rate of interest on the capital worked, would, to the uninitiated, bear the stamp of exaggeration. The directors, however, feel assured that the company will eventually assume such dimensions as to invest it with a most important character ; and that the development of the resources of Africa will do more than any thing else to hasten the extinction of the foreign slave-trade, an event not more desirable to philanthropy than to commerce."

Were it needful, we might speak of the "African Aid Society," and the "Cotton Supply Association," as organizations of a kindred character, all designed to draw out the resources of Africa, and to establish an extensive and lucrative commerce with her. Another company, known as the "Manchester Commercial Association," report very gratifying success in their experiments of cotton cultivation at Cape Coast Castle. Having spoken of the feasibility of the cultivation to any extent that should be demanded, the report continues :

"The cotton has been examined, and found very closely to resemble Brazilian, or rather Egyptian. It is of extremely good color, and fair short staple ; has been well cleaned (without injury) by saw-gin, and is worth fully 6d. per pound. The cost of its product and transit to Manchester is said not to have exceeded 3d. per pound ; a result strongly confirmatory of the assertion

that cotton cultivation in Africa may be rendered remunerative. As to the disposition of the native Africans,
they have been found in this instance to accept work on
the farm with absolute avidity, not only on account of
the readiness with which the wages asked were paid,
but apparently with an intense desire to imitate or assist
Europeans ; and they evinced pride in being brought
into connection with the whites. Men, as many as were
required in the clearing and preparatory operations,
worked diligently and regularly for two dollars a
month ; women for a dollar and a half ; and stout lads
for half a dollar, without rations in any case. According to the last accounts respecting the farm, men have
rarely been employed since the ' trees' have been planted,
the labor of women and children being found quite sufficient for all ordinary purposes. The hands worked
eight hours a day, and seemed thoroughly contented
with themselves and their masters. The example became contagious soon after the experimental farm was
cleared ; for so long since as October last, several European residents had started plantations on their own
account, and on one lot alone there were twenty thousand flourishing trees. The average yield has been
found to be most satisfactory. Now those who have
hitherto conducted the experiment so nobly originated
by a few gentlemen in Manchester, are desirous that
regularly trained persons should be sent out to superintend the several plantations which must ere this be in
existence. The originators are most desirous to see the
resources of the Cape Coast Castle district more fully
developed ; and we think we have stated enough to
show that while extended operations could not fail to
be highly advantageous to the trade of this district,

they would certainly return remunerative profits for any investments."—*Liverpool Times.*

I do not know that I can do the reader a better service than to lay before him an abstract of the third annual report of the "British Cotton Supply Association." It reveals some extraordinary facts, showing the energy and research of the association, determined to obtain a full supply of cotton in the future, without dependence on the product of slave labor. Though her increased consumption is very large, England already obtains nearly one-third of her supply from other places than the United States. And the prospect of a future supply is yet more encouraging. They state that there is not an inhabited cotton country in the world, to which their attention has not been directed. The following localities are reported as hopeful sources of a future supply :

" Through the influence of the British consuls, the cultivation of cotton in Turkey has been commenced under great promise. The Home Minister in Greece has introduced it into many departments ; and in the island of Cyprus an estate of 80,000 acres has been devoted to it. Cotton seed has been distributed among the farmers of the fertile valley of the Meander, in Asia Minor, with full instructions for planting and gathering the crop. Of Egypt, the committee report ' that they expect to increase the growth from 100,000 bales, to the large figure of 1,000,000.' In Tunis, the bey is using great exertions with his subjects to cultivate the ' great staple.' In Western Africa, at Sierra Leone, and Sherbro, cotton-gins have been introduced, and a profitable trade in the native cotton commenced. In Liberia and along the Gold Coast every exertion is being made, with every prospect of success. At Accra and Cape Coast Castle are Agricultural Societies which make cotton culture their specialty. A great quantity of cotton is raised in the adjacent countries. The Accra Agricultural Society have engaged with a Lincolnshire firm to purchase this cotton, which they buy in the seed, at less than a cent a pound. This cotton, cleaned, is worth in Liverpool fourteen cents a pound.

" From the interior an agent of the association reports that a large export trade will soon be realized, and that he saw 70,000 people busy in its growing, spinning, and weaving. The prospect is, that, in the numerous towns which stud the coast, cotton marts will soon be established, and furnish a large quantity.

"At Elmina, Benin, Old Calabar, and the Cameroone, a good beginning has been made by distribution of seed and cotton-gins. At Lagos a hopeful trade has been opened. Along the line of the river Niger it is proposed to establish trading stations. It is reported that immense quantities which can be bought for six cents, clean, on the Niger, is worth sixteen cents in Liverpool.

" In South Africa, the Government of Natal is stimulating the cotton culture. Numerous farmers there are planting it, and, as an illustration of their success, one of them reports ' that he has on hand 100,000 lbs.'

" In Eastern Africa, in the rich valley of the Shire, an European colony is being established for raising cotton.

" From the Feejee Islands the committee have received the most wonderful specimens of cotton growing wild there, and reproducing, for from ten to fifteen years! The samples are so valuable as to range from thirteen to twenty-four cents per pound ; they say ' that from no other part of the world has such a collection of graduated qualities been received.' It is calculated that from half the area of these islands might be raised 4,000,000 bales per annum.

"Australia has entered into the cultivation, and will soon export freely. Samples of the best quality have been received. But the committee say, from 'wondrous India' are they receiving the most flattering reports ; and this year it is estimated that her exports will reach 1,000,000 bales. In British Guiana the cultivation has also been undertaken, with the most encouraging prospects.

" In Jamaica, the 'British Cotton Company' report flattering progress. So much for England.

" In Havana, Cuba, great efforts are being made, and a new company has been established, called the ' Anglo-Spanish Cotton Company,' with a capital of $4,000,000, for raising cotton.

"It is evident from these facts, to the intelligent mind, that ' King Cotton' does not sit so firmly on that throne, before which so many bow and worship, as many may imagine or desire ; and it is certain that the day is not distant when the manufactories of Europe will draw their largest supply of cotton from the sources named. And that the American manufacturer will also be impressed with the belief (so soon as his sympathies for the interests of the Cotton States shall be refused and severed), as are the European manufacturers, that cheap labor should produce cheap cotton, and that in no other parts of the world can labor be found upon the right soil and in the right climate to compete with Africa and the East Indies, where more than 300,000,000 are waiting employment. To those parts of the world will the Northern States soon be led to look, by the energies and example of England, to supply their wants of cotton; and asked to join with the other 'civilized powers' of the earth in the protection and employment of free labor, and the suppression of those institutions antagonistic to the same.

"In this view, it is quite within the probabilities of the future that the Legislature of the State of Georgia, which ignores those immutable laws which govern trade, may deem it expedient to repeal that 'enlightened act' which she so recently passed, to wit:

"'That no citizen of the State of Georgia, under a penalty of a fine of $2,000, shall be allowed to sell a bale of cotton or a barrel of apples to any person north of Mason and Dixon's Line.'

"And it is, also, quite probable that she will realize the necessity, with the other Cotton States, of employing cheaper labor than she now employs, or will be forced to ask that protection on her cotton and rice which is now given to the sugar of Louisiana."

The prospect now appears fair, at least, that English manufacturers will never again need to suffer themselves to be dependent on the lordly planter and the unrequited toil of the negro, for a supply of the indispensable material. A single year will so increase the proportion of a supply from other sources as to give some fair promise of a speedy relief from her present undesirable, if not guilty, complicity with American slavery; and do much to seal the final doom of the "institution," which has for more than two centuries been a foul stigma on our otherwise fair escutcheon.

As nearly related to commerce, I may not pass unnoticed the contemplated line of steamships from the United States to the coast of Africa, in its bearing on the emancipation of Africa from her present evils. This will open a quick and frequent communication between the two countries, and we can scarcely be too sanguine as to its beneficial results on Africa. It would serve a three-fold purpose in reference to suppressing the slave-trade; it would more than serve the purpose of our present squadron there; it would extend the commerce of Africa, by bringing America into a healthful competition with England, and thereby greatly developing the native resources of Africa; and it would afford facilities, and hold out inducements to the colonization of our colored people. Hitherto America has received but the scanty gleanings of a commerce with Africa, and in return, Africa has enjoyed as scantily the benefits she might realize from America. A new commercial mart will be opened on the one side, and the most healthful moral and political influences will flow in from the other. The committee to which the subject of such a line of steamers was referred reported favorably, and it is to be ardently hoped that Congress will accede to the plan. It is a measure full of hope for Africa, while it opens a rich field of enterprise to American com-merce, and a yet richer hope of freedom and enterprise to the people of color in the United States. It is confi-dently believed that, if a quick and pleasant passage by steam vessels was provided, multitudes of free negroes could be induced to go who are now unwilling. The two countries, moreover, would be brought into a nearer proximity. Africa would become known to America, and her wants and her woes would draw out the tear of sympathy, and America would become known to Africa. Colonists would pass and repass—the exiled, suffering race of Ham in America would visit the land of their fathers, and report to their brethren in bonds of the goodness of the land. And when they there see thick lips speaking wisdom among senators, and the crisped hair basking in the sunshine of liberty, the ambition of the black man will be fired that he may realize in his child, at least, what he sees and admires in his race in his fatherland. In no other way will prejudices against African colonization be so effectually removed, and in no other way will there be so healthful a stimulant created to induce the free people of color to emigrate to their native land. Would we share with Great Britain in a lucrative and extensive trade? Would we extinguish the slave-trade? Would we, in the most effectual way possible, bless Africa with our civil and religious institutions to her very centre? We must bridge the Atlantic with a line of steamers so as to throw open that great land of darkness to the light of liberty, learning, and Christianity.

CHAPTER XIV.

The cure—The migrations of mankind—Their power—Colonization and the colonists.

II. CHRISTIAN COLONIES.—Another efficient means of Africa's regeneration is the planting of Christian colonies on her coast. Though I name this second in order, it is really the first in importance. There is scarcely a more interesting chapter in the records of Providence than that which relates to the migrations of mankind. The influence of these migrations on the destinies of the world has been vastly greater than the superficial reader of history is aware of. They have often, in ages gone by, quite changed the whole face of human affairs. God is wont to improve men, as he does animals or plants, by change of place. He breaks up old associations—brings a people under new influences—removes them from old ones. Abraham was called from the land of the Chaldees, a land of idols. Israel first migrates to Egypt, for their civil and perhaps for their religious benefit; and then they migrate from Egypt (the purpose being accomplished which took them thither) to Canaan, for their yet greater benefit, that they might there begin their national existence—there organize the Church on a more favorable basis than had ever been before. We have seen, in the instance of the Carthaginians, the wide-spread influence of one great migration into Africa. They were for generations the Anglo-Saxons of the continent. They were in their day the renovating race.

We are now, we believe, on the eve of another great influx into Africa. It is now the return of her own sons—first enslaved, then civilized and Christianized, and finally liberated from their bondage, and prepared to rear, in their fatherland, a nationality of a higher type than Africa has ever yet known.

The strong arm of Providence, as often as he has need, transplants whole masses of men—takes them up from one nation or continent, and puts them down in another, having fitted them to do a work and to carry out his purposes there. We have seen how civilization traveled into Greece through colonies from Egypt and Phœnicia ; and how Europe was indebted to Greek colonies for the arts and sciences and civilization ; and how the extraordinary progress made among the northern nations of Africa was the fruit of the colonizing policy of Phœnicia, and finally of Carthage. "The dawnings of Roman civilization and greatness received their chief impulses from Greek emigrants on the coast of Italy." Spain was settled by the Carthaginians, and "Marseilles in France was an offshoot from Greece." The Romans in turn extended their laws, their civilization and their language to their remotest provinces through the colonies which she sent thither. So again was the whole Roman empire at length revolutionized by the vast Gothic migrations which poured in upon her from the north. Or, more remarkable still, we see the teeming tribes of Arabia spreading themselves eastward and westward, and quite changing the whole aspect of human affairs. The western stream rolls along on both sides of the Mediterranean as far as the Pillars of Hercules, quite transforming the nations on either side ; the other sweeps in resistless torrent over the southern portions of Asia, into Hindoostan, and to the remotest East. Turbaned tribes of Arabia come like so many swarms of locusts, and devour every green tree. They overthrew governments, changed laws, and themselves took possession of the soil. To say nothing of that other overwhelming torrent which at a later date flowed out from Central and Eastern Asia, and run westward, prostrating the kingdoms of all Central Asia, China, Russia, Hindoostan, at one time; and Persia, Syria, Asia Minor, as far as Constantinople, on the one side of the Mediterranean, and over all north of Africa on the other. Such were Mogul and Tartar migrations in their days. Their descendants still hold possession of the Greek empire.

Extensive and influential as ancient migrations were, modern systems of colonization are more so. The present is most emphatically the migrating age, and it is doing more than ever before to change the aspect of the world. Four principal streams are now bearing their living burdens over a great part of earth's surface, each to fulfill his destined mission. One stream sets eastward from Europe into India and the East, freighted with intelligence, science, a higher type of civilization than is known there, and a pure, elevating, heart-transforming religion. The next stream is directing its course westward from Europe over the Atlantic into America. It carries with it, for the most part, ignorance, poverty, superstition, a base counterfeit of Christianity, and all the beggarly elements of civil and religious despotism— mostly vile ingredients, or, at best, some precious metal with much dross, all borne over the Atlantic to be cast into the crucible of our burning democracy, that its "hay, wood, and stubble" may be burned out, and its pure gold appear. And toward our west goes yet another stream, starting from the Atlantic shore, and coursing its way across the entire continent—beyond the Mississippi, beyond the Rocky Mountains, till it meets the land of gold and the placid waters of the Pacific, carrying with it the industry, the enterprise, the intelligence, education, virtue, and religion of the Atlantic States—yea, laden with the rich inheritance of the Pilgrim Fathers. And, lastly,; another stream is rolling back over the Atlantic from these United States to Africa. It is freighted with the sable sons of Ham. They are returning, with songs of joy, to their own fatherland—to the sunny clime of their sires—to the palm-tree and the vine where their fathers dwelt in peaceful simplicity before the destroyer came. They are captives set free. Their bosoms begin to heave with a glow of conscious manhood. New hopes—new aspirations fill their souls. They are going to a land where they may be men, and rear their sons for a destiny never thought of by their fathers.

But whence came this stream of Ethiopian hue? How came the fountain from which it flows to be in this land of liberty? This forces before our vision another stream of involuntary migration—and it is a stream more bitter than death. It takes its rise in Africa; amid shrieks and cries enough to pierce a stone—amid blood and carnage; wars, the most barbarous and exterminating; burning villages; flying inhabitants, and manacled captives dragged into slavery; families forever torn asunder, and atrocities of too deep a dye for aught but demons to commit. You trace this black, turbid, bloody stream, through the "middle passage" of the shadow of death, all the way vocal with sighs and groans that pierce all but a demon's heart, and all animate with an anguish that nowhere else wrings the human heart, till it empties itself, after awful deduction of mortality, into the great reservoir of human wrongs and sufferings, called slavery. And here, strange to tell, in this furnace of their affliction, there walks one like unto the Son of man. Their burdens are lightened, their heavy yoke is often eased by the consolations of our blessed religion, which, in a kind Providence, meets them here. In this weary land they find the balm of Gilead—as their sickening souls sink within them, they meet here the great Physician. In the troubled waters of this Bethesda many wash and are clean. From this great Stygian pool there is flowing back to Africa that purer stream which we were just now tracing. They are returning to the land of their fathers, with a bright presage of good to themselves, and laden with a greater good, eventually, to that whole continent.

There is little room for doubt that African colonization is destined to be a mighty lever by which to raise Africa from her present state of degradation. The results which we expect from this colonization, aside from opening an effectual door for the introduction of the Gospel, are principally three : The suppression of the slave-trade ; the benefit of the African continent ; and the benefit of the colonists. Nor is its bearing on the abolition of slavery to be overlooked. Though its influence as an emancipation instrument, at first, seems insignificant, yet it is not so. It emancipates, it is true, but by the score or the hundred, and the objector asks— How long, at this rate, it will take to manumit three millions of slaves ? But he must bear in mind that, narrow as this egress .from bondage is at present, it is nearly or quite the only safe and expedient one. It is yet to be shown that emancipation, under any other circumstances, has improved the condition of the negro in America. Are the negroes at the North or the South, or the newly formed colony of Canada, in a better condition, whether for this world or the next? A man freed to remain in this country is not half freed. He scarcely has more incitements to industry, or more to rouse his aspirations for a higher condition, than he had before. He can not rise here. The indomitable force of circumstances has decreed it. Or, perhaps, nearer the truth, to say, that God, in his providential arrangements, has decreed it. And, however, much any class of men, in their wisdom or benevolence, may wish to have it otherwise, they can not change it. And we, therefore, have no alternative but the migration of the colored man back to his native clime and soil, or his miserable dwindling and degradation among us. And the inadequacy of the present colonizing policy to compass the desired end lies only in the limited condition of its means; and the want of acquaintance with the advantages of the scheme, or the unrighteous prejudice which has been excited against it. Let our General Government and our different State Legislatures aid individual and philanthropic enterprise in opening a frequent, easy, and cheap communication with Africa, and at the same time increasing a hundred-fold the pecuniary means of colonization societies; and let no pains be spared to make African colonies all they should be, and to disabuse the mind of our colored people concerning them, and we should then see, if even the colossal structure of slavery will not crumble under the power of these combined efforts. As strong a tide of emigration would set in from this country to Africa as now flows hither from Europe.

We spoke of three principal influences resulting from the planting of Christian colonies on the coast of Africa, the check it imposes on the slave-trade, the benefit of the African continent, and the benefit of the colonist. We have in the colonies which already exist on the western coast of Africa, a beautiful illustration of each of these points.

Liberia, rather than Sierra Leone, is the kind of colony from which we more especially hope for the renovation of Africa. Sierra Leone colonized, not men who had been for years acquainted with and considerably imbued with the spirit of liberal institutions, and who are to a considerable extent educated and Christianized, as is the case in Liberia, but captured slaves principally, who have just been dragged by the ruthless hand of violence from the lowest depths of ignorance and degradation. Many of these remain in the colony (which is said to number 45,000 or 50,000 souls), where they are brought under Christian influences — taught the rudiments of useful learning—brought into the pale of civilization—and, through church, educational, and industrial appliances an incalculable good is conferred upon them. And that colony, no doubt, is (in despite of all the bitter waters that may mingle with it) a fountain destined to send out many a healthful stream into the surrounding desert, to make glad that solitary land. Yet the constitution and character of the Liberia colonies serve best our purposes for an illustration.

We regard the relation of Liberia to Africa very similar to that which the American republic holds to the broad land between the Atlantic and the Pacific.

In relation to social, civil, and religious institutions, she seems charged with some important mission to that whole continent.   And,

1. Taking Liberia as our model, what grounds have we to expect the suppression of the slave-trade from an efficient system of colonization?   As far as colonies hold and govern territory, which, in the case of Liberia, is 600 or 700 miles on the coast, the inhuman traffic is suppressed.   The power of the government is employed to put down the trade.   Their little naval force is kept on the alert for this purpose.   The example of the government and the citizens, goes to discourage and restrain all such traffic ; and, there is an exclusive social and moral influence that is exerted by such a colony, which is felt much beyond their own narrow bounds. It is a fact of great interest, that the slave-trade has been suppressed on more than one half of the whole western coast of Africa.   Of the 2,000 miles north of the equator, there remains but two points where slaves can be purchased.   "Colonization, in some form, has extinguished the traffic on about one half of the western coast of Africa."   Besides the well-known colonies of the Americans at Liberia, and the British at Sierra Leone, European nations, especially the British, which are opposed to the slave-trade, have forts or colonies of some sort, at different points on the coast, as at the mouth of the river Gambia, at Cape Palmas, and on the coast south of Cape Palmas, for some hundreds of miles.· This coast is said to be thickly set with forts, and trading posts belonging to different nations of Europe, mostly British, which exclude the slave-trade as far as Popo, a distance of about 700 miles.   Along this coast are many thousand native Africans living under

12

British jurisdiction. " In all cases this colonization has been rendered possible by the employment of men of African descent," the most efficient and successful instruments have been emancipated slaves.

One fact here is worthy of special notice. Slave-dealers from the first have felt that the Liberians were enemies to their traffic ; and no spirit has more uniformly characterized the colonists at Liberia than an uncompromising hostility to the slave-trade ; and nothing is clearer than that they have waged an exterminating war against it. Most of them have themselves felt the galling of the chains, and they are, to the heart's core, the sworn foes of the traffic. Hence the difference in this respect between Liberia and Sierra Leone. The whole influence of the Liberians, to the whole extent to which it reaches, is point blank against the slave-trade. The influence of the colony at Sierra Leone is scarcely felt at all. The reason no doubt lies in the fact that the Liberians are the best kind of anti-slavery Americans— Anglo-Saxonized republicans, and pledged, in life or in death, to hate oppression. The people of Sierra Leone are recaptured Africans, the offspring of ignorance, sottishness, and despotism, but just beginning to breathe the vital air of a higher state of existence. An intelligent gentleman, writing from Liberia, says :

" It is now universally admitted that settlements such as Liberia present the most effectual barrier to the slave-trade ; that, so far as their influence extends, the trade is wholly destroyed. In proportion, therefore, as the republic of Liberia increases in strength and influence ; in proportion as it extends its territory, and acquires strength to protect and suppress illicit traffic, in the same proportion will slavery be suppressed, and the ne-

cessity of keeping cruisers in the vicinity of the settlements be decreased."

2. We present colonization as a cure of bleeding
Africa, because of the rich and lasting benefit it is fitted
to confer on the whole African continent. Already
Liberia extends over a considerable territory, and every
year it is enlarging by purchase. Over this territory
extends a republican government, free institutions, the
habits and the fruits of industry, schools, and the benign influences of Christianity. President Roberts, in
a late message to the Legislature of Liberia, after
speaking of the very salutary influence already exerted
by the colonists (about 7,000 or 8,000 only) over the
native population, says the native Africans, already
embraced in the colonies, is not less than 200,000
(about a nucleus of 8,000 American colonists); that
they "are improving more rapidly at present than at
any previous time; there are more instances of laborious industry every returning year;" that "the chiefs of
several tribes within our jurisdiction have recently expressed to me an earnest wish to have missionaries and
schools established among their people, who, they say,
are anxious to receive them; and there is nothing to
prevent the sending of missionaries, and the establishing
of schools, except the want of the pecuniary means."
The President speaks, too, of the applications of other
native chiefs, "asking the protection of that government, and to be received within its jurisdiction by an-
nexation of the whole of their territory to the republic."
He then urges on the Legislature the adoption of the
most efficient measures, by means of education, the industrial arts, and especially the diffusion of a pure religion, to bring these native tribes, in the shortest possible

time, under the influence of the enlightened and Christian government of Liberia. We look on this republic, dropped by the hand of Providence on the border of that great continent, as the little leaven hid in the measures of meal. A thousand influences are working unseen, which will yet transpire. Not only the 200,000 who are inclosed within the boundaries of these salutary influences are benefited by them, but a great part of Western Africa, far into the interior, is benefited. One such well-regulated colony as Liberia is a tangible illustration of what are the legitimate fruits of good government, of education, industry, and honest, moral life, and a pure religion. Such an example can not but exert a considerable influence. The native tribes have a tangible illustration of what industry and sobriety will do to develop the resources of the soil and to promote the useful arts, and thereby surround a people with the comforts and elegances of life; and of what education and a sanctifying religion will do to elevate, refine, and truly bless a people.

In Liberia, the native tribes have before them an exemplification of what may be realized in their own race. They see men of their own hue and idiosyncrasy living in well-built and commodious houses, reared by their own hands, worshiping the true God in well-constructed temples raised by their own skill and industry, gathering in bounteous harvests from their own well-tilled farms, and reclining under the shadow of a government constructed by themselves; laws framed by senators of a black skin, and executed by men of their own hue; and justice dispensed by judges who need no crisped wigs; and an army and navy officered by men of the same color; with a complete learned corps of editors, authors, teachers, preachers, and men of all the learned professions, of the same ebon skin. Such an exhibition of advancement in his own race will supply a stimulant to the native mind, that he may imitate what he sees possible in men of his own kind. He will not long be satisfied to live a brute, when he sees it possible for him to live as a man. He will no longer barter the flesh and blood of his own kind, when he has learnt that his soil, his mines and forests produce articles of barter equally acceptable to foreign nations.

An important desideratum now is, the establishment of colonies in the interior of Africa, where there is a better soil, a better climate, and a better class of people. Such a scheme of colonization, though exceedingly promising of benefit to Africa, could not be entered upon by the limited means which any Colonization Society has at command at present. It must be a colonization on a large scale—hundreds of families would need to be combined in such a migration to make it efficient. A few families would probably be overwhelmed by the semi-barbarous natives, and prove of no avail. When Congress and State Legislatures shall put their hand to this work as it deserves, we may expect that the Anglo-Saxonized sons of Ham will spread themselves over the wide plain, and the rich and beautiful mountain valleys, and the great interior; and that there agriculture, and the arts, and the institutions of learning, freedom, and religion shall flourish.

A London paper says: "Liberia, of ten years' growth [in her national existence] is worth more [to the cause of civilization and human advancement in Africa] than all that has been effected by the European race in Africa in twenty-two centuries." This enterprise has, in all,

cost the friends of benevolence and philanthropy, including the purchase of 20,800 acres of land, $2,250,000, a
sum not sufficient to support the British squadron on the
coast of Africa a single year.   And I might here quote
a valuable testimony of Sir Charles Hotham, commander
of her British Majesty's naval forces on the coast of
Africa.   He says: "So long as the people of Liberia
observe their present system of government, both humanity and civilization are deeply concerned in its progress.   It is only through their means we can hope to
improve the African race."   This testimony is the more
valuable on account of the source from which it comes.
The people of Great Britain are at this time especially
interested to promote their own interests on the coast
of Africa. and would not be likely to make any gratuitous acknowledgments in favor of any American enterprise there.   Africa is now the point toward which
England is now particularly directing her attention for
new colonial and commercial aggrandizement.   And Sir
Charles is a high functionary of that Government to
protect and favor English interests there, and to carry
into execution their future plans.

The "New Republic" is deservedly exciting of late
much attention in England.   Statesmen, as well as philanthropists, are inquiring into the character of that
government, and especially into the causes that have
contributed to give Liberia an influence against the
slave-trade, and in favor of African civilization and
evangelization so different from any other colony on the
coast.   A committee was not long since raised in the
British House of Lords, to inquire into the condition of
Liberia—the causes of its prosperity and influence in
Africa, and for the suppression of the slave-trade.   The

replies to the following questions, put to the Rev. Mr. Miller, in his evidence before this committee, are much to our present purpose:

"Why does Liberia exercise such a wonderful influence in suppressing the slave-trade in its neighborhood, while the British, French, Dutch, Portuguese, and Spanish colonies exercise none whatever? Because Liberia is inhabited by a class of intelligent, Christianized American negroes, who have a mortal hatred of the accursed slave traffic, whilst the colony of Sierra Leone is inhabited by recaptured Africans, who are little removed from the state of barbarism and savageness in which they were found when taken out of the slavers by the British cruisers.

"Why does Liberia present the most successful example of a black settlement prosperous beyond measure, and likely to become a great empire, on which, during its existence of twenty-five years, only £250,000 have been expended, while the colony of Sierra Leone, on which millions of pounds have been lavished for more than fifty years, shows no signs of improvement, and little prospect of future prosperity? The reason is, that, in the first, the blacks govern themselves, and are consequently stimulated to every kind of improvement, while in the latter the whites are the rulers, between whom and the colored people there is no sympathy or cordiality of feeling; the whites sicken and die, and those that live are glad to get back to England as soon as possible."

Or I might here adduce the very valuable testimony of Capt. A. H. Foote, of the American Navy, and commander of the brig Perry, off the coast of Africa. Though he went to Africa with unfavorable impressions of Liberia, he speaks in the most glowing terms of the colony. He regards Liberia as the most efficient agency now in operation for the suppression of the slave-trade, and the only practical agency by which to civilize and evangelize Africa. And more confidently does he assert it to be the interest of the colored man in America to migrate thither.

Indeed, we may with propriety here ask, if the agencies and instrumentalities embodied in a community like Liberia be not suited to renovate Africa, where shall we look for our agents and instruments? White colonists and missionaries can not live there. The providence of God is very decisive that Africa must be regenerated, if at all, by the agency of colored men. In asserting this, Bishop Payne says: "During the twelve years of this mission's existence (American Episcopal), twenty white laborers, male and female, have been connected with it. Of these there remain in the field, at the present moment, myself—the only clergyman, my wife, and Doctor Perkins, three in all." And the history of other missions is perhaps not more favorable. A few live; but such is the mortality as to indicate that Africa is no home for the white man. At whatever cost, he has, in the incipient stages of the work for Africa's renovation, a very important work to do; yet the main agency should be of the colored man. But where shall we find such instruments? They are to come out of "great tribulation"—out of American slavery. This class of men, oppressed and abused as they have been, are a hundred years in advance of any other class of Africans anywhere else to be found. God has met them in their captivity, and blessed the anguish of their bodies to the joy of their souls, and here, in the school of affliction, fitted many of them to return and bless their fathers' land.

The conception in the mind of the noble Buxton, of the Niger expedition, was a grand one; yet it failed. Vast sums of money and many valuable lives were expended for an object which was truly a great one; yet it accomplished next to nothing. But shall its noble objects never be accomplished? Undoubtedly they shall. But not by white men. An expedition fitted out from Liberia, manned by the agriculturists, artisans, and savans of the ebony race, may accomplish more than ever Buxton dreamed of. Time shall accomplish what prematurely failed. All the pleasing hopes of English philanthropists, of a flourishing commerce on the Niger —of a civilized and Christian population cultivating the fertile plains and rich valleys of the interior—marts of trade and opulent cities with their institutions of learning and their sacred temples pointing the weary pilgrim to the skies, may yet be abundantly realized through the agency of a race whose the land is, and who seem destined to redeem it from its present waste.

Or we might, with the same propriety, ask what is to be the destiny of the present colored race of America— where is he to find a home and a resting-place, if not in Africa? His best condition here is that of slavery; and shall we be satisfied that he have no better? Must we look upon his bondage as his permanent condition? There is no fair hope of a better in this country Free him, and still you scarcely more than change his position in name: He is now in a position where it is lawful and possible for him to rise, but where it is almost certain that he will not rise. There is no hope, if there be a possibility, that two races so completely distinct

12*

should live on terms of equality. They must, as two distinct races, have two countries, two governments, and distinct classes of institutions. Shall we yield them America, or shall they take Africa—the home of their fathers, and that land which God gave to Ham, whose children they are?

The condition of the freed colored people is becoming every year more and more embarrassing. The Slave States are adopting every possible means, by legislation, public sentiment, and daily practice, to rid themselves of a population which have become exceedingly undesirable to them. They are consequently driven into the Free States. But here their presence is looked upon as more undesirable, if possible, than in the Slave States. Consequently, Indiana, Ohio, Illinois, Iowa, and I know not how many other States, have passed laws excluding the free negroes from their respective States; and States in the South, acting on the same policy, are passing laws prohibiting the emancipation of slaves at all, unless the slaves be removed beyond the bounds of the United States or territories. The tendency of the last is to discourage emancipation, if there be not a cheap and easy mode of colonization to Africa; and of the first, to impoverish, dishearten, and make vagabonds of the free people of color, and then to drive them, as a nuisance, into such States as have no laws to exclude them— which States, in self-defense, will feel obliged to pass such laws. And, then, whither shall they flee? To Canada? But there they can not live. The experiment has been tried, and signally failed. The negro is a tropical plant, and can not thrive in Canadian snows. The destiny of the colored race in this country seems to be approaching a crisis. He must either groan out a miserable existence as a slave, or go to Africa and be a man, or draw out the most miserable vagabond life, with no place on the bosom of mother earth to lay his head till he sleep in his obscure grave. There is hope for the race only in Africa.

And if these stubborn influences were not in operation, there are others no less sure that are working out the same result. The laboring Irish, Germans, and others, from Europe, are pouring into our land in inundating multitudes, and are occupying the position and doing the services which formerly fell to the colored people. They are, therefore, in another sense, driven from our country.

3. Colonization in its bearings on the colonists themselves. The best testimony we can have on this point is their own. Are they happy? Are they prosperous? Do they feel that they have bettered their condition by a removal to Africa? Or would they gladly return to the land from which they went? We have their testimony. They speak no equivocal language. A man from Congo, being asked if he did not wish to return to his own country replied: "No, no; if I go back to my country, they make me slave. I am here free; no one dare trouble me. I got my wife—my lands—my children learn book—all free—I am here a white man—me no go back."

The Rev. W. W. Findlay, Methodist and colonist at Liberia, writes: "I do thank God; I would not leave this for any country that I have ever seen; for here I have my liberty. I have been in Canada, and fourteen States of the Union, but Liberia I like better than any."

Another colonist gives utterance to the satisfaction

he feels in his present condition, in language like the following : " Thousands of poor colored men are foolish enough to remain in the United States, sighing for privileges they will never possess there, and many are foolish enough to abuse the colonization scheme which has placed us in possession of rights they will never enjoy in that country. I know by experience the depressing influence of the white man. Such was its effect on me, that I failed to improve my mind as I might have done, if the slightest hope of future usefulness could have been indulged. But every high and noble aspiration appeared to me, in that country, consummate folly, and I was thus induced to be satisfied in ignorance, there being no prospect of rising in the scale of being. But how altered is my condition in this country! Here, honors of which I never dreamed have been conferred on me by my fellow-citizens, and I have been treated as an equal by gentlemen from the United States ; and what makes me truly happy is the kind feelings I can entertain for the white man. The good effects of freedom on many who came off plantations are quite visible. Many fill responsible offices under Government, and perform their duties in a manner creditable to themselves and the country."

"Liberia," says another colonist, "is, in my estimation, pre-eminently congenial both to the physical and mental constitution of the colored man. Liberia, indeed, seems to have a transforming influence upon the minds of those who return to her shores, by rousing up those latent powers of the mind which slavery has kept inert. Here, then, is the home of our race ; here we find ourselves no longer doomed to look upon men of every grade and complexion as our superiors ; here we daily see ignorance, superstition, and vice disappear before us like the mist which rolls up the mountain-side before the rising glory of the morning sun ; here talent can attain the summit of perfection. If this be the true state of Liberia, who would not say—Let the man of color go to his native clime, where he will be free from oppression, the bane of human happiness ?"

: Another says : " I am thankful to my heavenly Parent for the inestimable blessing of casting my lot in a pleasant place, and that I can now say, my 'heritage' is a good one. We enjoy the rights of citizenship. Colonization, we owe it to thee !"

Or we may turn from the testimony which the colonists themselves give as to the benefits which they feel that they derive from their residence in Liberia, to the testimony given by other competent witnesses concerning them. "A larger proportion of the population of Liberia," says one, " are professors of religion than can be found in any other nation on the face of the earth." This speaks volumes for their moral condition, and, by way of inference, for their condition in every respect. And this is the section of country which, thirty years ago, was covered with the habitations of cruelty—and which, some years earlier, contained some of the worst slave marts on the coast of Africa. Another report says : " The progress of this colony has indeed been wonderful in all that concerns its material interests— but what shall we say of progress in all that relates to their moral and religious interests ? Impartial visitors represent this progress to have been still more remarkable." And the same unvarying testimony is borne by all classes of visitors to that oasis in the desert—by ministers, missionaries, naval officers, and private adventurers. There is a larger number of schools and churches, and a smaller number of dram-shops and places of amusements, than are anywhere else to be found among the same amount of population. Capt. Foote speaks of what he found to be the prevailing sentiment of the colonists. Though they are subjected more or less to the inconveniences, hardships, and privations incident to the settlement of a new country, he says: "The colonists generally prefer their present position to that which they held in the United States."

Here I may introduce the testimony of an intelligent colored man, who has studied well the subject of African colonization, and seems to have much at heart the welfare of his colored brethren. He says: "I have been unable to get rid of the conviction, long since entertained and often expressed, that if the colored people of this country ever find a home on earth for the development of their manhood and intellect, it will first be in Liberia, or in some part of Africa." * * * "Our servile and degraded condition in this country, the history of the past, and the light that is poured in upon me from every source, fully convinces me that this is our true, our highest, and happiest destiny, and the sooner we commence this glorious work the sooner will light spring up in darkness, and the wilderness and solitary place be glad, and the desert rejoice and blossom as the rose."

I might here quote another English testimony. *Chambers' Edinburgh Journal* says of African colonization: "It needs no other defense of its policy than to point to the spirit which has all along animated the black people who emigrated to Africa. One sentiment, viz., that it is worth while to encounter all possible hardships and dangers on a foreign strand for the sake of perfect freedom, appears in the whole, conduct of these men." * * * " We view it as the point of the wedge by which a Christian civilization, if ever, is to be introduced into Central Africa."

The view that has now been taken of Africa ought :

1. To engage our prayers and sympathies in behalf of that great, interesting, and truly unfortunate continent, and to secure our benefactions. Africa may demand this at our hands, as a matter of Christian charity. She is a suffering, destitute land. No land so dark, and so much needs the sun of righteousness to arise upon it. No land so debased, and so much needs the renovating power of truth. No land so full of the habitations of cruelty—a land of bondage, where there is no " flesh in man to feel for man, and so much needs the ever-blessed Gospel that preaches the acceptable year of the Lord—that unbinds the heavy burden—that opens the prison doors, and lets the captives go free." If there be a people on the whole face of the earth which may claim above all others the gracious interposition of Christian benevolence, that people is the long downtrodden sons of Ham ; and if the Gospel is especially a heaven-sent boon to the " poor ;" if it contemplate, as some of its richest trophies, those whom it shall redeem from the lowest depths of human suffering and sin, we may surely expect its choicest realization, when " Ethiopia shall stretch out her hands unto God." Fervent, then, be the prayers, profound the sympathies, bountiful the benefactions, when poor suffering Africa be the object !

Humanity demands, in self-defense, that we open wide the door of access to Africa. Pity pleads that we spare them from annihilation, by giving them a home in their native Africa. Where else can they go? Is there a spot within the limits of our country where there is any fair prospect that they may live, and be blessed? Other experiments are being tried. Will they succeed? We shall see.

2. If our views are correct as to what is a suitable and hopeful remedy for the wants and woes of Africa, schemes of colonization have claims on us, as philanthropists and Christians, inferior to no other claims for benevolent and philanthropic action. There is no hope for Africa, but in the religion of the cross; and we have shown, and the history of modern missions has shown, that there is no fair hope of the introduction of Christianity into Africa except through the door of Christian colonies on her coast. All attempts to introduce the Gospel otherwise have heretofore failed. If this be the channel designated by the finger of God, through which he will send the healing waters of the river of life over those great arid deserts, we must accept the Divine appointment, and make our feeble efforts to bless Africa harmonize with the Divine plan. God has (as has been shown elsewhere) remarkably prepared his instrumentalities for the moral renovation of Africa. In the depths of a cruel servitude he has been fitting a class of men for the very work in question. They are, with the native African himself, bone of his bone, and flesh of his flesh, and the only class of agents, as far as we know, that can extensively live in Africa, and labor for its redemption. It is the business of colored societies to seek out these men, to transport them to Africa, and thus put them in a position to do their destined work. Until Providence, therefore, shall point out some other mode

of blessing that continent, and choose some other instrumentality, the duty of every friend of the African race and of Africa, seems plain. He must allow the institutions whose special object it is to bless Africa and her races, to hold a prominent place in his prayers, his sympathies, and his alms.

CHAPTER XV.

The practicability of an extensive colonization—What has been done—The desirableness of colonization, and the testimony of colonists.

WE have spoken of colonization as the cure of Africa—at least, as the appointed channel through which the blessings of civilization and Christianity are likely to flow in upon that great continent. There is among the wise and the good an opinion, yearly gaining strength, that this is the method through which God will deign to bless and renovate Africa. An intelligent and shrewd writer* on Africa, and one who has resided in Liberia, and taken a deep interest in her affairs, says: "I believe that God intends that the moral and intellectual elevation of the benighted tribes of Africa is to be effected chiefly by her own returning civilized and Christianized children, bringing with them and introducing among the ignorant and degraded aborigines habits of civilized life and the glorious Gospel of salvation." Mysteriously has God overruled the connection with, and dependence of, the negro race upon the whites in this country, to the furtherance of the physical, intellectual, moral, and religious improvement of Africa. It is believed that enough has already been done to indicate the line of Divine Providence in respect to Africa, and to give some assurance of what the course of the Divine procedure shall be in time to come.

---

* Dr. J. W. Lunginbeel.

After what has been said of the value of colonization on the coast of Africa, and its bearing on the future destiny of the whole continent, some inquiries
may arise, which we would not pass over in silence.
Is the colonization of Americanized Africans on the
coast of Africa practicable to any such extent as to
bring relief to the great mass of free colored people in
our country, or to achieve any general and lasting
good to the continent of Africa and the African race?
What has been effected already, as a voucher of what
may be expected of colonization? What is the duty
of the American people—of every philanthropist and
Christian in our wide domain? What the relation
and duty of slaveholders in respect to the African
race among us, and in general? And what the duty
and interest of the sons of Ham, who are found scattered over our land, whether free or yet in bondage?
Each of these queries demand a few moments' attention.

1. The practicability of the present scheme of colonization. Can it be made extensive and efficient
enough to serve the desired purposes? We think it
can. These purposes are the extinction of a large
slave-trade, the transportation of the portion of the
people of color from America to Africa, and the planting of such colonies in Africa as shall essentially and
extensively benefit that continent. It has been altogether fashionable in certain quarters, of late years,
to decry all present schemes of colonization, as altogether inadequate to accomplish any such purposes.
I met an elderly gentleman not long since, who is still
in active life, though he treads hard on the verge of
his three-score years and ten, who told me, that when

he first left his home in New Jersey, to seek his fortune in the city of New York (sixty years ago), the only ferry-boat that plied from the Jersey shore to the great emporium of the empire State run from Elizabethport. This was an awkward sail-boat, called a "Perianger," which made but one trip a day, and carried from three to fifteen persons at a time. Indeed, it was thought to be a good business when it found itself loaded with a dozen passengers at a single trip. A few dozen a day comprised the whole amount of travel from the State of New Jersey, from Philadelphia, and the South. Suppose some keen-eyed seer could then have made to cross the field of his vision the moving multitudes which are now, after but sixty years, hourly pouring into the great city, from the same quarter. He could scarcely have conceived the present ample accommodations for their rapid transit every hour. Our young adventurer, when ten years old, was taken by a friend to Albany. Providing themselves with all the needfuls for the voyage, they set sail in a sloop, and not till they had, with many incidents of storm and calm, head-winds and opposing currents, made full thirteen days and nights, did they arrive at the place of their destination.*

It does not require so great a stretch of credulity, or of hopefulness, to conceive that the facilities of communication with Africa should be so increased as

---

* The same gentleman says he has been on the said ferry-boat when she was thirty-six hours making her distance from Elizabethport to New York. Contrary winds would compel them to put into Staten Island in the morning, along whose coast they would make their way during the day, as far as Mother Van Buskirk's tavern, on the northwest corner of the island. Here they would put in for the night and wait a favorable change of wind for the morning.

to convey thither some two or three millions of people, as it did then, that the teeming multitudes that come to and from New York should find the present ample and comfortable accommodation for locomotion. Europeans, all classes included, have for some years past, migrated to this country, at the rate of about half a million a year. This they do, for the most part, as a matter of individual enterprise. Impelled by the conviction that they can here better their condition in life—though generally extremely poor, they find the means of getting here. There is nothing impracticable in the idea that as broad and deep a stream of emigration should flow from America to Africa as now pours in upon us from Europe. Let as strong a conviction pervade the entire mind of our African population as prevails in Ireland that their own best interest demands their removal to Africa, and let all available facilities be employed, and all parties do their bounden duties on the subject, and there would be no difficulty in sending to Africa half a million of emigrants a year. All who ought, in right, and to whom it would be a privilege to go, might be sent out in less than five years. Or, suppose, as Mr. Webster does in the speech quoted in our last chapter, that 100,000 be sent out annually, the work would soon be done, and done quite as fast as the highest interests of all concerned would admit. For so large a number could not be found prepared to migrate; or, if prepared, the colonies would not be prepared to receive so large accessions.

Colonization to any extent necessary, in order to transplant in a very few years all the population now residing in this country that are fitted to go, or who can be benefited by such a change and are willing to go, is practicable in the course of a very few years. Let the mind of this unfortunate people be disabused in respect to the advantages to be derived by their removal to Africa; let them exert themselves to secure the means to go to the land of their fathers as the Irish do to come to this country; let individual efforts be made—let the North make as great pecuniary sacrifices to send the blacks to Africa as the South, at one period, showed themselves ready to, to free their slaves that they might be sent; let colonization societies co-operate with, and be liberally aided by, State and national benefactions, to forward one of the noblest efforts of modern days, and there can be no doubt of the successful result. Ethiopia would soon be seen to stretch out her hands to God in praise to Him who worketh all things after the counsels of his own will, and in gratitude to all, far and near, who shall have contributed to redeem them from a state of miserable bondage and degradation, and to raise them up and make them sit in heavenly places. Nothing more is needed but to give extension and efficiency to present schemes of colonization, and the desired object would be accomplished. Let the American Colonization Society receive from the hands of private charity $500,000, instead of $50,000; let a line of national steamers bridge the Atlantic from some southern port to Liberia, through which a quick and frequent intercourse would be kept up between the two countries, both to bring our colored population acquainted with the advantages of Liberia, and to afford them a cheap and easy passage thither; let private enterprise be encouraged, so that hundreds of colored people would emigrate to Africa through their own efforts, aided, if need be, by their own private friends; let State legislatures and the General Government make those liberal appropriations which they can well afford to make, whether it be regarded as an act of justice to the blacks, or as the interest of the whites, or in respect to the promotion of a stupendous scheme of philanthropy toward Africa; let the church of the living God exert the power of her puissant arm, through her prayers and benefactions, to raise Africa from her present abasement, by means of her regenerate sons restored to the bosom of their abused, lacerated mother, and we shall hear no more of the impracticability of present schemes of colonization. There is no impracticability, except that which has been created in the lack of pecuniary means, which, in all right, ought to be forthcoming; and in a wicked prejudice, which has been gendered in the breast of the colored man against African colonization. Aside from these two obstacles, we have reason to believe that the African race now found in America can be removed to Africa much faster than Africa would be prepared to receive them. Were all hands and all hearts combined to consummate this work before this generation should pass, we might expect the barbarous slave-trade would be suppressed, slavery become extinct, and a work of civilization and evangelization begun in Africa which should soon pervade the whole continent. The scheme is practicable.

2. Our next inquiry relates to what has already been done in the way of colonization on the coast of Africa. Can we point to any realization of the scheme which warrants the hope that colonization

shall produce any such fruits as has been intimated?
We think we can.

Within the short space of forty years, and with the
small aggregate sum of $2,000,000, the present colon-
ies of Americanized Africans have been planted on
the western coast of Africa. The time, when compared with the usual length of the infancy of nations,
is quite insignificant; and the money expended in the
enterprise is not more than individual enterprise
sometimes employs in commerce or trade—not more
than a fifth of the amount expended in the construction of the Hudson River Railroad. And what has been
accomplished? What have the friends of colonization
to show as the work of a single generation, and as the
result of the small expenditure I have named? They
can show, on the coast of Africa, a civilized, independent Christian nation, living under a constitution and
laws modeled after our own, yet administered by the
ebony sons of Ham—the printing press, in a prosperous tide of operation, sending its streams of living
light even into Africa's dark interior—the means of
education, schools and academies, not less abundant
or inferior to those enjoyed by any other people, and
a college in a hopeful state of progress. They can
show a population of some 7,000 or 8,000, who have
been transported here from the land, and many of
them from the shackles, of slavery, there made men;
and some 200,000 native Africans over whom the
broad ægis of a free government is extended, and who
are enjoying, through the colonies with which they
are incorporated, the blessings of free institutions,
and of a pure religion, and taking valuable lessons
daily in all the industrial arts of civilized life, which

have been introduced through the colonies. The slave-trade has been suppressed directly through these colonies along the coast for 700 miles, and indirectly, no doubt, to a much greater extent. A healthful commerce has been created with European nations, which, of itself, is a substitute and remedy for the slave-trade, and a fruitful source of prosperity to the nation. The industry, skill, and enterprise of the colonists have already, to a considerable extent, developed the natural resources of the soil, and thus laid the foundation for the future prosperity of Africa, and set an example to the native tribes which as they shall in time follow, it shall transform the entire physical condition of the African continent.

The seeds of civilization and of our holy religion are sown there—have taken root and are beginning to bear fruit. A great work is begun—the foundation laid—the tug of war past—the burden and heat of the day endured. The Church, the Sabbath, and the Bible, the embodiment of Christianity, are there—the mightiest elements of reform ever thrown into the deep and broad pool of human corruption. In not less than thirty churches the Word of God is preached every Sabbath day. Christian education, too, and the press, the other two mighties (though they attain not to the three mightiest), are doing their work.

But we have no occasion to confine ourselves to progress in Liberia. Africa is begirt with philanthropic and Christian agencies. Africa is on every side invaded by these benign influences. The combined influence of colonies, commerce, and Christian missions is telling delightfully upon that dark continent. "Bright Christian lights now begin to blaze up, at

13

intervals, along a line of sea-coast of more than 3,000 miles, where unbroken night formerly reigned. The everlasting Gospel is now preached in Kumari, and Abomi, the capitals respectively of Ashantee and Dahomey, two of the most barbarous kingdoms on the face of the earth. Christian missions are now being established all over the kingdom of Yoruba, a land once wholly given up to the slave-trade, and blood-shed. Along the banks of the far interior Niger, Christian lights are springing up. At Old Calabar, a place renowned in former times, not only for being one of the chief seats of the foreign slave-trade, but for unparalleled cruelties and barbarities of its people, the Gospel is not only preached, but the Spirit of God is poured out upon the debased people. On the heights of the Sierra del Crystal mountains, the Gos-pel has been preached to a people who had not only never before heard it, but who, themselves, were un-known to the Christian world until within a few years." *

Enough has been done (to say nothing of South and East Africa) to give a most pleasing assurance that the "time is not far distant when the light of the Gos-pel shall reach the darkest and the most remote cor-ner of that great continent."

Yes, we may expect the ingathering, at no distant day, of a great spiritual harvest. Nor is all this future. Already we see the first fruits, as a sure pledge of what shall come. We glean from the same source the following items: Within the last twenty-

---

* The "Princeton Review" as quoted in "Liberty's Offering," by E. W Blyden.

five years more than one hundred Christian churches have been organized in that country; and upward of 15,000 hopeful converts have been gathered into those churches. Nearly 200 schools are in full operation in connection with these various missions, and not less than 16,000 native youths are receiving a Christian training in those schools, at the present moment. More than twenty different dialects have been studied out, and reduced to writing, into many of which large portions of the sacred Scriptures, as well as other religious books, have been translated, printed, and circulated among the people; and, doubtless, we may with safety assume that some knowledge of the Christian salvation has been brought by direct or indirect means within the reach of at least 5,000,000 of immortal beings, who have never before heard of the blessed name of the Saviour.

But we are, for obvious reasons, more especially concerned to present Liberia as a realization of what Africans can do for themselves and for their colored race. The hope of Africa we seem to see bound up in the destiny of the Anglo-Africans of America. Looking upon them as the qualified and appointed agents of her renovation, we regard Liberia as the most hopeful door of entrance into those dark domains of spiritual death.

We may, therefore, name as another most hopeful feature, that a larger proportion of her population are church members than is to be met in any part of the United States, and a larger proportion of the children attend school, unless, possibly, New England be excepted. Liberia is, indeed, on the coast of Africa, a reproduction of New England—destined to do for that continent what the Plymouth colony has done for North America.

We are unwilling to dismiss this topic without calling attention to the exceedingly interesting position which the little State of Liberia at present holds. We refer here, not only to her relation to Africa and the slave-trade, but to American slavery, the free people of color in this country, and to our white population. Philanthropy and Christian benevolence has not four graver problems to solve than these : How shall Africa be brought within the pale of civilized and Christian nations? How the slave-trade be effectually and permanently suppressed? How American slavery be done away, so as to be the most advantageous to the enslaved? And, How our free people of color be rescued from a condition already truly wretched, and becoming every year worse, and soon must become intolerable? Liberia has an interesting relation to each of these objects. We have alluded to her as the radiating point of influences, principles, and institutions which are able to renovate all Africa, and which, in proportion as they shall be planted in that soil, shall eradicate the vile traffic in human flesh. We would speak now rather of the relation of Liberia to the other objects named.

Causes were said to be at work, before the outbreak of the present slaveholders' war, which some supposed would, in the course of a few years, bring slavery in this country to an end. If no other cause was in operation, it was believed that slavery was becoming so unprofitable that the strife with the master would soon be, not how he should hold his slaves, but how he should free himself of them. Already had the tide of Irish and German laborers threatened to supplant the negro, North and South; and it was becoming too obvious that free labor is the cheapest.

A large planter in Louisiana was heard to say: "I can make more money off my plantation by cutting it up into small farms, erecting little cottages, and renting them to these families of emigrants, they bringing to my sugar-house so much cane annually for the rent, thus relieving me from all the vexations, responsibilities, and expenses of providing for 150 slaves, that must be fed and clothed, and taken care of when sick, whether the crop fails or not; and the time is not far distant," added he, "when these experiments will be made, to the entire satisfaction of every southern man, thereby rendering slavery a pecuniary burden too grievous to be borne—and which must be thrown off." This, we are told, is but a specimen of changes going on in the public mind at the South.

The Rev. Dr. Sautelle, who, some years ago, traveled extensively at the South, met among a certain class of planters the same state of feeling. Speaking of the changes which had taken place, he says: "Only let them progress silently and steadily a little longer, and let things take their natural course, under the guidance of God's superintending providence, and ere long the anxious cry will be heard from the South, not, how shall we keep, but how shall we get rid of our slaves? Who will take them off our hands? Where is there a place provided for them? And, wonderful as it may seem, while God has been working these changes in the South, he has, at the same time, been working in the hearts of Christians and philanthropists, inciting them to prepare for the slave a home in the land of his fathers, and paving the way for a return to it. How delightful to recognize the hand of God in all this!

."With the eye turned to Liberia, and the heart lifted up to God, we are ready to exclaim : 'There is hope for the slave!' 'There is hope for Africa!' 'There is hope for our own country!' "

Recent events would seem but too clearly to indicate that the above views were, at best, but partial and limited, most readily yielding to the now prevalent idea of the "Divine right" of slavery, and to the consequent determination to hold on to it at all hazards.

The fact that the existing war has produced a complete revulsion of all such favorable feeling on the part of slaveholders, detracts nothing from our position that Liberia holds out a hope and a home to the exiled sons of Ham, not the less hopeful than she did before their oppressors rose, in their great wrath, and inaugurated this wicked war, with the avowed purpose of perpetuating, and, if possible, nationalizing negro slavery, and making it the corner-stone of their confederacy. We do not believe that the "slave master's rebellion" will in one jot or tittle turn aside, or hinder for a day, the great and good purposes which God has to accomplish through these exiled sons of Africa. The war may precipitate universal emancipation, and embarrass the work, by what may seem to us, too great haste. Or it may seem to retard the work by raising new and difficult issues, yet, we may be sure the end shall not be frustrated.

We do not feel that we are in danger of overrating the desirableness, that every facility and encouragement should be afforded our negro population, that they should secure a home and a nationality in Africa. Neither the character nor the condition of the free blacks in our country, is such as to give us a very strong hope that the emancipation of our slave population would greatly better their condition, if they must remain in this country, and be obliged to compete with the white race. The hope that the two races may live and thrive together, and, on any comfortable footing of equality, is a hope against hope— a hope against all experience—an attempt to join what God has put asunder.

Some, who have most strenuously opposed African colonization, are beginning to regard it as the only hope of the poor African. And we can not here but devoutly admire the gracious Providence which has, precisely at the right time, provided such an asylum for an exiled race. There, in their fatherland, they may find a home, forever secure from the all-monopolizing, all-absorbing foe, the white man; it is their own land; protected by a double wall, fever and death, as a flaming fire, from the old competitors of the seed of Japheth; the only country in the world where the white man can not follow him, and the country designated by the finger of God as the asylum and home of the sons of Ham. There, he may sit under his own vine and fig-tree, with none to molest; and there he may rear up his children as men, and not as chattels to be bought and sold.

Did we need further testimonials to the real worth of the republic of Liberia, as an agency to be used by Providence for the emancipation of Africa, we might produce them by the scores. Naval officers, ship captains, free adventurers, missionaries, intelligent colored men, who have gone there to examine the country, and its prospects in reference to the removal of their families thither, all speak essentially the same language. John, a respectable and intelligent colored man from Elizabeth City, N. C., who has recently returned from Liberia, where he had been to examine for himself, and if he liked it, to return for his family, and such of his friends, as, from his report, might be induced to accompany him, after spending six weeks in the country, makes a report, which is "in every respect favorable." He is completely disarmed of his prejudices, and is about to go to Liberia with his family and fifty emigrants.

Commodore Lavallette, in a letter to the *Philadelphia Inquirer*, says : "I have visited Bassa Cove, and all other settlements of the emigrants on the coast of Liberia. I find them prosperous and happy; and I believe, if it were generally known to the colored population of the United States that Liberia offered to them a home possessing incalculable advantages, and the means of transporting them were provided, few of them would remain in our country."

A writer in *Chambers' Edinburgh Journal*, who seems to know whereof he affirms, speaks in language no less decided. Passing by the comparative view which he takes of the obvious results of either the naval squadrons on the coast of Africa, or the abolition movement, or the colonization scheme, he says : "An humble and almost unnoticed association of emancipated negroes from the United States has been doing real work, by quietly planting itself along the African coast, and causing, wherever it set its foot, the slave-trade to disappear. Strange to say, it has done this, not as a primary object, but only secondary and incidental to a process of colonization, the prompting causes of which were of a different, and, as some might think, partly inconsistent nature. Whatever were the motives of the Colonization Society, the consequences of their acts are such as to give them no small ground for triumph. For any thing that we can see, their settling of Liberia has been the most unexceptionably good movement against slavery that has ever taken place. Perhaps, it has not been the worse, but rather the better, for that infusion of the wisdom of this world, which has discommended it so much to the abolitionists.

"It occurs to us that the Colonization Society needs no other defense for its policy than to point to the spirit which has all along animated the black people who have emigrated to Africa. One sentiment, that it was worth while to encounter all the possible hardships and dangers on a foreign strand for the sake of perfect freedom, appears in the whole conduct of these men. They appear to have been generally persons of decided piety, and the missionary spirit is conspicuous at every stage of their proceeding. Not less important, as a testimony to the same effect, has been the energetic contention which the colonists have kept up against the slave-dealing propensities of the native princes. These men felt, from the first, that the Liberians were enemies to that traffic which gave them their most valued luxuries, and here lay the great difficulty which the settlers had to encounter. Their early history is a series of martyrdoms visited upon them by the slave-trade."

13*

"On the whole," says the same writer, "Liberia is a thriving settlement, and its destiny appears to be one of no mean character." He calls it the point of the wedge by which a Christian civilization, if ever, is to be introduced into Central Africa.

An emancipated slave, writing from Liberia to his former master in Hanover, Va., says: "This country bids fair to be one of the greatest countries in the known world. We, with our feeble means, are growing coffee, sugar-cane, ginger, arrow-root, and cotton, in the greatest abundance, and in no far distant day will raise every necessary for our domestic comfort. You will tell all the people of color, who have it in their power, to come to this country, and be free; now is the time for them to come and give us their aid in restoring lost Africa to her former greatness and glory."

In his inaugural address, President Roberts says: "You have successfully warred against that curse of all curses, the detestable slave-trade, and by your exertions have aided in effectually driving from these shores those monsters in human shape who once infested this coast; you have relieved thousands from innumerable distresses, consequent upon the ravages of cruel wars instigated by heartless slave dealers, and, with other thousands, brought them within the pale of civilization. And, above all, from Liberia has gone forth the light of Christianity, penetrating the very depths of heathen superstition and idolatry, so that in every direction may be seen the sons of the forest giving earnest heed to the story of the cross."

Again, the governor says: "And no country presents to them a more inviting field for industrious enterprise than the land of their ancestors; no country possesses greater natural resources than this—rich in minerals of the greatest value, and a soil unsurpassed in fertility and productiveness. Indeed, nothing is required in Liberia to make her powerful and her citizens respectable, wealthy, and happy, but cheerful hearts and willing hands." `

CHAPTER XVI.

Duty of the American people ; of slaveholders ; of the colored people of this country.

WE can by no possibility, if we would, dodge the question—What shall be done with the negro ? We have had too much to do with him already to hope for exemption now. We must, *volentes nolentes*, have much to do with him yet. For pride and gain, with cruelty and barbarous inhumanity, we have brought him into his present position, and God will hold us responsible, not only to deliver him from bondage, but to recompense him for the wrong.

The singular apathy of our Government and of the American people to press forward every feasible scheme of colonization at this critical juncture may be the occasion of another negro nationality, which we may not altogether relish—a nationality in our own country. Every consideration of fitness, of interest, of duty, would seem to urge their settlement in their fatherland. While we are relucting, Providence is moving. He is breaking every yoke, setting the captives free ; and now as freemen they must have a name and a place, a country and a home ; and if we, as their constituted guardians and protectors, do not hasten to give them the helping hand, and guide them back to the land of their fathers, the heart that pities them, the hand that is stretched out for their succor, will take from us and give to them some portion of a country which they have earned by their unrequited toil, and watered for long and weary years with the tears of anguish. But we pass to inquire :

3. What duty do the American people owe to Africa, and the present scheme of African colonization ? Much, every way ; but chiefly because of the wrongs which, as a people, we have inflicted on Africa. Our obligation is three-fold : we are debtors as Christians, as philanthropists, and as wrong-doers. Africa is a great pagan continent, and, as Christians, we are bound to send there the Gospel. Her people must be told of a Saviour ; and as intelligent Christians, and obedient, willing servants of our Divine Master, we must watch the movements of Providence, and work where he works, and in the manner indicated by the Divine working. Some nations are converted through missionary operations, some purely through providential agency. War in one instance opens the way for the introduction of the Gospel ; peace, in another. One people are brought to an acquaintance with Christianity by receiving Christian colonies into her bosom, and learning of them ; another, by means of her people, either voluntarily, or otherwise, going to a Christian people, and dwelling with them, so as to learn of them what be the truth in Jesus. In the establishment and extension of Christianity, the Great Head of the Church has pursued no one course to the exclusion of others. It is wisdom on the part of the Christian to discern the mode of the Divine proceeding in any given case ; and it is obedience to make his prayers, labors, and benefactions harmonize with the Divine mode of operation.

God is successfully introducing the Gospel, and establishing his Church in Africa through Christian colonies. We must accept this way of working, and work with it.

It is therefore our duty, as Christians, to favor, by every means in our power, the present scheme of colonization, as the appointed means of evangelizing Africa. We are debtors to her, not only in the sense that all who have the Gospel are bound by a Divine injunction to give it to those who have it not, till all nations shall be evangelized, but we are under some special obligation to Africa. We have been confederate with them who have spoiled Africa, and are therefore laid under some special obligation to make her such a return as shall in a special sense bless her. We can never wash the deep blood-stains from our skirts, yet we may become to her the almoners of Heaven's richest gift to man. Though we may never repay the wrong we have done, we may staunch her bleeding wounds; we may pour into her lacerated heart the balm in Gilead; we may bring to her aid the Great Physician.

While, therefore, it is undoubtedly the duty of our General Government and of our State Legislatures to make liberal appropriations to send to Africa every colored man who is willing and fitted to go, and to do every thing which money and influence can do to make the condition of the returned African comfortable to himself, and useful to his kindred, and the duty of the whole American people to favor, by every means in their power, so worthy an enterprise, it is most evidently the duty of the professed Christian to make Africa the object of especial interest. But what shall he do? He must watch the finger of Providence, and work in the way indicated thereby. Through Christian colonies there a wide and effectual door has been opened, through which Christianity and all its rich concomitant blessings may be made to flow in upon that desert land.

But I shall not repeat here what has already been, on this subject, either directly or impliedly said. It is enough to add, that a vast continent—a teeming population of 150,000,000 pagan souls, are now, in the providence of God, fairly laid at the feet of the Church of Christ. The time for their gracious visitation seems to have come. Access is open to them, and thousands of agents are prepared for the work. No pains should be spared—no sacrifices thought too expensive by which to carry out purposes so philanthropic and benevolent as the rescue of Africa from her present state of bondage and spiritual death.

I shall at present speak of but one feature of the scheme which, in my humble estimation, is at this time a very important desideratum in the hoped-for renovation of Africa. I mean a provision for establishing, in this country, a literary institution where intelligent, enterprising colored young men may obtain a thorough education. A paramount duty which we owe to our colored population, and one clearly indicated by the providence of God, is the preparation of this people, in the shortest possible time, to return to their fatherland, that they may there accomplish the mission assigned them. Provision is being made for the endowment of such an institution in Liberia. The Liberian College is already in successful operation. This is as it should be; but such provision in Africa can not meet the demand for a similar institution in America. If the exodus of the African race from this country were already accomplished, or on the eve of a speedy accomplishment, the case would be different. Schools and higher institutions of learning in Liberia can not be too highly valued. They will meet a very important demand there. Without such institutions, well sustained, colonization will quite fail of its objects. They are indispensable both to the permanence and prosperity of the colonies, and to the greater benefit of the native tribes.

But the greatest good of Africa equally demands similar institutions in this country. The first and chief desideratum is, not how we shall send the greatest possible number of blacks to Africa, but rather how those who may be sent shall be qualified, and how the mass of our colored population in this country shall be qualified, at an early day, to migrate to and fulfill their destined mission in Africa. It would be quite possible to inundate Liberia with a class of emigrants which should curse, rather than bless, her. A suitable preparation, in this country, of the people of color is a vital feature in our scheme for renovating Africa. The rising generation in Liberia, and the young who may migrate thither, should doubtless be educated in Liberian schools. Yet a college and schools in Liberia, though important in their place, do not meet the necessities of the case in this country. The importation to her shores of ignorance and vice can not possibly benefit Africa, nor can the ignorant and vicious derive any advantage from transportation. Colonization is desirable only in proportion to the preparedness of the proposed colonists to emigrate.

Preparation in this country, then, is vital to the whole scheme. Before our African population should be fitted for their exodus and their profitable colonization on the coast of Africa, they must have their Moses and Aaron, their scribes and priests, their skillful laborers and cunning artificers. The utility and efficiency of such colonies depends on the social, civil, and moral resources which, as a body politic, they may possess. These resources they must carry with them, or they will fail to fulfill their mission. Our colored population must therefore be educated. Very few of them are yet fitted for the enjoyment of liberty. The mass must be elevated and enlightened. But what is no less important, there must be a class among them of more highly educated men. Such a class of colored men is needed more, perhaps, for the purpose of acting on the African race in this country, and preparing them to emigrate, than for the sake of going themselves to Africa.

But how shall this be done? Is there any fair hope that any considerable number—a number by any means adequate to the demand, shall be educated in our present institutions of learning? Practically few of our higher schools are open to the colored man. But if open—if he may enter, if he please, and graduate at one of our colleges, is the mere permission to do so much better, in the circumstances of the case, than a practical prohibition? The permission amounts to just about as much as the permission of the Romish hierarchy does, when they allow the mass of the laity to own and read the Bible. The disabilities in the case quite neutralize the permission. Few of our colored people can meet the expense of a liberal education, whatever school may be accessible to them, and a still smaller number are able to surmount the difficulties which they would most certainly meet in such an attempt. But give them an institution of their own, provide for them a cheap, and in most cases a gratuitous education, and how differently they would feel and act. Young men of native talent would soon be collected there, and bleeding Africa would soon not be without a class of her own educated sons, who should supply with educated men, and a ministry of a higher order, her own exiled sons in this country, and act as their leaders in preparing them for that other and better country beyond the floods, and become their companions and their guides thither.

They who desire and pray for Africa's speedy renovation can not do a better thing, or more effectually compass their object, than by the establishment in this country of a high school and college for the education of such of our colored population as shall be found to have the talents and enterprise to seek an education. In no other way, perhaps, could they so permanently and extensively benefit that waiting continent.

Our home duties to this people, are at this moment greatly increased by the events of the present war. Tens of thousands are now thrown upon us. They are fugitives from oppression. They stand at our doors asking aid, present protection, advice, and guidance. They come poor, ignorant, destitute of employment, and homeless. They are used to work—are willing to work—expect to work, but lack the place, the patronage, the opportunity. They are in a transition state— passing from the house of bondage to the land of promise. It is their wilderness state; and we must be to them the manna from heaven, the water from the rock, and a defense from the enemy. God has risen up to break every yoke, and to let his captives go free; and we, as his people, must see to it that we be found in hearty and happy co-operation with our God.

The mass of this people should undoubtedly, for a considerable time, remain with us. They are not yet fitted for their nationality. Many are not willing to go. Adequate means are not yet available to transport them hence, and to settle them abroad ; and our African colonies could not at once bear so great an influx of population. The more immediate and temporary destiny of the mass is to remain in this country as laborers, not as slaves, but as free men. They need the training of an honorable and compensated labor. We need the labor. They should be left in their own " sunny South," with every encouragement which industry, honesty, and sobriety can hold out, to make themselves men in every honorable pursuit of life, and to prepare themselves in the shortest possible time, for their own higher and better condition in their fatherland.

4. We come to inquire next, What is the duty of the slaveholding portion of our population in respect to Africa and African colonization? We should not stop here to raise any question as to the moral character of slavery, and the blameworthiness of the slaveholder. Be it enough, that they have in their possession an unfortunate people, toward whom they hold some peculiar relations, and whom they have it in their power greatly to bless, and through whom they may confer incalculable blessings on Africa. No class of men, perhaps, on the whole face of the earth have it in their power, at the present time, to do so stupendous a work of philanthropy and Christian benevolence as the present generation of American slaveholders.

Africa is fast becoming the great field for missionary enterprise. Americanized Africans, trained in the rigid school of slavery, are, as we have seen, undoubtedly to be the chief agents in bringing Africa within the pale of civilization and Christianity. To prepare these agents for their destined work, and to transplant them to their destined field of labor, is peculiarly the work of the southern slaveholder. Every American citizen, and every philanthropist and Christian the world over, has an interest here, and should liberally bear any share of the burden which may fall to him. But it is pecu-liarly the work of the South, and much of it can be done only there. After the South should have qualified their slaves for removal, and emancipated them, the North may transport them to the promised land, and settle them, and give the facilities to execute there their destined mission. But this is but a small part of the whole work. The people of the South will have done the greater share before. I speak, for the moment, for-getting the unhappy conflict between the two-sections of our country. I speak of things as they should be, and as I hope in God they ere long will be, and not as they unhappily are.

Never did a people have it in their power to do a nobler work. It is, first, a work of justice, the redress of a wrong, the restoration to a race of what is dearer than life. And, then, it is a work of mercy and benevo-lence. While it will give liberty to the captives of a temporal bondage, it will confer on a wretched conti-nent an infinite good.

It is most cheerfully conceded, that a portion of our slaveholding population were nobly doing their duty in this respect. They were doing much, and making great sacrifices, as we have shown elsewhere,* to pre-pare their slaves for freedom, and then to emancipate them and send them to Africa, where they might enjoy the blessing of a new life, and do much to confer the same blessings on the suffering race of Ham. What

---

* "Hand of God in History," chap. xvi.

the few were doing, the many ought to do. A whole heathen continent lies at their feet—a continent teeming with immortal souls, and abounding in all sorts of natural resources—capable of becoming one of the richest and most beautiful provinces of Immanuel's empire. Christians at the South hold in their hands the agents—have the training of the men, who, under God, are to achieve the redemption of that great continent, and subject it, with all its resources, to the rule of the great King.

There were men at the South, and we hope are still, who feel this solemn weight of responsibility pressing upon them, and who will nobly meet it. There are more who have no just appreciation either of the duties that in this respect devolve upon them, or of the honor and privileges which, through their providential position, they may enjoy; but through a cold-blooded avarice, and reckless of all providential intimation, determine to keep their slaves the victims of their selfishness. To such we would raise the voice of kind entreaty and of caution. How sad, that they who, in the arrangements of a wise and gracious Providence, stand in the most interesting relation to Africa, and have it in their power to do her an inestimable good, while at the same time they should confer a priceless individual good on their own slaves, should choose to act the part of oppressors rather than benefactors! But all success and a rich reflex blessing be on the heads of those noble men and women, who, with praiseworthy sacrifice in time and money and care, are doing so much to prepare their colored people for their freedom, and, then, at a yet greater sacrifice, are restoring them to the bosom of their motherland. No class of men are doing a better or a greater work. May Heaven smile on them!

The above paragraph was written before the out-break of this dreadful rebellion, and we choose to let it stand as a pleasant monument of the past, rather than to mar the picture by the indelible stigma of the the present.

5. Finally, we would say a word to the sons and daughters of Ham who are scattered up and down through the length and breadth of our land. Africa is their natural home, and both duty and interest urge their speedy return thither. Could it be shown that the condition of the slave or the free black in this country is not likely to be benefited, personally, by a removal to Africa, still strong reasons urge him to remove. To say nothing of the duty he owes to his fatherland and to his native race, he owes it to his children to deliver them from the thousand disabilities of their position in this country, and to place them in circumstances of hope in another land. The condition of the colored man in this country is, to make the best of it, a hope-less condition, and every day it is becoming worse. They that advise them to remain in this country are bad friends. They advise them to act against their best interests. Their right to remain and enjoy a happy equality with the whites may be undisputed, and the disabilities under which they live may be founded in unrighteousness; yet such is their condi-tion, and such in the nature of the case will it most certainly remain, that it is only cruelty to the colored man to prolong his stay here. He may go where he may be a man—where he may rear his children as freemen—where they shall have stimulants to indus-

try, and may aspire to the highest and best condition of manhood. Some of their best friends,* though long strenuously opposed to every scheme of removing the blacks from this country, have recently come out in favor of colonization on the coast of Africa. There is no hope that the two races shall prosper together in this land. One will and must have the ascendency. And which shall it be? God has, by a series of most signal providences, designated these United States as the habitation and theatre of action for the white man, and as signally has he pointed out Africa as the home of the black man. Such is her physical condition, especially in respect to climate, as virtually to exclude the white races. He has reserved one continent as the land of Ham, where he will display toward that long-forsaken race the greatness of his power and the riches of his grace.

Many of that unfortunate race have been wickedly wrested from their native home, and doomed to a foreign bondage. Yet this very bondage, as we have seen, forms one of the most interesting chapters in their providential history. Their restoration to their native home shall be as life from the dead, to the putrid corpse of Africa. Why, then, will they linger in a land where slavery, with all its wrongs, and oppressions and depressions, is their best condition? In Africa, alone, is there hope for the colored man. Say what we will, do what we can, and their condition is a hopeless one. They can not rise—they can not prosper here. Try as you will, you can not rear

---

* See the late address of James G. Burney to the colored people of the United States.

thrifty, fruitful plants beneath the thick foliage of a wide-spreading tree, not till you bring them out and allow them to breathe heaven's natural air, and bask in the rays of an unobstructed sun, and be exposed to the genial showers, will they grow and prosper. Every interest, every hope, of the negro is over-shadowed by the predominance of the white races.

It is, therefore, the only hope, the highest interest, and, consequently, the imperative duty of the colored man to return, if possible, to his own native Africa.

But all this may pass as the opinion of an outsider. Let us then hear what men, who, as a race and as individuals, are personally interested, say. I quote from a multitude of like kind the following testimonials of residents in Liberia, who have exchanged their condition in America for their present home and position in Africa. It was at a public meeting held by citizens of Monrovia, for the purpose of declaring and making known to the world their free sentiments and opinions concerning African colonization. This interesting meeting was addressed by several citizens of the colony, under a deep sense of obligation to the Colonization Society; and with an enthusiasm and eloquence worthy of the cause they had assembled to promote. Said one: "I arrived in Africa on the 24th of May, 1823. My object in coming was liberty, and under the firm conviction that Africa is the only place, in existing circumstances, where the man of color can enjoy the inestimable blessings of liberty and equality, I feel grateful beyond expression to the American Colonization Society for preparing this peaceful asylum."

Said another: "I thank God that ever he put it into

the hearts of the Colonization Society to seek out this free soil on which I have been so honored as to set my feet. I and my family were born in Charleston, S. C., under the appellation of free people ; but freedom I never knew, until, by the benevolence of this society, we were conveyed to the shores of Africa. My language is too poor to express the gratitude I entertain toward the American Colonization Society."

Said a third : "I came to Liberia in 1832. My place of residence was the city of Washington, D. C., where I passed for a free man. But I can now say that I was never free until I landed on the shores of Africa. I further state, that Africa, as far as I am acquainted with the world, is the only place where the people of color can enjoy true and rational liberty."

Said a fourth : "I beg leave to state that my situation is greatly altered for the better by coming to Africa. My political knowledge is far superior to what it would have been had I remained in America 1,000 years. I therefore seize this chance to present my thanks to the American Colonization Society for enabling me to come to this colony, which they have so benevolently established."

The following resolutions, among others, were then passed, as expressive of the sense of the meeting :

"That this meeting entertain the warmest gratitude for what the American Colonization Society has done for the people of color, and for us particularly ; and that we regard the scheme entitled to the highest confidence of every colored man.

"That this meeting regard the colonization as one of the highest, holiest, and most benevolent enterprises of the present day. That, as a plan for the melioration of the condition of the colored race, it takes the precedence of all that have been presented to the attention of the modern world. That in its operations, it is peaceful and safe—its tendencies benevolent and advantageous. That it is entitled to the highest veneration and unbounded confidence of every man of color. That what it has already accomplished demands our devout thanks and gratitude to those noble and disinterested philanthropists who compose it, as being, under God, the greatest earthly benefactors of a despised and oppressed portion of the human family.

"Whereas, it has been widely and maliciously circulated in the United States of America, that the inhabitants of this colony are unhappy in their condition and anxious to return: *Resolved*, That the report is false and malicious, and originated only in a design to injure the colony by calling off the support and sympathy of its friends; that, so far from having a desire to return, we should regard such an event the greatest calamity that could befall us."

CHAPTER XVII.

Ought the negroes to emigrate? — Prejudice — A negro nationality—Their destiny—The intimations of Providence.

WE have spoken of the practicability of a scheme of colonization which shall be broad enough to transport the whole colored population of America to the fatherland, and settle them there in comfort. But is it expedient that they should go? Is it for their interest—is it for ours? And if once transferred there, are they capable of self-culture, of self-protection, and support? Have they the capabilities to form and sustain a negro nationality—to so conduct matters of state, of church, of education, and jurisprudence, as to make their independent condition any real improvement on their long-protracted servile condition? Has their education, their training and discipline, during their long bondage, been such as to warrant any such expectations? And all these things being granted, ought the colored people of this country to be urged to leave the land of their birth and adoption, and even voluntarily to exile themselves to a country which is to them a foreign land? And if they are willing and wish to go, is it good policy in us to have them go? Do we not need them all here as laborers, not as slaves, but as free men?

Such queries give rise to a variety of considerations which we shall do well to canvass.

As touching these several points, four things must

be assumed. The race in question, if they will ever rise from their present depressed condition, and attain to the position we have supposed : 1. Must be able to disenthrall themselves from the inveterate prejudice which, in this land, like a deadly incubus, crushes them to the earth. 2. They must secure to themselves a negro nationality. 3. They must go where they can be men, and not chattels or tools; only associated with property. 4. It is important that they should, as an undying incentive to energy and perseverance, be inspired with the conviction that the finger of God is pointing them to that land— that they have a great mission to fulfill there—that the strong hand of Providence is stretched out to bring them to their promised land—that the land is kept in reserve, waiting for its rightful occupants— that they are the heaven-appointed agents for the accomplishment of Heaven's purposes toward that long forsaken continent. A brief consideration of these points will be a sufficient answer to our queries.

1. The prejudice. We may denounce it as an unreasonable prejudice—a wicked prejudice. But it is a stubborn fact; indelible, ineffaceable as the color of the Ethiopian's skin. Right or wrong, for more than two centuries it has existed in this country, unabated, unmitigated by time. We are not discussing the right or wrong of it, but the stubborn fact. Of this the negro but too well knows its power. Few, if any, have been able to overcome it. It should be removed —it should not exist. But it does exist; and it will exist. The negro, therefore, has only to yield to the hard pressure and succumb to the subordinate condition which it, as a general condition, implies; or he

must shake off the incubus, and cast in his lot among the people of his own nation and color, where he can stand up in the pride and independence of his own manhood. And is not this as heaven would have it? True it is, that God "hath made of one blood all nations of men for to dwell on all the face of the earth;" and equally true, that he hath "determined the bounds of their habitation." God sacredly regards nationalities, and does not smile upon that violence which ruptures the distinctive branches into which he has been pleased to divide the one great family of man. Whether the distinctive mark of each branch be the color of the skin, or the contour of the face, he would have the nationality respected.

What marvel, then, if we meet with an instinctive something, call it prejudice, if you please, which jealously guards these national boundaries. The Hebrews met it in Egypt, and have met it now for the last eighteen centuries, and, it is this that has preserved them a distinct people for the great and good purposes which Heaven designs. Though in no other case, perhaps, so marked as between the Caucasian and the negro, yet the prejudice exists toward the Chinese, the Malays, the North American Indian. Nationalities are of Divine appointment; and, these appointments are made with special reference to his chosen people—his Church, and the progress of the work of redemption. We have the record: "When the Most High divided to the nations their inheritance, when he separated the sons of Adam, he set the bounds of the people according to the number of the children of Israel."—Deut. xxxii. 8.

No people may lightly esteem their nationality.

Their life-mission is to be executed through this nationality. I was about to say, that it was the negro's right to remain in this country, but his interest to unite his destiny with his brethren in Africa. Better to say it is his right only in a subordinate sense. As the land of his birth, the land of his toil and his sufferings, he has a right to remain as he is. As touching his relations to his human oppressors, he has the best right to stay. He has enriched the land by his toils; he has watered the soil with his tears. He has rights. But a higher interest, a higher duty, demands that he forego these rights. His God, his kindred according to the flesh, the claims of nationality, present a higher duty, a louder call, and bid him hasten his escape from a land of oppression and incorrigible prejudice, to the land of hope, where, unembarrassed, he may arise and assert his manhood—enjoy the smiles of Heaven, and, by blessing himself, bless his race.

Is it, then, expedient, is it right, and their duty to migrate to Africa? Undoubtedly it is. Interest, duty, the unerring finger of God, all seem pointing in that direction. An unmistakable, unremitting prejudice seems to say: "This is the way, walk ye in it." Whether it is for our interest as Americans to have them leave us, is quite another question; and one that might receive quite a different answer. While I can see reasons enough why, for their own sake, they should go, I see no reason why we should wish them to go—why we should thrust them out, save the reason assigned by the Egyptians why they should hasten away the Israelites. A righteous retribution had become too severe for endurance; and they wished those who had been the innocent occasion of it should be removed out of their sight. They yielded to the necessity, hoping to escape a further judgment. On any other ground, it is not easy to see why we should wish their departure. Of all laborers they are the best adapted to the fields of their former toil—they are needed there—and our interest would dictate that they remain.

We are amazed at the deep-rooted prejudice against the whole negro race which the present war has developed. The thoughts of many hearts are revealed. It is more than a prejudice. It is with a large party a hate, a satanic determination to keep the whole race in question crushed beneath the same iron heel of slavery which has kept them crushed for the last two centuries. It repudiates all idea of a common brotherhood in the race—all idea of right for the negro—all opportunity, if not all capability, of rising above his present low level. It is a feeling evoked, strengthened, and confirmed, by the present war. Whatever view we may take of the war, as seen from a northern standpoint, the instigators of it at the South do not disguise the fact that it is a war urged for the vindication and perpetuation of the enslavement of the African race. Principles had been promulgated and urged on the public attention at the North, which, if persisted in and successful, would peril the existence of the "peculiar institution." It was to meet this, and forever to crush the hope of any future attempt to abolish the system of human bondage, that the war was waged; and for the same reason it is prosecuted with a desperation and madness, which none but a people reared in the atmosphere of human servitude could wage.

Our amazement is not so much that southern slaveholders display such an inveterate determination to keep the victims of their pride and avarice in a perpetual and hopeless bondage ; for they profess nothing better ; and their leaders of public opinion, grave divines, and sapient statesmen have fortified them in the dreadful delusion. But our astonishment is, that so large a party at the North should manifest, in no mistakable manner, sympathies with the slaveholder, and prejudices against the negro race, which would, if possible, forge their chains stronger than ever.

Our conclusion from all this is, that prejudice is too strong to admit of any fair hope that the two races may ever live together and prosper on the same field of activity. Their separation is, not only expedient, but indispensable to the prosperity of the African race. We conclude then,

2. That there is no well-founded hope for the colored men of our land but in a negro nationality. "The bounds of his habitation must be determined." Would they successfully achieve, as a race, the great struggle of national life, they must have a " basis." They must have a home—a local habitation, where the family and school—where social influences and motives to acquire property and position—shall act upon them. They must have rights, social and religious, to stimulate them to activity and respectability. They must be where they shall feel the power of society and the incentives of patriotism. It is not enough that they are subjects of a government, and acquire the wholesome discipline of obedience. It must be their own government, of which they shall be an integral part—not only be competent to vote, but to be voted for—eligible to any office for which they may be deemed competent.

Liberia holds out the offer of such a nationality. No one, perhaps, will question that the negro has no fair prospect of rising, except by securing for himself the rights and privileges of a nationality. He can never develop his manhood while deprived of such rights and privileges. You may emancipate him from slavery, and make him own himself, but if you do not give him the opportunity to use himself, body, mind, and soul, in the various relations in which they are made to be used, you have gone but a little way toward conferring any real benefit on the man. Facts do but too stubbornly show that the larger number of negroes who have from time to time, been emancipated in this country, and left to seek their fortune as best they could, have not been able to make for themselves a better position than they left in their servitude. They secured the consciousness of being free, and that is about all. But give them social, civil, and religious rights—give them a nationality of their own, and, then, if they will not rise, and thrive, and expand into being, and vindicate their claims to a status among the nations, we will hand them over to the tender mercies of their traducers.

But do they, at the present moment, indicate, by any aptitudes, qualifications, or capabilities—or does the providence of God, by his present dispensations, indicate any such destiny for these sons of Ham? Have we any fair ground for the hope that they shall become a great, and good, and prosperous, and highly useful nation—getting good to themselves, and imparting a greater good to the benighted tribes of that unfortunate continent? I think we have, and I shall state some of the grounds of such a hope.

Admiral Foote, than whom few men are better versed
14*

in the question before us, said in a recent public address : "There never can be peace in the world until the status of the negro is defined. Where shall he live? How shall he be instructed? What shall be his social position? What are his capacities? What his rights, natural and civil? These are questions that agitate the world. Statesmen, as well as philanthropists, are engaged in solving this problem." The flippant may ridicule, the profane may sneer, the demagogue may rant, but the "nigger question" is the great question of the age. As well might Pharaoh and his host have ignored the Hebrew question of their day. God was in it, and he had a great and a far-reaching purpose to accomplish through it. The deliverance of the captive Hebrews was the first great necessary step to their establishment and expansion into one of the most important nationalities that ever existed.

Does the material exist—does the present generation of Anglo-Africans in this country possess capabilities and qualifications, suited to build up and sustain such a nationality in Africa as shall essentially benefit themselves and bless Africa? From their past training and education what encouragement do we derive that they may constitute such a state as we have supposed? We have already adduced instances not a few to show that, in spite of the most formidable disadvantages, colored men have become statesmen, scholars, writers, and men of wealth and position—that they are respectably represented in the learned professions, and lack not artists, poets, and orators. The only marvel is, that they have made laudable progress under so forbidding circumstances. We may safely say, that, as far as we know, no people apply themselves to learning, when they do have the opportunity, with so much eagerness, or, according to their opportunities, make a more rapid progress, than this very race, as examples already quoted abundantly attest. No class of children and youth show a more hearty desire to learn, or, under the same circumstances, make a more satisfactory proficiency. Most interesting examples are now constantly being reported of the large class of negroes that are, at the present moment, continually falling into our hands, called "contrabands." Their eagerness to be taught, and the progress which they make, adults as well as children, fully verify the remarks I have made.

We are quite justified, then, in the conclusion, that all they need is the adequate opportunity to fit them to occupy the position we have supposed. But it is rather to their religious training and fitness to which I would direct attention. Do we see any special presage for good here?

While the negro is not lacking, as we have seen, in the development of the intellectual and physical elements needful to the building of a nationality of his own, yet more especially does his fitness appear in the development of his religious susceptibilities, indicating the character of the mission he is to execute on the broad field of the African continent. If we mistake not the divinely appointed agents for the conversion of Africa to Christianity, are Americanized negroes. This we infer, more especially, from the singular religious history of this people during the last fifty years, when taken in connection with their no less singular religious proclivities. The first dawning of hope to the American negro appeared near the beginning of the present century, in the abolition of the slave-trade, followed in a few years, as a natural and happy sequence, by the successive emancipation of the blacks in the West Indies, and throughout nearly every civilized nation. This gave them an impulse onward and upward—cast the first decisive ray of hope over the dark waters of their servitude, and bid them rise and assert their rights as men. The most distinctive sign of a sure resurrection appeared in the development of the religious elements—the mightiest, surest element by which to work out a people's renovation.

Previous to the period I have named, "the negro race had been left in a state of almost absolute spiritual neglect." Along the whole line of the west coast of Africa, not a mission had been commenced, not a temple of Christianity pointed its spire to the skies. In America and in the West Indies the masses of the colored population were in a state of heathenism, though surrounded by Christian institutions. Indeed, their oppressors were not yet well decided whether they were susceptible of religious improvement, or had immortal souls.

Africa's degradation had now reached a crisis. From this point a marked reaction followed. Henceforward her suffering sons, aroused from their long and deep slumber, showed a singular disposition to receive and be profited by religious instruction; and, as corresponding with this, there sprung into existence about the same time a disposition, equally strange and unprecedented, to come to the rescue of this long-benighted, degraded race. This feeling soon clothed itself in the overt act, and at length became embodied in certain philanthropic and benevolent societies, the design of which is the evangelization of the enslaved and the recently emancipated; and through them, the evangelization of Africa. We refer to such associations as "The Ladies' Negro Education Society" of England; a society in the island of Barbadoes, under the patronage of the governor and bishop; a society in England, under the patronage of the Archbishop of Canterbury and the leaders of the Church and of the State; our own Colonization Society, and Missionary Societies of every name and nation. These are but the movings of the great heart of Christianity toward the long-benighted and down-trodden sons of Africa.

And, in correspondence with this again, slaveholders in America, who had heretofore scarcely thought more of providing religious teachings for their slaves than for their horses, now begin to erect chapels, build schoolhouses, employ teachers and preachers; and themselves and families often contributing to, and participating in, the noble work. And in beautiful harmony with this, the Spirit of God, poured out from on high, has accompanied these teachings, simple as they oftentimes are; and never, perhaps, in the history of Christianity, was the same amount of means made effectual to the production of so great results, and this, whether numbers are brought into the account, or the character, the spirituality, of the converts; never has the same amount of means, and means characterized by so moderate intellectual power, savingly and permanently effected so large a proportion of a community, or been followed by so high an order of genuine spirituality.

We have seen various statements of the number of southern slaves in connection with Christian churches. We give the following from the *Educational Journal*, of Forsyth, Ga. :

Connected with the Methodist Church South,
    are.................................... 200,000
Methodist North, in Virginia and Maryland.. 15,000
Missionary and Hard-Shell Baptists 175,000
Old-School Presbyterians 12,000
New   "   "   (U. Synod) supposed 6,000
Cumberland........................ 20,000
Protestant Episcopalians............ 7,000
Campbellites or Christian Churches........ 10,000
All other sects combined.................. 20,000

Total colored membership, South....... 465,000

"It is a safe calculation," remarks the same journal, " to say that three for every one connected with the churches attend Divine service on the Lord's Day. In the extreme Southern States there are more, for the owners and overseers require them, in many instances, to turn out to preaching. Then 465,000 multiplied by 3, gives us 1,395,000 slaves in attendance on Divine service in the South every Sabbath."

No missionary scheme acting in any quarter of the globe presents any thing like such results. All the missionary societies of all branches of the Evangelical Christian Church do not exhibit so large a list of converts during the same time.

But what kind of Christians are they? We do not speak of their intelligence, of their social influence, or of their pecuniary ability. Yet we often marvel at the intellectual attainments which they actually acquire while yet in slavery. It is the spiritual caste of their religion that we now inquire after. What is the character of these half million of slave Christians as to genuine heart-felt piety?

We may here quote, as a fair specimen of the many testimonials we have from the same quarter, the "testimony of a pastor" of one of their churches at the South : " In the church I serve," he says. " there are some of the most beautiful specimens of Christian character I ever saw. Often have I witnessed the calm, intelligent, triumphant death-bed scene, and said in my soul : I shall not be fit to sit at the feet of these in heaven." Those who have been present at their services in their own churches at the South, bear the most willing testimony to the peculiar fervency of their prayers—to the godly simplicity of their worship—to the pathos, humility, and single heartedness of their religion. There is about it a meekness and lowliness of mind ; a renunciation of self ; · a drawing near to, and a casting one's self upon, God ; an obedient, dependent, and filial spirit, which we are sure bears a nearer resemblance to the apostolic religion —bears more indubitable marks of a heavenly origin, than any form of religion with which we are acquainted. It takes hold on God. It engages the hand and heart of God in its behalf. The High and Holy One that inhabiteth eternity, whose name is Holy, dwells with him that is of a contrite heart and a humble spirit.

Mighty agencies, terrific agencies, are engaged at the present moment to carry forward the war which this great African question has originated in our land. Armies, navies, military strategy, vast pecuniary resources, are engaged. But there is an agency at work infinitely mightier than they all. We meet it in the filial and undying reliance of the abused ones on Israel's God. We meet it in their humble, importunate prayers, and strong cries and tears, as in the iron furnace they sigh for deliverance. Their oppressors may defy northern

steel, and northern men and money ; but in their negro's
prayers they are sure to meet a power which is altogether too hard for them.   They take hold on the omnipotent arm ; and he that resists shall perish.

Here lies our hope, here the power, that shall deliver
them from their present thraldom, and make them a great
and good nation in their native Africa ; and make
them, in turn, the great and paramount agency for the
civilization and evangelization of that great continent.
We think we see substantial grounds for such a hope in
the singular susceptibilities, and readiness in the colored
man to cultivate a religious character ; in the singular
disposition manifested by white Christians to bring religious teachings within their reach ; and the no less
extraordinary manner in which the Spirit has been
poured out from on high and given efficacy to these
teachings.

But a query here arises, which we would not suppress.
It relates to the apparent inadequacy of the means to
the result.   We are wont to expect spiritual results
only in proportion as the appointed means of grace are
applied, in proportion to the amount of truth presented
and enforced on the heart and conscience.   In the case
before us, we meet with this disparity strikingly prominent.   Our negroes at the South are generally without
the Bible, and without the ability to read if they had
the book ; much of the preaching and religious teaching
which they enjoy is of a very meagre character, imparting but very little knowledge of the truth.   And their
opportunities for verbal instruction, owing to their associations being almost entirely confined to persons as
ignorant as themselves, are scanty and few ; and if these
advantages were multiplied and of a high order, their

lack of time and opportunity—their peculiar condition, as slaves, chattels, tools—would, we should suppose, very much hinder the due improvement of the means of spiritual profiting. Yet, as a most interesting matter of fact, they have an amount of religious knowledge— have a Christian experience, thorough, shrewd, discriminating—which far transcends any thing we are led to expect in the circumstances. In the matter of a humble, heartfelt, experimental religion, they have a depth of experience, a drawing near to God, and a childlike familiarity and confidence, which give no doubtful evidence that they are, indeed, taught of God. Constrained to acknowledge that these outcasts among men, but honored of God, have drunk deep in Divine philosophy, many an intelligent white Christian does not disdain to sit at their feet, and be taught the wonderful things of God. But whence have these men letters, never having learned ?

We seem shut up to the conclusion, that men in this condition are taught by a direct and special revelation from God. The class in question would seem to furnish abundant evidence that they are thus taught. The idea is brought out in an extract before me, taken from a paper by Dr. Floy, a Methodist clergyman-of New York. The interest of the subject will excuse the length of the extract. He says :

"He finds in South Carolina the most extraordinary knowledge of Divine things among the slaves. They are ignorant, they are not much taught ; and he is clearly of the opinion that they have not derived this knowledge, either from reading the Bible, or from the oral instruction of Christians. He asks how they get it ; and he answers the question by saying that he believes God reveals it to them. I believe so too. But does he reveal it to everybody that does not know it? No; not to those that can find it out for themselves. But take a mind, and let it hunger and thirst after righteousness ; let a mind that is in darkness be pressing toward moral truth, and yearning for it, without the power of obtain-. ing it, and then I believe that God will reveal that truth to him.

"Now the African mind is essentially a religious mind, and it has had culture enough to know that there is a heaven, and that there is a Jesus Christ that died for men. It understands the great outlines of truth, and yearns toward it, and feels after it ; and I see nothing in philosophy or religion that renders it difficult to believe that to souls that have no light of God's Word, from which they are shut out by penal enactments, that have little or no religious instruction, and that are blindly groping to find God, he does send light enough to let them know which way to walk. Is it harder for God to teach a poor African than a poor old Jew, like Isaiah? Is it harder now for God to teach some old Dinah than, in olden times, it was for him to teach a Hannah? And if there is a good purpose for it, I do not know why he should not do in these later times what he did in earlier days.

" But, it is said, ' The canon is closed, and we are not to add to, or take away from, the Word of God.' Who pretends to add to God's Word, or to take away from it? I do not say that God makes the Bible longer. What I say is, that there is no evidence that he does not still reveal the truth to a man that is dying for it.

" This is not, however, to foreclose moral education. It is not to discourage the use of our faculties. These revelations, these inspirations, at any rate, are not for you, nor for me; they are for those around about the gate of heaven who are willing to work and to suffer, but who have not the means of helping themselves, and who cry : 'Lord, send a beam of light to guide our souls to thee.' I believe that God carries emancipation to the souls of men by the Holy Ghost shed abroad.

" And I believe that God ministers his truth to some persons who are not in servitude. I believe that poor sailors on the deck, and ignorant men in the outskirts of society, whose circumstances are such that they can not themselves obtain a knowledge of God, often have him revealed to them. I believe that some vicious criminals, that are neglected and cast away, have given to them in their dying moments the illumination of God's Spirit.

" Times of need are God's throne. He sits in the times of need of the poor human soul, and out of his great beneficence and grace sends forth royal decrees of emancipation : Not to every man, but according to his own good pleasure."

Have we not shown that there is ample material, and material of the very best kind, of which to form a negro nationality in Africa ? And does it not follow, as an obvious sequence, that every man of this class, who is fitted for such a noble work, and who is so circumstanced that he can go, should immediately put on the harness, repair to the arena of action, and contribute his quota to the great work. This being conceded, we shall press the argument in yet another form :

3. If our colored friends would ever rise from their present degradation, they must go where they can be men. We have conceded their right to remain in this

country; but would persuade them of their interest to go. We have alluded to the insuperable disability which precludes the rise of the negro in this land. Call it prejudice against color.; call it the tyranical interdict of a wicked public opinion; call it what you will, it is a law which no legislation can repeal. It is the virtual disfranchisement of the Free, no less than of the Slave States. With a single and almost accidental exception, not a man of them, so far as my knowledge extends, holds any civil office, from the St. John's to the farthest West." Do you say this is a cruel proscription? It is admitted. But so it is. Such is their actual condition, and such it has been for two centuries. Suppose they remain among us, can they calculate on any such change in public sentiment as shall secure for them a fair competition with their white neighbors? Such is a forlorn hope. Experience is against it. The controlling tendencies are all the other way. The whole history of the world is against it. No two races, differing so much as the Caucasian and the African do, ever dwelt together in the enjoyment of equal consideration, rights, and privileges. So long as these marked distinctions exist, one or the other will have the ascendancy. Nothing but amalgamation can prevent it, and who, in his senses, will plead for that?

By giving different constitutions and complexions to great branches of the human family, God evidently intended they should be kept separate. The unhappy state of things in the United States has grown out of the enormously wicked infringement of this Divine allotment. The black man ought never to have been brought to America. They do not belong here. God gave them a better home in Africa.

But here they are, and it is a question of stupendous moment, what shall be done with them? Our interest replies, emancipate them from their involuntary servitude, and let them remain here as free laborers. We need them. They are better adapted than any other class of laborers to all the southern sections of our country. Selfishness would retain them—not as slaves, but as freemen—not as equals, but as a menial class of laborers; for above this, as a class, they can never rise. Philanthropy, humanity—the only hope we ean see for poor Africa—the only reasonable expectation we can indulge for the proscribed race among us, is that they should be disenthralled from their present disabilities, and, by opening to them the privileges and incentives of a nationality, put them in a position to display to the world whatever of manhood they possess.

It will give force to the argument to give it in the words of an intelligent writer and a thoroughly educated colored man who has resided twelve years in Africa, and has carefully studied the capabilities of the negro for improvement—has had ample opportunity to witness what, in the incipient stages of his nationality, he has already accomplished, and what he is in a fair way to accomplish. He has had ample opportunities, too, to become acquainted with the resources of the country, with the facilities there furnished and the opportunities there offered for the growth and expansion of his manhood. I refer to the Rev. Edward W. Blyden, professor in the Liberian College.

In a recent address, in this country, he advocates the colonization of his colored brethren on the coast of Africa as the only scheme for their real elevation. He will not accept, as the true friends of his kindred, those whose whole zeal is exhausted when they see them de-livered from the bonds of servitude, but do not give them a home, a name, and a nation of their own. "Many of the strong advocates for the abolition of slavery," he says, " manifest no special desire to see negroes form themselves into an independent community. In fact, many of them do not believe that the negro is fit for any other than a subordinate position. They expect that after slavery is abolished, and the country rescued from that foul blot on its character, the negro will find his position among the free laborers of the land. They never think of assigning him any other part than that of the Gibeonite. He is to be, though free, always the ob-ject of pity and patronage, to be assisted and held up, never to stand alone. They do not conceive how na-tionality and independence can be at all objects to us. They suppose that after they have given us meat for food, houses for shelter, and raiment to cover us, there is nothing else that· we desire, or are fit to enjoy. These men do not know us, or they would understand that we have souls as well as they. They would know that our hearts are made of the same material as theirs ; that we can feel as well as they ; and that the words ' nationality' and 'independence' possess as much charm and music for us as for them."

On the other hand, the founders of the Liberian re-public, and the patrons of colonization, he says : " show a truer appreciation of us, in aiding us to deliver our-selves from all this overshadowing and dwarfing patron-age, and to enjoy a field of action where we have the whole battle to wage for ourselves, and where thousands this day feel themselves happier in the resources of their own individual industry—limited as those resources may be—than they could possibly have felt in all the provisions which could have been made for them, if they had remained in this country.

"The founders of Liberia looked upon the negro as a man, needing, for his healthful growth, all the encouragement of social and political equality. They provided for him, therefore, a home in Africa, his own fatherland. And while a partial and narrow sympathy was pouring out its complaints and issuing its invectives against their operations, they were sowing the seeds of African nationality, and rearing on those barbarous shores the spectacle we now behold of a thriving, well-conditioned, and independent-negro State."

- Mr. Blyden does but utter the sentiment of every intelligent Liberian. Rev. Mr. Crummell, professor in the same college, bears a like testimony to the transforming and elevating influences of the Liberian nationality on his native race. "When I went to Liberia," he says, "my views and purposes were almost entirely missionary in their character, and very much alien from any thing civil or national; but I had not been in the country three days when such was the manliness I saw exhibited, so great was the capacity I saw developed, and so many were the signs of thrift, energy, and national life which showed themselves, that all my governmental indifference at once vanished; aspirations after citizenship and nationality rose in my bosom, and I was impelled to go to the magistrate, take the oath of allegiance, and thus become a citizen of Liberia. For myself and my children, Liberia shall be my country and my home." Again he says : "In every department of life and labor in Liberia, there are unmistakable evidences of growth. I feel the assurance to affirm here, that, in every quarter, the most casual observer can perceive strength, confidence, self-reliance, development, increase of wealth, and great hardiment of character." But we had not done with our last witness. Mr. Blyden shall be heard through. He adds :

"The superior advantages which our position in Liberia gives us have never been fully set forth in all the eulogiums of colonization papers. They can never be expressed. As soon as the black man of soul lands in Liberia, and finds himself surrounded by his own people, taking the lead in every social, political, educational, and industrial enterprise, he feels himself a different man. He feels that he is placed in the high attitude of an actor, that his words and deeds will now be felt by those around him. A consciousness of individual importance, which he never experienced before, comes over him. The share which he is obliged to take in the affairs of the country brings him information of various kinds, and has an expanding effect upon his mind. His soul grows lustier. He becomes a more cultivated and intellectual being than formerly. His character receives a higher tone. Every sentiment which his new position inspires is on the side of independence and manliness. In a word, he becomes a full man — a distinction to which he can never arrive in this country.

"When I say that the negro can never attain in this country to the distinction of true manhood, I say so deliberately and from a heartfelt conviction. I am aware that there are many who are enduring their disabilities in this land with great fortitude, in view of the future. Their tranquil hearts, drilled into a most undignified contentment, are cherishing a better prospect, and reposing on the sure anticipation of happier days in this land of their thraldom. They hope that the growth of free institutions and the progress of Christian sentiment will eradicate the intolerant prejudice against them. Such advance and progress may have that effect, but by that time the negro will have passed away, victimized and absorbed by the Caucasian."

And here it is but justice to allow the new republic to be the expounder of her own purposes of nationality. A single paragraph from her Declaration of Independence indicates what were the designs of her founders— what they expect to accomplish for the colonists ; and what is the character of the influence we may expect they will exert on the native tribes beyond them. In the following declarations we discover, as a leading idea, the purpose to develop, through their national organization, a noble manhood :

"Liberia is an asylum from the most grinding oppression.

"In coming to the shores of Africa, we indulged the pleasing hope that we would be permitted to exercise and improve those faculties which impart to man his dignity—to nourish in our own hearts the flame of honorable ambition, to cherish and indulge those aspirations which a beneficent Creator had implanted in every human heart, and to evince to all who despise, ridicule, and oppress our race, that we possess with them a common nature, are with them susceptible of equal refinement, and capable of equal advancement in all that adorns and dignifies man."

4. But there remains one other aspect in which we would contemplate the idea of a negro nationality in Africa, and the duty of our colored population in rela-

15

tion to it. It is the providential aspect. Are there grounds for the conviction that the finger of God is pointing them to that land?—that they have a great mission to fulfill there—that the strong hand of Providence is stretched out to bring them to their promised land—that that land is kept in reserve, waiting for its rightful occupants—that they are the heaven-appointed agents for the accomplishment of Heaven's purposes toward that long-forsaken continent.

1. There has been a note-worthy preparation on the part of Africa. Ethiopia is stretching out her hands for aid. Most wonderfully has the hand of God wrought, during the last fifty years, to prepare that continent to receive the rich boon of civilization and a pure Christianity. From various motives, travelers, explorers, adventurers, have been moved to bring Africa out from the dense, dark cloud that has so long enshrouded her, and to make known to Christian nations her woes and her wants, that they in turn should be moved to come to her relief. Christian travelers have here done a great and a good work. They are the best explorers of an unfrequented country, for the double reason that we have, in the character of the men and in the motives which prompt their travels, a guarantee of trustworthy accounts; and that they are not transient travelers or simply sojourners in the land, but residents, who have free intercourse with the people in their own native tongue, and every facility for a thorough acquaintance with the manners, customs, religion, and general resources of the country and its people. Scientific explorers have done a service scarcely less valuable. Governmental expeditions for discovery, have forced their way up the great rivers of Africa, and exposed to

the view of the other nations the resources of her interior. Commerce has followed in their wake, and been as the strong arm of Providence to prepare Africa to receive into her wounded bosom the "oil and the wine" which the good Samaritan waits to pour in.

And what is yet more worthy of our admiration and gratitude, is the wonderful readiness to receive the Gospel. Like Cornelius and his "kinsmen and friends," they are "waiting"—" to hear all things commanded of God." We have the concurrent testimony of all missionaries to the readiness, the eagerness, of the native Africans to receive the Gospel. If the missionary is but a transient traveler in their tribe, they entreat him to come and take up his abode among them. They hold out every inducement in their power. They employ strategy to retain him. Ethiopia thus stands in the posture of outstretched arms, hungering for that bread which came down from heaven. But,

2. Do we discover any movements of Providence corresponding to this; preparing the agencies and the agents to meet such a state of preparedness on the part of Africa? Most undoubtedly we do. We have seen what an irrepressible desire for instruction has, within the last generation, sprung up even among our slave population; and how that, in spite of disadvantages that would seem insuperable, many have risen, not only to respectability, but to eminence, and fitted themselves to be just the kind of agents which Africa is prepared to appreciate and be profited by. Africa stands in a waiting posture to receive them—with outstretched arms to welcome them to her embrace. She is famishing for the bread of life; and her Americanized sons are the only almoners on earth fitted to supply her need. The mis-

sion is theirs, heaven-ordained ; theirs, because heaven has adapted them alone to it.

The opinion expressed above is abundantly confirmed by a recent traveler in the South, who states a " few facts," as the result of his observation, which mark the signs of the times on this subject: " In no period since the existence of slavery has there been such attention paid to the religious instruction of slaves as in the last ten years ; and in no part of the world have there been gathered richer fruits to encourage the laborer. It is also worthy of special notice that, while our country generally has been suffering a spiritual death, the colored population of the Southern States have been sharing largely in the gracious influences of God's converting Spirit. Now, if we connect these facts with the foregoing, and mark their coincidence—the instruction that is now being-given them—the outpouring of the Spirit, and converting them to God, together with the brightening prospects of Liberia—what other interpretation can be given to all this, but that God, in his own way and in his own time, is raising up and preparing missionaries, school-teachers, and statesmen for that infant but growing republic, that is beginning to attract the attention and admiration of the civilized world ? During my present tour, I have taken especial pains to obtain information respecting the amount and extent of religious instruction among the slaves ; and it is truly surprising and cheering to witness the almost universal feeling and interest on this subject, and the extent to which they have carried out their plans, in establishing schools and churches, and obtaining missionaries and teachers for the sole benefit of the colored people. Some of the church edifices, that are neat and costly, are owned by the slaves themselves, with regularly organized churches, large and orderly congregations, where they enact their own laws, have their own pastor, and worship in their own way."

And the same din of preparation is heard—the same training of agents for the renovation of Africa—the same yearning to bless their fatherland in the emancipated thousands of the West Indies, and among the recaptured Africans taken to Sierra Leone. These last, " civilized and Christianized, feel all of a sudden an irresistible desire to return to the land of their birth. They charter vessels, and a large number go down the coast a thousand miles and more, bearing the Gospel to Abbeokuta."

3. And in correspondence with all this, and outside of all, we meet mighty auxiliary agencies which Providence has furnished, by which to bring into action and to make effectual the facilities and resources I have named. Philanthropy and Christian benevolence were never more effectively roused than at the present moment in respect to Africa. Already (and this all within a few years) is Africa begirt with Christian missions. Nearly every Missionary Society is represented. On the west, the south, and the east, this efficient agency is at work, and every year does but deepen the interest felt in Africa.

No question is of so momentous import as that which relates to the negro. It is the great question of the day. It shakes England to her very centre. It agitates all Europe. It has burst on the American Union like a thunderbolt, and, with a furor that knows no bounds, threatens its dissolution. Nations, not a few— nations, great and mighty, seem likely to become actors in the great drama, and arbiters of the fate of Africa. Never before did the world witness the mighty movements of Providence so concentrating on one great arena as we now do in relation to Africa. Commerce is turning thither her keen eye, and extending her puissant arm toward that long-neglected land, developing her resources, demanding industry, evoking enterprise, and giving sure promise that thrift, light, knowledge, civilization, nationality, and Christianity shall follow in her wake.

Never did a people have stronger inducements to decisive and energetic action. Would they be men and not things—free men and not chattels—citizens and not a race of menials, they must go where alone the opportunity of asserting and maintaining their manhood is offered. And would they not prove recreant to the noble mission given them to fulfill, not to a tribe, but to a continent, toward which the unerring finger of God is pointing, they must, in obedience to the heavenly behest, go to them who are ready to perish. Never did a people have spread out before them so extensive, so inviting, and so promising a field.

CHAPTER XVIII.

Wherein more especially lies our hope for Africa—In the peculiar character of the agency provided for their renovation—No inveterate system of false religion to encounter—The present war and its bearings on Africa.

WE have said there is hope for Africa. We come now to inquire after the reasons of such a hope. To many, it seems a hope against hope, that a people so long debased, so long preyed upon by every evil man or devil could invent, and who have so long lain helpless under such an accumulation of evils, should at length emerge and shake herself from the dust of her debasement, and sit among the nations clothed and in her right mind. Shall she, who hath "lain among the pots, be as the wings of a dove covered with silver, and her feathers with yellow gold."

But on what, especially, do we predicate our hopes for Africa? As already said, we have a confident hope for the amelioration of that benighted land, through the colonies which are directing their course thither. These streams of a kindred humanity, improved and elevated by a hard culture under Anglo-Saxon discipline, are thus flowing back to bless the fatherland. They go richly laden with some of Heaven's best blessings. They carry with them the English language, which is the language of liberty, the language of civilization, of progress, of the arts and sciences, of Protestantism, and, more than all, it is the language of an evangelical Christianity. They carry with them a civilization of a higher grade than Africa, as a whole, ever yet knew, and of a vastly higher grade than she knows now. They go endowed with a practical knowledge of the business of every-day life—with industry, common education, and many of them with that higher grade of education which will not fail to give a controlling influence to the right formation of social, civil, and national character. And, better than all, they carry with them Christianity; and Christianity of that peculiar type which obtained its growth, vigor, and spirit in circumstances of a humiliation and debasement, which gives it more of a dependence on God, humility, filial trust, patience, lowliness of mind, love, and forbearance, than is often met among those whose religion has been cultivated under circumstances widely different.

From such colonists we hope much—especially when we recall what we have seen to be true of the peculiar field on which they are to act. We here refer more especially to the readiness of the tribes beyond them to receive the Gospel—to acquire the habits and to appropriate the advantages of civilization, and to become incorporated in the same body politic with the colonists —to adopt their manners, customs, and religion, and to come under their benign influence.

Again: we see hope for Africa in the extended and rapidly extending commerce which is being pushed into every harbor on the coast, and up every river into her rich interior. We see in this the no distant extinction of the slave-trade, her deadliest bane; the quickening of her enterprise and industry, and the consequent development of her soil, her mines, her forests, and rivers; the growing intelligence and elevation of her people through the intercourse which trade with the more civilized nations will promote; the accumulation of wealth, which gives character and prestige, as well as ministers to general well-being, and is the precursor and the messenger that prepares the way for the angel having the everlasting Gospel to preach—opening the way for its introduction, and providing the means for its support and extension to pagan tribes beyond. We have seen commerce already working a mighty revolution in Africa, and we are in no danger of disappointment that its auspicious beginnings shall deceive our hopes of yet more comprehensive results. Its influence is not likely to abate till it work out the social and civil renovation of the whole continent.

Other grounds of hope for Africa we meet in the peculiar character of the agency which Providence has raised up and prepared for this work; in the peculiar type of Christianity which the African seems capable of; in the success which has already attended Christian missions in that country, and the promise of yet greater success; in the remarkable readiness of the native Africans to receive Christian teachings—yea, their eagerness to be taught. Again: the fact that no systematic, time-honored, and inveterate form of idolatry or false religion so preoccupies their minds and engrosses their hearts as to present obstacles the most formidable to the reception of the Gospel. And again: have we not some fair ground to hope that a people, who have themselves so recently escaped, some from the galling bonds of servitude, and all from the scarcely less cruel and oppressive thraldom of caste and prejudice, will, while yet in the spring-time of their national existence, be impelled, by every generous and benevolent motive, to impart the rich boon they have received, till

15*

tribe after tribe, and nation after nation, shall be brought under the same happy influences, and all Africa shall be saved? To some of these points we have already referred. We would now corroborate our assertions by the testimony of persons who have personally seen and known the things whereof they affirm.

No barbarous people were ever civilized and evangelized by foreign aid alone. Others must begin the work —Christianity must be carried to them and its institutions established. But the details of the work, its burdens and consummation must be by the people themselves. In the British Isles, centuries elapsed in the slow process of preparing the men that should fabricate their then future, but now present nationality. Indeed, centuries were required to bring them up to the point where the New England colonists, or the colonists from this country to Liberia, begun. In their training for their work, the founders of Liberia were not unlike the Pilgrim Fathers, or the founders of the Hebrew Commonwealth. In character, training, and experience they were centuries in advance of the founders of States, which have, after a protracted period, risen to eminence. In relation to government, liberty, free institutions, and right educational views, Liberia is this day in advance of almost every nation of continental Europe. They have not yet reached the point where they begun. Why, then, should we not hope for Africa?

The same hope we predicate again on the peculiar type of Christianity which we have seen to characterize our black Christians, and that higher order of civilization which the most intelligent writers on the race, concede them to be capable of. The Rev. J. L. Wilson, for eighteen years a missionary in Africa, and late Secretary of the Presbyterian Board of Foreign Missions, does but speak the language of such writers as Pritchard, Smythe, and Morton when he says : "The African, when brought under the benign influence of Christianity, exemplifies the beauty and consistency of his religion more than any other human being on the face of the earth. And the time may come when they may be held up to all the rest of the world as examples of the purest and most elevated virtue."

A kindred sentiment is expressed by the *Westminster Review*. We quote it rather for the sake of a quotation it contains of an American writer, which is peculiarly apposite to our subject. We must bear in mind, as he remarks, that "Africa has never yet been seen fairly exposed to civilizing influences except in the condition of a servant—the only condition, it may be added, in which he could well be placed in contact with civilization at all. His character is believed to be rather that of the infancy of civilized, than the maturity of savage, life. As to his intellect, it appears to be quick and ready, but not strong ; imitative, but not original. It is wanting in the daring, enterprising, stern, persevering qualities with which the European mind is endowed. The two races are not less distinctively marked in moral attributes. The European is vehement, energetic, proud, tenacious, and revengeful ; the African is docile, gentle, humble, grateful, and commonly forgiving. The one is ambitious and easily aroused ; the other meek, easily contented, and easily subdued. Christianity itself has not yet infused its milder influence thoroughly into the stubborn elements of the Caucasian race."

In connection with these general reasonings, the *Review* quotes a passage from an American work, entitled

" Some Lectures on Man," delivered by the author in Cincinnati in 1839. The work alluded to is a profound philosophical production, by Alexander Rimmont, who died in Cincinnati before his book was published The book is but too little known. The following passages are quoted by the *Westminster :*

" When the epoch of the civilization of the negro family arrives in the lapse of ages, they will display in their native land some very peculiar and interesting traits of character, of which we, a distinct branch of the human family, can at present form no conception. It will be—indeed, it must be—a civilization of a peculiar stamp ; perhaps we may venture to conjecture, not so much distinguished by art as by a certain beautiful nature ; not so marked or adorned by science, as exalted and refined by new and lovely theology—a reflection of the light of heaven more perfect and endearing than that which the intellects of the Caucasian race have ever yet exhibited. There is more of the child, more of unsophisticated nature, in the negro race than in the European.

" The peninsula of Africa is the home of the negro, and the appropriate and distinct seat of his future glory and civilization—a civilization which we will not fear to predict will be as distinct in all its features from that of all other races as his complexion and natural temperament and genius are different. If the Caucasian race is destined, as would appear from the precocity of their genius and natural quickness and extreme aptitude for the arts, to reflect the lustre of the Divine wisdom, or, to speak more properly, of the Divine science, shall we envy the negro if a later, but far nobler, civilization await him—to return the splendor of the Divine attri-

butes of mercy and benevolence in the practice and exhibition of the milder and gentler virtues ? * * * *
The sweeter graces of the Christian religion appear almost too tropical and tender plants to grow in the soil of the Caucasian mind ; they require a character of human nature of which you can see the rude lineaments in the Ethiopian to be implanted in, and grow naturally and beautifully withal." ·

We quote yet another writer, who alludes to one element in the religion of the negro, and, indeed, in his civilization, which is too characteristic to be passed unnoticed. It is music. There is a softening, a subduing influence—a devotion—an absorption of soul—a lifting up of the heart to God—in the sacred songs of this people, which has not failed to arrest the attention of all serious persons who have had the privilege to attend on their worshiping assemblies, and which, I am sure, is met in the same degree nowhere else. The writer says :

"The tastes and tendencies of the African mind in that region seem, however, to tend (as it does in this country) toward music and the softer arts, rather than toward the scientific and stronger developments of intellect. If this be the ultimate tendency of African tastes and developments, then it may be a very desirable and beautiful civilization which that country will ultimately attain ; but one which will never counteract the domination of the Gothic, or, as it is now called, the Anglo-Saxon superiority. It is only the scientific development of the human mind which can ever wield power.

"Africa is probably destined to receive a civilization as soft and luxurious as ancient Asia ; but raised to a far higher level by the genius of Christianity. Christianity is itself mild, peaceful, and softening, and may therefore ultimately find in Africa, and in eastern climes, a soil congenial and peculiar to itself. Amid the world's overturning and revolutions, it may happen that Europe will be darkened and defiled by a gross infidelity, while America and Africa may become the residence of the purest and brightest Christianity! Such a revolution would be no more marvelous than that Babylon and Tyre have become ruins, and returned to barbarism. The world is but a complex scene of ruin, revolution, and restoration. The day is dawning for Africa, and even the blackness of her night will pass away before the renewing influence of Christian civilization."

The strong religious tendencies of the colored race— perhaps stronger in the slave than in the free negro— appear in the fact so well known, that, when employ- ed at their labors, they alleviate their hard bondage with their sacred songs. Or if you overhear their con- versation, as they are assembled in groups after their labors have closed, you will discover religion is the topic. No people are so readily moved by religious motives.

And there has been within a few years past an " un- usual solicitude everywhere manifest in the negro race —a stirring up in the spiritual desires and yearnings of this race such as was never before witnessed." From every side, says an intelligent colored writer, we hear the earnest cry from yearning hearts for Christian light. There is no quarter of the globe where the children of Africa are gathered together, but where we see this trait of character more discovered than any other. Religious susceptibility and moral dispositions are the more marked characteristics of the negro family. Where the white man goes he first builds a bank, or a trading-house. The first effort of the black man is to erect a meeting-house.

"During the last few years there has been a more than usual—a most marked expression of these features of character. We have the testimony of West Indian pastors, missionaries, and teachers to the eager craving of the African peasantry for instruction. In America the gravest hinderances can not repress this desire; and among the free black population I can testify, from personal acquaintance and observation, that this, the religious solicitude, is the master principle of that people." And of Africa, he says : " I doubt much whether, if ever, the history of missions has discovered such a wide-spread and earnest seeking for Christian knowledge as is seen among the pagan tribes on that suffering coast. A missionary on his way down the coast lands at a certain spot. The news of a God-man, as they term him, having come, flies like lightning through the neighborhood. Three kings visit him ; several chiefs bring him their sons, and desire him to take them under his care for instruction ; numbers of the people assemble, all expressing their sorrow that he will not abide with them and teach them. When Mr. Freeman went some two hundred miles into the interior to visit the King of Ashantee, the whole kingdom was thrown into excitement. Thousands of troops attended him on his approach to the sable monarch, and in the midst of the grossest superstition and most cruel rites, the ambassador of Christ was received with the most marked respect; and full permission was given him to establish Christian institutions in the capital of the kingdom. All along the coast where missions are established, kings and princes and great men are bringing their children forward to be trained in our holy faith." *

Parents come with their children from the far interior ; and so numerous are these requests, that the missionaries are frequently obliged to decline receiving them. The missionary, wherever he goes, is sure to get a large, patient, inquiring auditory. Sometimes "the chief of a tribe refuses an escort through a neighboring town, lest the missionary should stay with the other people, and not come back to him and his people." At times it is both ludicrous and tearful to hear of a missionary being kept captive by a heathen king, for fear, should he suffer him to depart, he might never return. Only last year the people of a village formed a strategy to keep a traveling missionary to themselves. They attempted to bribe the boatmen to go away, so that he would be obliged to remain with them. And such is the desire for the Gospel which comes from every quarter. Surely, is there not hope for Africa ? Ethiopia is already stretching out her hands unto God. She is famishing ; she feels her need ; she begs the bread of life at our hands. Shall we say her, nay ?

Nor is the day of Africa's redemption afar off. It seems to draw near, vast and extensive as the work may be, indications are that it shall be a rapid one. Since the abolition of the slave-trade the improvement of this race has been remarkably accelerated, and the intimations are that the evangelization will be equally rapid. We have such an intimation, I think, in the noted prediction : "Ethiopia shall soon stretch forth her hands unto God." Not by the long and protracted progress

* "The Future of Africa," by Rev. Alexander Crummell, p. 303-4.

by which other people have been renovated and brought into the pale of Christianity, but she shall come readily, suddenly, unexpectedly. She shall yield a ready response to the kindly invitations of the Gospel—shall eagerly embrace its gracious overtures as soon as made. Not only " soon;" in point of time, shall they embrace, with outstretched arm, the unfading riches of Christ, but most promptly and gladly shall they hear the voice of the Son of man, and come forth from the long slumber of spiritual death.

May we not expect God will make a short work with Africa ? The preparation has been a long and dreary one. Not " four hundred years," like as preceded the outgoing and the uplifting of the children of Israel, but for 4,000 years have these devoted sons of Ham been kept in the iron furnace of preparation, with only an occasional gleaming up of the light through the thick darkness ; just enough to keep the world apprised of the existence of such a race, and of their capabilities to rise and act their past in the world's great drama, when the curtain shall rise. But how events were hastened when God arose with outstretched arm for their deliverance ! In a few months—perhaps only a few weeks —and a most remarkable series of events took place in Egypt, resulting in the overthrow of Pharaoh and his army, in the " spoiling of the Egyptians," and the triumphant deliverance of Egypt's bondmen. Yet, their deliverance was not followed by their immediate settlement in the promised land, and the consummation of their nationality. Forty long and wearisome years, years of conflict, war, privation, temptation, and manifold trials, were appointed them before they should realize the high destiny which awaited them. To the superficial observer—to all who had not an unwavering faith in Israel's God, more than thirty-nine of these forty years seemed lost, worse than lost ; for Israel now seemed removed further from the realization of their hopes than on their immediate release from bondage. The most formidable part of their work now seemed before them.   Great and mighty nations were to be overcome, and dispossessed of their lands before Israel could enter.   Yet in a few weeks it was all done—more apparently done in these few weeks than in the forty previous years.

And may we not trace a parallel in that great nation of bondmen of whom we are speaking? Long and weary, and, to all human ken, hopeless have been the years—the centuries—of severe preparation.   Most rigorous has been their discipline—painfully protracted their anguish and ignominy.   But how easy, how speedy and triumphant their deliverance when the mighty arm of God is stretched out for them !   A thousand years are with God as one day.   In a day he may do the work of a thousand years.   He is graciously responding to the earnest yearnings of a depressed people.

Another ground of the hope we indulge of the speedy renovation of Africa, and her conversion to Christianity, we find in the absence of any ancient, well-organized, venerated system of false religion, preoccupying the minds of the people, and constituting the most formidable obstacle to the introduction of Christianity.   There is idolatry, there is superstition enough there.   Yet, as our missionary author says, "there is no well-defined system of false religion which is generally received by the people.   There are a few leading notions or outlines of a system that prevail in all parts of the country, but all the details necessary to fill up these outlines are left to each man's fancy, and the answers given to inquirers are almost as various as the characters of the persons to whom they are submitted." So far from indulging pride or confidence in their religion, and fortifying themselves in it as a barrier against the reception of the true religion, the natives manifest "an extreme reluctance to make known their superstitious notions."

Like all ignorant people, the Africans are exceedingly superstitious. The leading, prominent form of their religion is fetichism and demonolatry. A fetich is little else than a charm or amulet, carried about the person, or set up in a convenient place, to guard against some evil or to procure some good. One is to guard against sickness; another against drought; a third against the disasters of war; or, to protect against fire, or pestilence, or witchcraft; to secure good luck in some way, or to escape evil.

Strictly speaking, the Africans have no system of idolatry, or image worship. They believe in the existence of one supreme God and in a future state. Yet they have no correct idea of the character and attributes of God. Having made the world, they believe God retired into some corner of the universe, and left the affairs of the world to the control of evil spirits. Hence the chief object of their religious worship is to conciliate these evil spirits, and to deprecate their displeasure. All they really have that deserves the name of religion is what seems to be some fragmentary vestiges which have been preserved of Judaism, or rather of the patriarchal religion, which ages of ignorance and superstition have never quite obliterated.

Is it not obvious, then, that, when compared with the

old pagan countries of Asia, there are few hinderances in the way of the evangelization of Africa—less rubbish is to be removed? No inveterate system of false religion has grown with the growth, and strengthened with the strength, of the nation's depravity; and become, as it were, a part and parcel of the mental and moral constitution of the people. The soil is comparatively unincumbered with noxious growth, and is waiting to receive the good seed. And may we not expect a ready reception, and a speedy and abundand harvest? Already the reapers seem to say : " the fields are white, ready to harvest."

Again : we discover hope for Africa through the dark cloud of war, which now hangs over our beloved country. Amid the thunderings and lightnings which in terror gleam out from this cloud—amid the carnage of the battle-field and the wide-spread desolations of the conflict, we descry a presage for good to that afflicted race. - The dreadful war that is now raging we believe is more effectually working out the great negro problem than all the arts of peace could do. - As the pages of the faithful historian shall record the annals of the present period, the " slaveholders' rebellion" will, no doubt, mark one of the most remarkable eras, not in the history of America alone, but, perhaps, especially in the history of Africa. We can not explain in a word what we believe will be the bearings, and what the results, of this wicked rebellion and dreadful war upon the future of Africa. All that it shall do, and precisely what it shall do, to bring succor to that benighted continent— to deliver her from her present degradation—to lift her up and give her a name, and a place among the nations, we shall not pretend to say.

A brief review of the cause, the character, and the probable results of the present war, will indicate the connection it has with the welfare and final destiny of the negro. And first :

The cause and character of the war. All will concede that, directly or indirectly, southern slavery is the cause. Whatever the North may agree to install as its cause, and the object for which they fight ; the South, that inaugurated the war, and ought to be allowed to know for what, have no hesitation of giving it the most open and vigorous prosecution as a war for slavery. It is for the support of its institutions, and for the wrongs or fancied wrongs they have suffered in connection with the system, that they have risen up in deadly combat. When stripped of a few adventitious circumstances, as of trade or tariff, or fancied abuse, it will go down to posterity as the slaveholders' revolt, for slavery's sake, against a government that never did the malcontents any thing but good—a war the most unnatural, suicidal, and brutal, waged, to all intents and purposes, to defend and perpetuate negro slavery.

We should need to go far back to detect the ulterior workings of the final cause of the war. A strong antagonism to human bondage has been working in the mind of Christendom for the last century, gathering strength with each revolving year. The light of the nineteenth century ; the course of human events ; the onward march of an irresistible Providence ; the latent workings of liberty in the great mind of the civilized world ; the pulsations of the great heart of humanity ; and the outspoken conviction of all Christendom, have decreed that man shall be free ; and, especially, have they decreed that man shall no longer buy and sell his brother, and thereby disown his man-hood, and reduce him to a mere chattelship.

It has been a long conflict—an "irrepressible con-flict," which has at length gathered strengh and reached a crisis. The wise and patriotic framers of our Consti-tution felt the incongruity of incorporating a system of human bondage into an instrument which should stand before the world as the magna charter of our liberties. Yet, in the hope of its early extinction, they extended to it a present toleration. Hence the " compromises of the Constitution." The northern portion of the origin-al confederacy continued to treat the institution of slavery as the framers of the Constitution evidently in-tended it should be treated, and, consequently, State after State became free. The southern portion pursued an opposite course, and established and perpetuated slavery ; and have, at length, found a priesthood who have canonized it as of Divine right.

These two antagonistic elements have been in active conflict (though suppressed), and gathering strength for more than four-score years, and have now burst forth into open hostility. The one strikes for freedom ; the other wages an uncompromising war for the extension and perpetuation of slavery. For a long time it was a war of opinion, of the ballot-box, of the pulpit and the rostrum—at length the appeal is to the sword ; and we wait in awful suspense the result. Will the just, the good, the merciful God smile upon and bless a confeder-acy confessedly founded on negro slavery as its corner-stone ; or, by giving success to our arms, will he vindi-cate our cause, and establish us such a nation as, in his providence, he indicated he would establish in this west-ern world ?

Apprehensions for the security and the perpetuation of slavery, arising from the more determined conviction of the North and an equally strong conviction on the part of the whole civilized world that every system of human bondage ought to be done away, gradually led, not only to drawing tighter the bonds of the system, making that to be good which they once conceded to be evil, but the same apprehensions, united with a strong self-interest and feudal pride, rapidly fostered a sentiment of hostility to the North. Hence the determined uprising of the South for the defense of their darling institution and for its extension and nationalization.

The conviction prevailed throughout the entire South that the institution of slavery was no longer secure in the hands of men who recognized neither its Divine right, nor its economic or humane policy. Hence it became a necessity, with all such as felt slavery to be a necessity, that the administrative power of our government should be in their hands. They did not feel that their institutions were safe in other hands. Such a feeling has, in a measure prevailed at the South from the beginning, but it has from year to year gained strength, till at length it is demonstrated in an open resistance to the ballot-box ; and we are plunged into a dreadful war because a fair majority declared in favor of a northern President. Of the seventy-two years from the inauguration of George Washington to the inauguration of Abraham Lincoln as President of the United States, southern men had occupied the Presidential chair fifty-two years ; and two or three of our northern Presidents were " northern men with southern principles," extending an unduly liberal patronage to the South. And not even this undue proportion measures the share of governmental power and patronage, which, in other respects, have been accorded to southern men. Such undue balance of power have they deemed it needful that they should hold in our National Legislature and in the Presidential mansion in order to preserve intact and inviolable the peculiar institutions of the South.

But even this would no longer do. The opposing tide from the North, backed by the united sentiment of the whole civilized world, still rolled on. It seemed to carry in it the portentous decree of universal emancipation, and it must and should be resisted, and as no other Government on earth would lend its support to the system, the Government of the United States should. Hence the uncompromising determination to force their own Government to a nationalization of slavery, and hence the necessity felt that the friends and supporters of slavery should hold the Government of the country at their own control. This seemed to them a matter of life and death. Had the election four years previous terminated in the election of a non-slaveholding candidate, war was then equally inevitable, though with a four years' less vengeance.

Our present conflict is eminently a war for human freedom ; for the emancipation of man from the thraldom of his fellow-man. It is the last great strike for liberty. If unsuccessful, it shall proclaim liberty to the captives and the opening of the prisons to them that are bound. If successful ; if they who offer to the world as a " model republic" for the times—a republic founded on negro slavery as its corner-stone—shall succeed, then we are thrown back into a barbarous age ; the tide of human progress is averted and turned back a century, and hopelessly may we look soon again to see the fair form of Liberty rise and attain its present stately proportions.

Such being the causes and such the character of the present war, we may very properly institute the inquiry as to the results—rather its bearing on Africa and the Africans. We have called it the "Slaveholders' Rebellion." We believe it will, in the end, be the slaves' emancipation.

War, we must bear in mind, is one of the dread agencies of Providence used, more commonly than any other form of agency, to break down and move out of the way the great hinderances to human progress. It is the millstone to grind to powder the great systems, organizations, and confederacies which the arch enemy of man erects as the strongholds of his empire. Modern wars are, perhaps, more especially overruled for such a purpose. What may we expect as the issue of the present war? If waged for the purposes we have alleged, we may expect it will have much to do in solving the great problem of the negro's destiny. There is, indeed, a very confident expectation that this war will not end but in the entire emancipation of our whole slave population. Though not entered upon by our Government with such an intent, and though there has been the greatest reluctance on the part of both the Government and people of the North to make the war a war of emancipation, yet the conviction is everywhere and every day gathering strength that it will be so ; that it must be so ; that Heaven has decreed it, and therefore it must be. In every form and mode, unmistakable utterance is given to the feeling that the day of redemption to our captives draws nigh ; the year of jubilee is at hand. A shrewd writer of the day, signing himself "a Veteran Ob-

16

server," may be taken as a representative of the sentiment. "We may dodge the point," says he, "as much
as we can, but slavery is the cause of the war, and the
war will be the *commencement de la fin* to slavery. The
time has come when the problem of the day, beyond all
others will be : What shall we do with the negro?"

And not only at home and abroad has a strange impression possessed the mind of the friends of freedom
that the day of general emancipation is at hand—that the
present war shall secure a consummation so devoutly to
be wished, but there is also, throughout the dark domains of slavery, the same longing hope and confident
expectation that the tocsin of liberty will so be heard
through all their fields and cabins, and the long-op-
pressed tribes shall rejoice that the day of their redemption has at length come.

How these things shall be we may not be able to say ;
but that such is the purpose of God in the war, and that
such shall be the result to the slave, we can not doubt.
Whatever disasters may first betide, and try our faith,
and humble our pride, and rebuke our extravagance and
self-dependence and boasting, we fully believe the issue
of the war will be such as abundantly to vindicate, in the
eyes of the world, the strength, stability, and superiority
of our free institutions, to wipe away the stigma that has
rested upon us, and to proclaim a year of jubilee to all
that are still bound.

But what bearing has this on Africa? Much, we
think. We expect it shall inaugurate a new era of development in connection with the whole African race.
The enslavement and general debasement of that race is
one of the great facts of history. Great results have
already been brought out of it, and what has been is,

probably, but the beginning of the end. So important an item as their singular transfer to, and their long bondage in, America, can not but have a connection with their future history of stupendous interest. What it shall be we can scarcely more than conjecture. Marvellous it would seem that a race should undergo so long, rigorous, and remarkable a discipline, yet for no adequate purpose. God is not wont so to work. Judging from the character and the amount of the preparation, we should expect a correspondingly far-reaching and lasting a result.

The shrewd observer of human affairs, 3,300 years ago, might have predicted with some degree of certainty, from the peculiar dealings of Providence, in conveying the children of Israel into Egypt, subjecting them to bondage there, giving them there a peculiar experience and training, from the deliverance he wrought for them in the land of Ham, and the judgments he afflicted on their enemies and oppressors; from such things as these it might have been predicted that the future history of that people would be signalized in a manner corresponding to their singular training. This is precisely what we expect, at least of that portion of the African race which have served in " durance vile," in America. Their bondage here has been their school-master, to train them for the position they are yet to occupy among the nations of the earth—for their nationality, whenever that shall be—and to train them for the Church and the peculiar type of Christianity and civilization which they are to illustrate. No people at the present day present a more interesting study for the philosophic historian, and none a more interesting field for honest conjecture.

Possibly it may strike the reader that we have over-stated the longing of the enslaved for their freedom. It has been extensively claimed by their masters, and reiterated by northern sympathizers with their masters, that they are generally quite contented with their lot, and really have no yearnings after freedom, and if left unbiased, would scarcely accept it if offered. We have represented them as earnestly desiring freedom—as making it from year to year the burden of their prayers—as waiting for the outstretched arm of God for deliverance —like the bondmen of Pharaoh, as " sighing by reason of their bondage"—as " crying," and God hearing their "groaning." We are happy to be able to confirm what we have said, by a living witness—or, rather, through him, to let the bondmen now set free, speak for themselves. The Rev. L. C. Lockwood, after " a year's experience among the ex-slaves," has furnished an exceedingly interesting article on the capacity of these people for freedom. We quote, as apposite to our present purpose, the head, entitled : " The desire of the slave for freedom a preparation for it."

"Even slavery can not quite crush out that instinctive love for freedom which is an inseparable part of manhood. It was the writer's privilege, after initiating the Emigrant Aid movement in New York City, to accompany the pioneer band to Kansas ; and during my stay at Kansas City I had communications with a slave seventy-five years of age, who was provided for by a kind master, and permitted to spend the remainder of his days in leisure, at home or abroad. I inquired of him if he would accept his freedom at that age, provided his master would give it to him. ' Oh yes,' said he ; ' I would be glad to have it.' ' Why, you might find difficulty now in providing for yourself ?' ' Oh, master, freedom is sweet." Ay, freedom is sweet ; for it seems to one like a badge of humanity, as distinguishing the man from the brute ; and therefore the spirit that prompts one to make sacrifices to obtain it, betokens a fitness for it.

" At Fortress Monroe I found that the slaves had for many years possessed an increasingly intense and prayerful desire for freedom, and strong faith in the coming blessing.

" The prayers of the ex-slaves all show that they have been familiar with earnest outgushings for deliverance. I wish all my readers could have been melted, as I and a number of soldier-friends and others were, by the simple petition of Mary Banks : ' Good Master,' she cried, ' please take a gentle peep down into these low grounds, where sorrows grow and every pleasure dies, and see your suffering children and hear their groans ; and oh, look upon those far, *far*, FAR away ; and if we never meet again here, may we meet where parting is no more. Please, Master, *please*, PLEASE,' uttered in plaintiff wail, in which all joined with indescribable effect. And they all told me that freedom had been the burden of their prayers, and especially for fifty years past. Ethiopia has thus been stretching out her hands to God for help. And they had prayed in faith. They knew not that they would live to see the day, but that day they were assured would come. They had a deep impression that they were the second children of Israel. And many of their songs were inspired by the spirit of liberty. I give one, sung by the slaves fifty years ago, arranged by myself and Rev. H. Highland Garnett, pastor of the colored Presbyterian church in New York City, who says he heard his father and grandfather sing it when he was a boy in Maryland :

> Stolen we were from Africa,
> Transported to America.
>
> CHORUS:
>> There's a better day a coming,
>> Will you go along with me?
>> There's a better day-a-coming,
>> Go, sound the Jubilee.
>
> See wives and husbands sold apart!
> Their children scream—it breaks my heart !
>> (Still faith said)
>> There's a better day a-coming, etc.
>
> They'll never see old Virginia more,
> They're sold away to Georgia's shore.
>> There's a better day a-coming, etc.
>
> Good Lord ! good Lord ! when shall it be
> That we, poor souls, shall all be free ?
>> There's a better day a-coming, etc.
>
> Our father's toiled and passed away,
> But we shall live to see the day.
>> There's a better day a-coming, etc.
>> (And some have lived to see it.)
>
> In eighteen hundred and thirty-three,
> 'Tis said the people will be free.
>
> CHORUS :
>> Lord, break the tyrant's power ;
>> Come, go along with me ;
>> There's a better day a-coming,
>> Go sound the Jubilee !

" In the last stanzas, the slaves' faith simply went ahead of time thirty years. It was sixty-three, instead of thirty-three. This jubilee hymn was one of the slaves' Marseillaises. Sometimes, to deceive the ears of any white listener that might be within hearing, the last stanza, as I was told, was sung in this wise :

> " In the eighteenth verse of thirty-three,
> 'Tis written the people shall be free."

But the slaves themselves understood it, and caught its enthusiasm.

There is another liberty song, that I brought north a year ago, and had published by Horace Waters, entitled " Let My People Go," a song more familiar to many, beginning :

> " The Lord by Moses to Pharaoh said,
>   Oh, let my people go !
> If not, I'll smite your first-born dead,
>   Then let my people go.
>   Oh, go down, Moses,
>   Away down to Egypt's land,
>   And tell King Pharaoh
>   To let my people go."

" This song, sung by the slaves for thirty or fifty years, has now rung in the ears of the nation, and its spirit has touched the heart of Abraham Lincoln, and he has said : " I will let the people go." And for that act all lovers of liberty must say : " God bless Abraham Lincoln !" When the President's proclamation of September 22d was issued, they considered it a signal answer to the prayers of generations, and they had faith in it. And in anticipation, they appointed a watch-night for New Year's Eve, to watch the old year of slavery out and the new year of freedom in. And at the hour of twelve, in imitation of their West India brethren, they resolved to receive the boon of freedom on their knees, as the gift of God, though through the administration of man, and then pour forth their souls in thanksgiving till morning, and keep New Year's Day a jubilee. Though dispirited somewhat by the exception of Fortress Monroe, Norfolk, and vicinity, in the Proclamation of the first instant, they do not falter in their faith in regard to the ultimate issue. They give full credence to the sentiment that

> " Right is right, since God is God,
> And right the day will win ;
> To doubt would be disloyalty,
> To falter would be sin."

On no one thing do we predicate so strong a hope for the no distant disinthrallment of these captives, as in their " strong cries and prayers to God" for their deliverance. Arguments and armies and navies may do 'something for their emancipation ; but all these are impotent compared with the simple-hearted, sincere, childlike, outgushing prayers of these bondmen. There is in them a feeling, a pathos, a filial taking hold on God, which is all prevalent. Surely God has heard their " groaning," is come down to deliver them out of the hands of their oppressors, and he " will bring them to a good land, and large," and one, if not " flowing with milk and honey," yet a land abounding in all the rich resources of nature, where they may dwell, every man under his own vine and fig tree, a man and not a thing.

You concede they desire to be free, and doubt not pray very earnestly for it ; but are they fitted for freedom ? Is not slavery their best condition ? Will they work as freemen ? Are they capable of caring for themselves ? What shall we do with them, if free ? We have answered, by saying : " Let them alone." Give them work. Give them an equal chance for life. Remove all impediments to their onward and upward progress, and see whether they will work and live, or sit idle and die. If they refuse to work, leave them to learn of the wise man of Tarsus, who says : " If any will not work, neither shall he eat." Simply subject him to the same law of demand and supply which rules in every other case. There is nothing like the pinchings of hunger to nerve the muscles for work. The negro, we fancy, simply follows the laws of reluctant nature—not negro nature, but human nature—when he only works when he has an impelling motive. We are not prepared to concede that all the motives held out by freedom—motives to rear and rightly to educate a family ; to vindicate the right and capability to be free, and to gather about him present comforts and provide for future wants—are not as operative and effective with the negro as with the white man. Who believes that motives such as these could not secure his thrift and industry quite as effectually as the compulsion or lash of the " overseer ?" He did work as a slave ; why should he not as a freeman ?

16*

CHAPTER XIX.

The future of Africa—A higher type of Christianity and civilization—Hope in her protracted afflictions — The great negro problem of world-wide interest—What prophecy, history, analogy, and the signs of the times warrant us to expect—Nothing to fear from emancipated slaves—The West Indies—Emancipation Day.

WE have already spoken of the peculiar readiness of the native Africans to receive the Gospel. We cite a few instances more, as nothing is so truly indicative of that high religious character, which we believe belongs to the future of Africa. The unprecedented facility with which they seize upon the truth is truly an auspicious omen of the rich spiritual future which remains in reserve for that people. Such yearnings, such outstretching of the hands for spiritual treasures, are not the innate movings of man's fallen nature. They are the inspirations of the Almighty, not the vain upheavings of an oppressed soul, but the moving on the face of the dark waters of the ever-blessed Spirit, betokening a new life, the new spiritual creation which shall emerge from the thick darkness of the past. God, her God, seems to be saying: "Let there be light!"

A missionary traveler, the Rev. Mr. Wilson says: "Indeed, the very demand for our labor obstructs our progress. We can not go far into the interior without passing over communities that say they have the first right to us, and who can not see why we should pass them to go to others. They ask if the people beyond are of more value, or have more need than they. In one case, two missionaries were traveling in the inte-

AFRICA AS SHE SHALL BE—See page 370.

rior, and stopped at one village, and called the people together, and preached, and gave as good an idea as they could of the Gospel and of their views in publishing it. And having finished, they asked the chief what he thought of the subject. He was silent for a while. Then he lifted up his eyes to a forest, and said: 'Suppose a man was lost there, and in the darkness of night, and you should go to him with a light, and offer to guide him home, do you suppose he would refuse? Suppose he were hungry, and you should offer him bread; would he refuse to eat?' and further than this he answered not a word. And yet this man represents the condition of millions."

The Rev. Beverly R. Wilson, a colored Methodist missionary, stationed of late at Sinou, brings from thence cheering intelligence as to the desire of the interior tribes to have education and the Christian religion established among them. There is a wonderful movement, he remarks, in this direction. All along, interior from the coast, for scores of miles, the heathen seem agitated with desire. Messengers are flocking to the Christian settlements, specially commissioned by kings and head men, begging for teachers and missionaries to be sent immediately to them. Their petitions are reiterated and importunate, admitting of no denial. Again and again they came to him, with the injunction not to return until they should succeed in their embassy; and in one, at least, touching instance, when the messenger had been sent back with painful declarations of his inability to gratify them, in a few days he was returned with positive injunctions not to come home, but to sit down at Mr. Wilson's until he should obtain from him a teacher or a missionary.

And of the same purport is the testimony of Rev.
I. J. Bowen. He hails from Yoruba, and has traveled
more extensively in the interior than almost any missionary. The Africans, he says, are the most docile
and friendly people on the globe. To the missionary
they are doubly interesting, because of the intense
eagerness with which they often listen to the Gospel.
No missionary has been, even for a few days, in an interior town without preaching to deeply interested
people; and no one has preached for two or three
months without gaining some converts. He has known
cases of those who believed under the first sermon,
and has met with people from the remote interior who
believed in Christ and renounced idolatry from hearing missionaries only a few times nearer the coast.

Mr. Bowen's testimony is the more valuable, as it
brings to light some facts respecting the interior and
from the centre of the Great Desert, which to most
people are new and of surprising interest. He found
there a condition of life, and a people of a character,
not even suspected to exist on that outcast continent.
When these are made to appear before us, we instinct-
ively feel that Africa has the elements within herself
for as glorious a future as the most sanguine are dis-
posed to claim for her. As essential as are her Ameri-
can-trained agents, her " black Yankees," to work out
her renovation, she has a well-capacitated agency within herself, which ere long shall come into play. In a
recent lecture in New York, Mr. Bowen states, that the
Great Desert, instead of being a vast desolation, as is
generally supposed, is extensively inhabited, containing two great republics, having a literature among
the oldest in existence, planted by the Saracens seven

hundred years ago, while the arts and sciences possessed at a remote age are still retained. The natives of the interior are large and muscular, the men being seldom under five feet ten inches in height, and generally over six feet, with Roman noses, thin lips, and a decidedly European cast of countenance. The woolly hair is universal, but the thick lips and flat noses are peculiar to the more degraded tribes on the sea-coast. They are distinguished for their sterling honesty, kindness, and affection, as well as for the qualities constituting force, stability, and endurance of character.

While traveling among them, Mr. Bowen was in the habit of instructing them first in the precepts of Christianity, and afterward in some of the arts of civilized life; and it frequently happened that on meeting natives months and even years afterward, they would inform him that from the time of hearing him, they had thrown away their idols and worshiped the Christian's God. Some of the tribes have retained through many centuries valuable religious truths derived from some unknown source. Strange as it may seem, there are Christian Africans scattered over the continent, who worship Jesus as God, calling him Yazu.

A spirit of improvement and reform is now pervading the tribes of Africa, and could they be brought under civilizing and Christianizing influences, they would develop powers that would astonish the world. The labors of missionaries have already resulted in great good, and the power of idolatry and Mohammedanism are waning before the teachings of the Gospel. Let the Christian missionary hasten to enter and occupy this land, so full of promise, and the prophecy will speedily be fulfilled : " Ethiopia shall soon stretch out her hands unto God."

This intense desire to receive the Gospel, and the very ready response they give to its teachings, we may receive as a no doubtful prognostic of the future moral condition of Africa. But this idea finds a more satisfactory confirmation in the peculiar caste of Christianity which seems there developing itself. We have said, but have been at no pains to establish the assertion, that we might expect in the future of the negro a higher type of Christianity and a better order of civilization than the world has heretofore witnessed. This we have inferred principally from the peculiar religious instincts of the people, and the facility with which they receive religious teachings.

The religious instinct of the negro is everywhere noticeable. He seizes the good seed of the Word with an avidity common to no other race; and his rude soul offers a ready soil to its acceptance. As in coming ages the spirituality of our religion shall become yet more developed, the negro races, if we mistake not, will be found the happiest illustrations. Their moral susceptibilities, or their susceptibilities to exemplify the more purely moral element of our religion, seem quite peculiar to themselves. There is, as we have said, in the negro a simplicity, a pathos, a lifting up of the soul to God, a bringing of heaven and earth to meet, which we discover in the religion of no other people. They will understand what I mean better than I can express it, who have had the privilege to join in their worship, and especially to lift up the heart with them in prayer and the song, in some church of the colored people at the South. Such a scene not only illustrates the point in question—the susceptibility of the negro for a higher order of spiritual life, and a religion of a type better suited to that future and higher condition of Christianity which we hope and pray for—but it brings to our minds a delightful evidence of the great condescending love of God, in vouchsafing to them so richly of Heaven's treasures, as a compensation to the lonely and humble, to the outcast and down-trodden.

1. Our expectation, that coming generations shall witness in Africa nationalities of a higher order than have heretofore existed, is predicated chiefly on the fact of the religious susceptibilities of her people being of a high order. The life, the vigor, the only reliable element of strength and permanency in a nation, is her religion. And that life is healthful, wholesome, useful, and long continued, in proportion to the character of that religion. Righteousness alone exalteth a nation. No nation can live and permanently prosper in which truth, that is, a correct idea of God and of duty, does not enter. It is as true of a nation as it is of an individual, that in Him is life. Commerce, wealth, refinement—laws, institutions, great men, are but the adjuncts of a great nation; these may exist, and yet a nation may crumble into nothingness and be no more. Could riches, power, extent of territory have saved a nation from dissolution, Babylon would have been saved. Could commerce avail to spare a great nation from an untimely end, Carthage would have survived until the present day. And Greece and Rome would have outlived the devastations of time, if power or luxury or learning could have spared her from going the way of all kingdoms.

These nations had the elements of permanency no further than they had the elements of truth and righteousness. They perished, because God was not in them.

If this be so, we see not why a nation, if fully imbued with these elements of life—life in Him, who giveth all life—should ever decay or perish. This seems to be the purport of the promise to Israel. If he would keep his covenant with his God, he should, as a nation, live forever. "Know, therefore, that the Lord thy God, he is God, the faithful God, which keepeth covenant and mercy with them that love him and keep his commandments to a thousand generations." Fidelity on the part of the people, love, obedience, loyalty toward God, were the sole and sure conditions of their continuance as a nation for a thousand generations, that is indefinitely.

But all ancient nations, you say, did decay and die; and all subsequent nations have followed the law of rise, growth, and dissolution. And why shall not existing and future nations yield to the same law? The reason is obvious. A new element of power and preservation is now introduced into the life of nations— an indestructive element, which is the *elixir vitæ* of the body politic, as it is the immortality of the individual's spiritual existence. We mean the mighty element of Christianity. A nation, fully permeated with this leaven, is as permanent as time, as imperishable as the everlasting hills. The nation, whose government, laws, civil institutions, commerce, social habits, and science, are under the all-controlling influence of Christianity, and whose leading minds and common minds are subjected to the same benign control, has its seed within itself, that it shall live forever.

But did not the nations of antiquity live to a good old age, and flourish, though destitute of the Christian element? We are by no means sure that they flourished a whit beyond the measure of the patriarchal religion, which entered into their origin. It was some centuries after the Deluge before the power of this religion was exhausted. Indeed, indelible traces of it appear unto this day. Every system of modern Paganism, in its very perversions, bears the marks of the original truths of which it is a perversion. It remains to be shown if Assyria, Babylon, Carthage, did not lose all there was in them of true greatness, power, and real worth, and verge onward to decay, in proportion as they lost a knowledge of, and ceased to be influenced by, those great radical truths which descended to them from the patriarchs. The only reliable guarantee for an abiding, vigorous national life is to be sought in the power of a true religion.

This being so, we are confirmed in our confidence that the negro nationality, which we see rising on the western coast of Africa, has the stamina to be a great and enduring nationality; and this greatness and endurance we predicate on the peculiar religious susceptibilities which we have seen the African to be possessed of, and the development among the race of a high order of Christianity. If their national life shall be a true reflection of their spiritual life, we may anticipate for them a degree of prosperity and permanence which has not heretofore fallen to the lot of any people. The strength of their religious character will determine the value of their civil position.

God propitiated, God on their side, his favor secured by an active and permanent obedience, and
they will not fail to be owned and honored of Heaven.
But if, like Israel, they shall forget the God of their
fathers, and turn aside after strange gods — if the
power of a living religion shall cease to permeate their
laws, their institutions, their learning, and their business avocations—and their every-day life, their glory
will depart—they will be shorn of the locks of their
strength, and become weak as other men.

2. We see light for Africa, a pleasing promise for
her future, in the very thick dark cloud which has so
long hung over her. It is light through her darkness;
enlargement through manifold sufferings; elevation
through sore depression.   The long endurance and
suffering of Africa—the severe ordeal through which
she has been made to pass, warrants the expectation
of the corresponding favor of Heaven.   It is no more
true of individuals than of nations, that "whom the
Lord loveth he chasteneth;" and he abases them that
he will exalt. When he has brought a people or a
nation very low, or continued the depression for a
long time, he will make his mercy abound toward
them in proportion as he has afflicted them. So God
has done, and so he will do in time to come.

Nations have their birth-pangs, their throes, and
painful struggles, which precede their national existence.   Oftentimes these are protracted and severe,
and seem more like death-struggles than birth-pains;
yet they usher in, and are preparatory to, a long and
prosperous life.

We need recur but for a moment to the early
history of a few well-known States to confirm what

has been intimated. What commotions and wars, and, perchance, famines and pestilences—what struggles for life and mountain-like hinderances—had to be met and overcome by the Assyrian, the Egyptian, and the Ethiopian empires, no historical mirror reflects! Analogy suggests they were subjected to the alternations of hope and fear—that they travailed in pain many long years before they stood forth before the world in their national manhood.

The oldest State, of which we have authentic records, is the Hebrew Commonwealth. The great founder of this State was called of God, and given every possible assurance of the high and long-continued prosperity which should bless his descendants. Yet, more than four centuries elapse before they are even organized as a nation, and take possession of the promised land. And what hardships and hard fighting, and disheartening rebuffs, afterward betide! The Canaanite still dwelt in the land ; and more than another period of four centuries elapse before the kingdom, under Solomon, in peace and prosperity, reached its full manhood. Neither Abraham, Isaac, nor Jacob had, in their respective generations, a fixed habitation or a national prestige. Four hundred years was the nation travailing in pain waiting to be delivered, and four centuries more was she struggling in her childhood and minority.

Or take Christianity as a kingdom : and what a rigorous and prolonged pupilage did she undergo! If we go back to the beginning of Christianity and contemplate the preparatory work which gave it birth, and then inaugurated it as a great power in the world, we should needs go back to the "promise" in Eden.

and bring into the account the entire history of the four thousand years which preceded the Incarnation— all the events and revolutions—all the wars and commotions—all the blessings of peace and the curses of war—the good and the bad, as overruled by the Almighty Hand to the furtherance of that great scheme. And since the Advent, has followed a conflict of centuries—already more than eighteen—centuries of persecutions, wars, an unremitting struggle against the general current of this world—a conflict with the powers that be ; with the manners, customs and spirit of the world—an uncompromising warfare with mighty confederacies of false religions.

Nor does Christianity yet stand forth in the strength of manhood. It is yet in a state of pupilage, has all this time been preparing through manifold suffering for a glorious career, but is yet scarcely entered upon it: "is as a bridegroom coming out of his chamber, and rejoiceth as a strong man to run a race." Every pang is a progress.

Another great power arose in the world in the sixteenth century. It was the Reformation. This notable event has been very justly denominated " a vast effort of the human mind to achieve its freedom." Though it burst upon the world at the appointed time, yet it had been preparing a thousand years. It was heralded—it was wrought out by wars and commotions ; by civil strifes ; by the incessant struggle of Christian communities to stem the torrent of invading floods of error and wickedness ; by all sorts of conflicts, civil, social, and religious, which often seemed to be bringing only disaster and dissolution, but which were really conducing most effectually to that great intellectual emancipation and religious deliverance, and advancement which we call the Reformation.

"The sagacious eye of the world's wisdom could not but have seen that mighty events were struggling in the womb of Providence. The Reformation was a necessary consequence of what preceded. Internal fires were burning, the earth heaving, and soon there must come vent. Had not the irruption been in Germany, it must soon have been elsewhere. Had not Luther led, it must ere long have been conducted by another." *

In like manner, we may speak of England and the English. You fix on a point far back into the misty morning of that great empire ; and from this point of sheer barbarism trace, step by step, the progress of that people ; through wars, conquests, and defeats ; through all their civil struggles, and hard battling against ignorance, prejudice, and corruption ; all the alternations of freedom and despotism ; all struggles, revolutions, and reachings after deliverance from thraldom ; from the ponderous foot of despotism raised to crush them : it was in this rough, untilled soil that England took root, and grew to a sightly tree, and sent forth her branches till she has overshadowed the whole world ; so that the sun never sets where Britannia bears not rule. How sterile and stormy ; often how unpropitious, protracted, and hopeless was her beginning, her history is the faithful voucher.

And need I more than allude to the early history of our Pilgrim Fathers—to the rigorous discipline they passed through in England ; to their training in Ger-

---

* " God in History," vol. i., p. 77.

many; to their hardships, and indomitable persever-ance in New England; to perils in the wilderness, and cruel conflicts with savages. And when they had secured a home, and a sanctuary, and a country, they were at length compelled to assert and defend their liberties through a seven years' disastrous and ex-hausting war.

Nor is the victory yet won. Liberty still cries for her final emancipation. She is yet in bonds with them that are bound. Our glorious revolutionary struggle broke the yoke of civil thraldom, but left the chains of social and domestic bondage still to fester in human flesh, and to chafe the immortal mind, till at length they have culminated in the lurid flames of war. And now a contest, harder and hotter than ever before, is making the last great strike for liberty. And may we not look that Liberty shall ere long emerge from the cloud of war and the dense smoke of the battle-field, fairer than before, more resplendent, and pledged for a loftier flight. And then, having been nurtured in the school of adversity, she shall pass from the gristle of youth into a more mature manhood.

Or the same idea finds an illustration in the work of modern missions. In how many instances, as in the case of Greenland and the South Sea Islands, do wind and tide—the whole course of nature and of sin, the waywardness of the heathen, the insalubrity of climate, and defection among brethren, all seem to preclude the hope of success; and when the missionary is about to yield in despair, the tide turns. God appears for him, and the work of years seems done in a day. And now they see that all those long, dreary years of waiting, were but the winter season of hope, effectually preparing the issues of spring and the fruits of autumn.

Or we might, at the outset, have cited the origin of imperial Rome. The Bard of Mantua has sung the wars, the wanderings, the struggles of the noble Æneas; the toils and strifes before the earliest foundation of Rome could be laid. Troy must be founded—must rise, flourish, be besieged and destroyed, that a chosen remnant, who should escape, might, after untold perils by sea and by land, be driven to the Italian shore, and there found the mighty Rome. And the great Carthage was little more than the stepping-stone to Rome's final greatness. Of Æneas, the immediate founder of Rome, and of his wanderings and toils, Virgil sings:

> " Seven long years the unhappy wandering train
> Were tossed by storms, and scattered through the main ;
> Such time, such toil, required the Roman name,
> Such length of labor for so vast a fame."

But why so extend our illustration? It is that we may concede the same in our expectations of Africa. Long and dreary has been her night; cruel her oppressions; profound her degradation. " Deep calleth to deep:" the depth of her humiliations to the depth of the Divine compassion. And will not He, whose ear is always open to the cry of the lowly, hear? And will he not come to their succor? " Whom he loveth, he chasteneth, and scourgeth every son whom he receiveth."

We think we see in the very peculiar dealings of God with Africa a presage and a promise of a future, which shall be as distinguished for the Divine favor, as the past has been for Divine malediction.   Whom God has especially abased, he will especially exalt. "God's method," says a popular writer, "is one of antagonism and conflicts.   Every step of progression in this world is a birth-pang.   Every step of development has been by throes."   The first and chief ground of hope, then, we find in the long, low, and extreme oppression of the African.   Herein they have the unfailing promise of God, the guarantee of Heaven, that the down-trodden shall yet sit in the high places of the earth.   God will surely lift up the heads that hang down "give them rule over them that hated them," and "reward them double" for all the dishonor which has been put upon them.   God will surely take the part of the oppressed, and put to shame· the pride of the oppressor.

But we have something yet more direct: we have promises, and the sure word of prophecy.   "Behold Philistia and Tyre, with Ethiopia; this man was born there.   The labor of Egypt and merchandise of Ethiopia and of the Sabians, men of stature shall come unto thee, and they shall be thine."   "Princes shall come out of Egypt.   Ethiopia shall soon stretch out her hands unto God."   Isaiah says: that Midian and Ephah and Sheba shall come, "bringing gold and incense," to "show forth the praises of the Lord."   And the. tents of Kedar and of Nebaioth shall be represented too.   And do we not seem to have a pledge for the evangelization of Africa in the early conversion, and reception into the Christian church, of the eunuch of Candace, Queen of Ethiopia; and a yet surer pledge in the interesting fact that the infant Saviour seeks in the land of Ham an asylum from persecution?   When he comes to receive his kingdom, will he not remember the land of his affliction? Identified in his first suffering, so shall she be when he shall come in his glory.

Nor are we here without another delightful pledge. Who is it that I see approaching the Man of Nazareth at the moment of his extremest humiliation? The scenes of Gethsemane are passed; the indignities of the Jewish sanhedrim and the scourging before Pilate have been endured; and now, when he is ready to sink from exhaustion and extreme suffering, they lay on him the cross, and compell him to bear it up the hill of Calvary. But as he sinks beneath the load, who is this that appears—receives the burden, and relieves the Sufferer in the time of his extremest need? It was Simon the Cyrenian, the African. His last sufferings on earth, as well as his first, were thus singularly identified with the land of Ham. The right hand may forget its cunning, the woman may forget her sucking child, but tell me not that that Babe of Bethlehem, that Man of Calvary, will ever forget the race who were thus engraven on his heart at the moment of his profoundest humiliation? In their afflictions he will most surely feel afflicted, and will not leave them in their time of need.

3. Again: the signs of the times are significant in relation to Africa. The great negro problem is of world-wide interest. England feels it to her very centre. France is moved by it in some of her most vital interests. All Europe is deeply concerned in its solution, and it is shaking from centre to circumference all that was, and all that is, the United States of America. No question, at the present moment, possesses, with all classes in our country, a more absorb-

17

ing interest. Is the negro the cause of the war? Are we fighting for him? Shall he be free? Ought he to be free? If freed what shall be done with him? What shall be his future destiny? They that hate the negro, hate him more cordially. They would bind him in chains never to be broken. They invoke all the sanctions of their religion to their aid. They call on their God to bind faster the chains of the bondmen. Slavery is made a constituent part of their theology— a part of their training for the sacred office and a *sine qua non* in the teachings of the sanctuary. He that speaks not according to these oracles can have no place at their altars.

On the other hand the friends of the negro have re-doubled their interest. They have discerned the mighty hand of God stretched out in his behalf. They fear to take part against him. There is among all such a singular harmony as touching the negro's future destiny. They write; they print; they wait, work and pray; they would enter any open door where their influence might be felt, or their co-opera-tion be effective, in working out that destiny. Not only do current events seem to foreshadow the idea I have supposed, but discerning minds, who have direct-ed their attention to Africa and the Africans, seem singularly impressed with the conviction, that a good time is coming to that long-neglected land. I shall cite the opinions of a few who have had the most favorable opportunities to form a judgment, and these will serve to confirm our expectation of an auspicious future for that race. Says one, " though chains and slavery yet fill the ears and appal the hearts of many, yet there is a very general conviction that some great development of Providence with regard to the African race may be approaching. Never could slavery have existed so long amid such influences of Christianity as prevail in this country, and such efforts of the southern people to abolish it, were it not that God intends to use these enslaved ones as the instruments of good to the African race."

After this manner discourses another good authority: "The African race has peculiarities yet to be unfolded in the light of civilization and Christianity, which, if not the same as those of the Anglo-Saxon, may prove to be morally of even a higher type. The Anglo-Saxon race has been intrusted with the destinies of the world, during its pioneer period of struggle and conflict. To that mission its stern, inflexible, energetic elements are well adapted. But as a Christian, I look for another era to arise. On its borders, I trust, we stand; and the throes that now convulse the nations are, to my hope, but the birth-pangs of an hour of universal peace and brotherhood.* When Africa shall, in turn, "figure in the great drama of human improvement," says the same author, "life will awake there with a gorgeousness and splendor of which our old western tribes faintly have conceived. In that far-off land of gold, and gems, and spices, and waving palms, and wondrous flowers, and miraculous fertility, will awake new forms of art, new styles of splendor ; and the negro race, no longer despised and trodden down, will, perhaps, show forth some of the latest and most magnificent revelations of human life ; certainly they will in their gentleness, their lowly

---

* " Uncle Tom's Cabin." By Harriet Beecher Stowe.

docility of heart, their aptitude to repose on a superior mind and rest on a higher power, their childlike simplicity of affection, and facility of forgiveness. In all these they will exhibit the highest form of the peculiarly Christian life; and, perhaps, as God chasteneth whom he loveth, he hath chosen poor Africa in the furnace of affliction to make her the highest and noblest in that kingdom which he will set up when every other kingdom has been tried and failed : for the first shall be last and the last first."

The last prognostic that Africa is about to enter upon a new glorious future, we seem to see in the late Emancipation Proclamation of President Lincoln; a trumpet which gives no uncertain sound. It proclaimed liberty to the captives. And the fact that they are, for reasons we can not see, kept back from an immediate and joyful response by one great and simultaneous movement from the house of their bondage, should not for a moment impair our confidence that the God of the oppressed will vindicate his ways, and in the end, and at no distant day, the more triumphantly set his captives free.

Already do we see the kind hand of God in the delay. Had there been, as we hoped, a simultaneous exodus of four millions of the emancipated, it would have imperiled the whole work, if not been a disastrous defeat. We think we are safe in affirming that emancipation has been, and is likely to be, quite as rapid as the best interests and the final welfare of the emancipated would allow. Few had anticipated the difficulties of the transit of four millions of souls from a state of bondage to a state of freedom—how much preparatory work must be done before they should be fitted for their new position—how the aid of Government and the charity of the nation must be taxed, to clothe, feed, school, and evangelize them, and fit for liberty and self-support those hitherto dependent and helpless myriads. We are sure they have come quite as fast as we have been able to meet them, and faster than we have adequately met them.

The National Freedmen's Relief Association and other kindred Institutions are doing much to meet this imperative demand. They are doing a great and a most praiseworthy work, and deserve a ready and liberal co-operation. By schools and colportage, and the direct preaching of the Gospel, as well as by large benefactions to meet the bodily wants of the destitute multitudes that seek an asylum within our borders, they are largely contributing to the work in hand, and challenge the aid of every patriotic and liberal mind.

We can in no way so well illustrate how the slaves received the announcement of their freedom, and how they really feel, as by quoting a notice which recently appeared of a jubilee meeting of ex-slaves on New Year's Eve, 1863. We accept the record as an item of our nation's history, which, we believe, will never disappear from our annals. Yea, it shall be transmitted to future generations as the great event of our age:

"At seven o'clock in the evening of Thursday, Dr. Nichols send a bellman round to the contraband quarters, to let them know that he would read the Proclamation of Emancipation to them at the camp. Several hundred came together, and they first sang a hymn, lined out by an old negro, who is called by all his friends in the camp 'John the Baptist.' One of the

pro-slavery journals alluded to, which have endeavored
to extract amusement from the 'negro meetings,' contains the following striking paragraphs.   Speaking of
the hymn, it says:

"'It was "lined out" by "John de Baptis." He
seemed to be the recognized leader of the contrabands
in their religious exercises, and altogether a good deal
of a character. He is perhaps sixty years of age, with
rugged features not unintelligent, grizzled locks, and a
somewhat martial bearing from his erect carriage and
the military overcoat worn by him. The hymn, or
"hime," was sung in full chorus, the women, who were
mostly congregated by themselves, keeping time by
that wide-swaying motion familiar to those who have
witnessed a negro camp-meeting, and the venerable
leader, as he sung, extending his arms over the crowd
in a sort of wild enthusiasm.'

"And again :

"'An old colored woman then took up the theme,
and raised their so popular hymn, "Go Down Moses"
(keeping time with head, hand, and foot), which piece
was sung with a fervor that indicated that there may
be truth in what has been intimated, that this piece is
the negro Marseillaise, or National (if not revolutionary) Hymn.

"'It was quite evident through the exercises of the
day and night that the negroes regard the condition
of the Israelites in Egypt as typical of their own condition in slavery, and the allusions to Moses, Pharaoh,
the Egyptian task-masters, and the unhappy condition of the captive Israelites, were continuous ; and
any reference to the triumphant escape of the Israelites across the Red Sea, and the destruction of their

pursuing masters, was certain to bring out a strong "Amen."'

"Perhaps the most striking scene in the whole performance was when Dr. Nichols explained to the poor creatures what States, and even counties in States, were rendered free by the Proclamation. For instance, when he told them that North Carolina was free, quite a number manifested their delight by raising their black arms and shouting. When certain counties in Virginia were spoken of as under the Proclamation, men and women would spring to their feet and exclaim, 'Dat's me!' 'Dar's whar I'se cum from!' 'Bress God! Oh, bress de God for dat!'

"After the reading of the Proclamation, William Beverly, a contraband, led in prayer, and some of his expressions were infinitely touching. Here are some of the sentences:

"'Let thy blessing rest on every thing belonging to the United States President, who has bestowed such gifts on us this night. We were bound as slaves. Chains on our hands. We have seen our people bound in chains, and carried away. Some got mothers in foreign lands. Some got fathers in foreign lands. Jesus! bless the President. Lay down with him this night, I pray God; rise in the morning with him! God bless the Union army wherever it may be. God Almighty, go with our people; lead us along in this dark, howling wilderness! Make us good. We pray for our brothers still in the South. Jesus, stan' by dem! Lord, be with dem in the most particular moment. Lord Almighty, make us willing to obey the United States President as much as do the soldiers as come to break our chains. We were bruised and dragged about. Let us lay down our lives for those who break slavery chains from our necks. Let de war be pushed on. Bress dem who have just run away and cum here—and bress all.'

"These words were from the lips of a man made free by the Proclamation. Who can read them and accuse him afterward of wanting in genuine appreciation of the gift bestowed upon him by the 'United States President?' The grateful expressions of the prayer will touch any heart not made of stone.

"The songs sung by the contrabands added much to the intensity of the scene. And old man, with a deep, hollow voice, struck up the song, 'I'm a freeman now; Jesus Christ has made me free!' and in five minutes three hundred voices were joined with his in chorus. A woman led off with a new song, 'There will be no more task-masters,' and in a very few moments the contrabands caught music and words, and sang with powerful effect.

"I have given but a fragmentary sketch of a scene worthy of Mrs. Stowe's pen, and the most joyful scene of New Year's Day in all the land. The Proclamation may be set down by white editors as a mere bit of paper, without effect, but the slave does not think so. He is upon his knees, thanking God and the President for it. To him New Year's Day was Emancipation Day!

"The day was fit for the promulgation of a decree of emancipation. There was not a cloud in the sky, and the temperature was that of October. It seemed as if Heaven smiled upon the act, and Heaven will smile upon it hereafter.

Is emancipation safe? Will not these freedmen

"deluge the land in blood, wrap it in flames?" No; never has there been any thing of the sort in the history of the negro. And it is not in his nature to do it. The notice just quoted does but bear testimony in harmony with the record of Emancipation Day in the West Indies. Facts demolish all fears here. Let us see how it was in Antigua. The negro had no revenge to take there. He has none here.

"On the night of the 31st of July, 1834, with the first stroke of the bell, as it tolled the hour of twelve, nearly 30,000 slaves in the island of Antigua became on the moment free. How this sudden transition was received, whether with fire and blood or not, the following extract from Thorne and Kimball's 'West Indies' will show:

"'The Wesleyans kept "Watch-night" in all their chapels. One of the missionaries gave us an account of the watch meeting at the chapel in St. John's. The spacious house was filled with candidates for liberty. All was animation and eagerness. A mighty chorus of voices swelled the song of expectation and joy; and, as they united in prayer, the voice of the leader was drowned in the universal acclamations of thanksgivings, and praise, and blessing, and honor, and glory to God, who had come down for their deliverance. In such exercises the evening was spent, until the hour of twelve approached. The missionary then proposed that when the cathedral clock should begin to strike, the whole congregation should fall on their knees, and receive the boon of freedom in silence. Accordingly, as the loud bell tolled its first note, the crowded assembly prostrated themselves. All was silence, save the quivering, half-stifled breath of the

17 *

struggling spirit. Slowly the tones of the clock fell upon the waiting multitude. Peal on peal, peal on peal, rolled over the prostrate throng, like angels' voices, thrilling their weary heart-strings. Scarcely had the last tone sounded, when lightning flashed vividly, and a loud peal of thunder rolled through the sky. It was God's pillar of fire! His trump of jubilee! It was followed by a moment of profound silence. Then came the outburst! They shouted "Glory! Hallelujah!" They clapped their hands, they leaped up, they fell down, they clasped each other in their free arms, they cried, they laughed, they went to and fro, throwing upward their unfettered hands. High above all, a mighty sound ever and anon swelled up. It was the utterance of gratitude to God, in broken negro dialect.

"In the days of slavery it had always been customary to order out the militia during the Christmas holidays, when the negroes were in the habit of congregating in large numbers to enjoy the festivities of the season. But the December after emancipation, the Governor issued a proclamation that "in consequence of the abolition of slavery" there was no further need of taking that precaution. And it is a fact, that there have been no soldiers out at Christmas from that day to this."

A correspondent describes his visit to the "contrabands," five hundred of whom he found quartered in a long stable, each group over a fire cooking rations. He says:

"It is amusing to hear the discussions among the men on the subject of their present distressed condition. One says: 'Bredren, we's come to de Red

Sea, dat is jes where we am : de 'Giptians is behind us, de river is afore us. Now what we wants is de rod ; dat is, de prayers of Christians, to take us over de river. Unbelief is great, but God will speak by-and-by through Massa Linkum, and say, "Go forward"— den we'll march. We must have patience.'"

It will gladden the hearts of these humble men to know that, at length, God has spoken through Mr. Lincoln, saying : "Let my people go." May God have them in his holy keeping!

There does not seem the least occasion to fear a servile insurrection. One of the most remarkable features of the war is the patient waiting of the negro. He is hoping, praying, agonizing for his liberty, fully conscious that the boon awaits him. Yet still he waits—trusting God and biding his time. Nowhere else at the present moment do we meet a more implicit belief, a profounder, a more simple faith. And whatever else may come out of the present war, sure we may be that the God of battles will hear the cries of his afflicted ones, and bring deliverance.

We think we discover in these things the most encouraging premonitions of the future highly favored destiny of this singular people. God is engaged for them—man is engaged for them. And shall not, philanthropy and religion—the church and the ministry—shall not we, as individuals, contribute our mite of influence, time, or substance to speed these millions of captives, not only to the desired goal of freedom, but to the fulfillment of their high commission as Heaven's chosen agents to scatter the dark cloud that hangs over Africa, to begirt it with the light of heaven, and to convert its great moral desert into the garden of the Lord. Let us only be careful that, on this great question of the day, we be found on the side of the Lord. They know not what they do, who throw a single straw in the way of the emancipation of this people, and their transference to their fatherland just as fast as the providence of God shall indicate it to be practicable. Yea, more, let us see to it that our prayers, influence, and benefactions shall contribute as efficiently as possible to the carrying out of this great and beneficent scheme.

But woe to them that set themselves to hinder this work! God is in it; the best, the most humane and benevolent portion of humanity is in it. And shall puny man resist? His recompense of reward is before him. Let him remember Pharaoh and his host: Egypt desolated by ten plagues and the Egyptians "spoiled." Let him remember the Red Sea, and the chariots and horsemen buried beneath its waves. Let them fear, for God will surely take the part of the oppressed; he will surely visit them that are afflicted and long time cast down. Though he chasten, he will not forsake them.

And not the good and benevolent only, not the haters of oppression and the lovers of liberty alone are favoring this great result; but bad men are unconsciously and indirectly doing the same. Our sorry sympathizers with the oppressor—the rage and madness of the oppressors themselves, are made to favor the very result which they so madly deprecate. Unconscious of its application in our present conflict, Watts expresses the idea in the following simple stanza:

" When God, in his own sovereign ways,
    Comes down to save the oppressed,
The wrath of man shall work his praise,
    And he'll restrain the rest."

Finally, what is the conclusion of the whole matter? What the solution of our problem? We find a solution in the universal emancipation of the negro race from bondage; in the singular training of that race while yet in bonds—especially in their religious culture, fitting them to be the very agents needed for the renovation of Africa, and in a corresponding readiness on the part of Africa to receive her regenerators. We discover the same solution in a negro nationality in Africa, fashioned after the Anglo-Saxon mould and vitalized by a living Christianity; in an enlightened commerce and an extensive colonization; in the physical development and the moral regeneration of Africa by her own redeemed children. In these various agencies we find the solution of our problem, because implied in them are all the elements of a healthful progress: Christianity, civilization, industry, enterprise; the education of the masses, and all the higher departments of learning. For these are all of the Anglo-Saxon type of life.

In a word, our hope for Africa lies chiefly in the hope of a negro nationality that shall be highly vitalized with the religion of the New Testament. This is the only living, enduring element of a nation's life. Commerce, learning, civilization, wealth, industry, enterprise, are but the mere adjuncts or manifestations of that life in a nation. Her real life is hid in the sanctuary of a pure and undefiled religion.

" PRINCES SHALL COME OUT OF EGYPT; ETHIOPIA SHALL SOON STRETCH OUT HER HANDS UNTO GOD."

CHAPTER XX.

The Interior of Africa—Recent developments—Their bearings on the future
- of Africa—British trade—The Liberia College.

OUR survey of Africa and estimate of her present
condition, and our anticipations of her future, would be
confessedly incomplete if we did not advert, at least, to
the recently developed features and resources of Africa's great interior.   Our notions of that great continent are derived very much from an acquaintance only
with her coasts, and more especially with her western
coast.   Such is altogether an inadequate view, and
essentially erroneous.   Perhaps no people have so severely suffered from intercourse with foreigners as the
people of Western Africa. First, a most demoralizing
system of piracies desolated the coast.   Then followed
an avalanche of Portuguese adventurers, who, like the
devouring locusts, swept over the land, and then, for
many a grievous year, ate up every green thing.   The
wiles and corruption, the avarice and despotism of
Rome never had a more unrestrained and luxuriant development.   All here found a befitting field—a house
" swept and garnished," for habitation. Those blighting piracies had but prepared the way for a more withering blight.   An ignorant, confiding people became the
victims of a wicked and designing priestcraft ; and
Rome never rioted in a more congenial soil.
    These two waves passed, a third, more blighting,
more prolonged and deadly in its bitter fruits, followed

in their wake with intensified virulence. What piracies began, and the contaminating rule of the Portuguese advanced to a fearful consummation, the slave-trade finished. No traffic was ever so impoverishing to the country, so demoralizing to the people. Instead of the civilizing, enriching, enlightening influences of a legitimate commerce, and the salutary influences which usually characterize intercourse with foreign peoples, this trade, in the vile pre-eminence it attained, has won the epithet, the "summation of all villainies." It, more nearly than any other device of the great adversary, obliterates from man the last vestige of humanity.

We may not, then, form any just estimate of the real character and capabilities of Africa and African races from the specimens which appear most conspicuously before us. Nor do we gain from the same quarter any juster apprehensions of what are the actual resources of the country, what the climate, or the future destiny of the people. A most withering sirocco has swept over the entire coast, and left behind it but one unbroken desolation. Morally, socially, and commercially, all is desolate. Man is there no longer man, but a wild beast preying on his fellow-man. The humanizing, ennobling, civilizing mission of commerce is made but the mission of degradation and death. "A fire devoureth before them ; behind them a flame burneth : the land is as the garden of Eden before them, and behind them a desolate wilderness ; yea, and nothing escapes them."

Never did so many and such malignant influences combine to crush a single people. The resources of commerce which are wont to develop the thrift, the talent, enterprise, and industry of a people, and to advance them in knowledge, wealth, and social position,

and to work out their general amelioration, have there
served only to spread distrust among men—to debase
and impoverish—and to make man fear and avoid his
fellow-man, and, consequently to repel all social intercourse and improvement.   It is a commerce before
which goes conflagration and war; and behind which is
left but ruin and devastation.   The impoverishment,
distrust, and general demoralization engendered by the
slave-trade, furnish reasons enough for the present depressed and abject condition of that portion of the African race with which we are the best acquainted.

But as we penetrate into the interior of that continent we meet a different country, a different people,
climate, and natural resources.   The researches of late
travelers represent Central Africa as one of the finest
countries in the world.   Instead of the low, level surface of the coast, an almost impenetrable jungle—fertile,
it is true, in soil, yet more fertile in malarious disease—
we meet " a high table-land, rolling, mountainous, and
consequently healthy," presenting, in all its natural features, a salubrious, fertile, and delightful land.*   What
was suspected thirty years ago by our early missionaries, as a fair matter of conjecture, has been verified by
recent tourists.   Facts soon confirmed the conjecture
that the great unknown interior of Africa was not, as
had been so generally conceded, a great desert.   Large
rivers were known to emerge from those supposed arid
wastes, and they said "there can not be large rivers
unless there be mountains; and, if mountains, then
inland lakes."   Other facts, which gave rise to the same
conjecture, were, that the Arabs, in large caravans, are

* Rev. A. A. Constantine, late missionary in Western Africa.

known to traverse those regions from year to year, in a manner it would be impossible on the supposition it was an unbroken desert. Large cities are known to exist there. The French are constructing a railway from Algiers to Timbucto ; an enterprise quite absurd, if the interior of Africa is a desert. They are extending thither improvements, such as they would only do in a country capable of improvement.

Researches of modern travelers have done much to correct the misconceptions of former days. Where it was supposed there would be met only arid sands and bleak barrenness, and a people poor, stupid, and abject, Dr. Livingston found himself amid hills and dales, mountains and rivers ; well-watered, well-cultivated, and fertile fields ; villages, towns, and cities ; communities of people so much superior to the inhabitants of the coasts, as to give them a fair claim to be called civilized. Those were regions of vast natural resources, rich in mines of gold and silver, and the useful metals. He found intelligence, a good degree of thrift, some well-organized governments, schools, and unmistakable, though not well-developed, vestiges of the true religion ; not only the relics of a patriarchal religion, recognizing one Supreme God, but vestiges of Christianity, which had, probably, found its way thither through Abyssinia, where it had obtained a foothold in the days of the apostles, and where, to the present day, it has never ceased to exist.

All this, and more too, is confirmed by other travelers. Captains Speke and Grant have deserved and received the thanks of the whole civilized world for their late successful researches. We can here no more than quote a few paragraphs indicating some of the general features of the parts of Central Africa which they visited. They represent that the interior of Africa is really "a great elevated water-basin, often abounding in rich lands, its large lakes being fed by numerous streams from adjacent ridges; and its waters escaping to the sea by fissures and depressions in the highest surrounding lands."

"I believe," says Speke, "I have discovered a zone of wonderful fertility in Africa. It is in a line with the equator, east and west, and its fertility perfectly astonishes me." This region is represented by him to be between 3,000 and 4,000 feet in altitude, watered by rains the entire year, fertilizing the adjoining regions with a temperature as mild as that of England in summer, and the most healthy of all the countries through which he traveled. Arab merchants, and others, say that there is no place so healthy as the equatorial regions. No part of the world, these travelers believe, holds out such promise to the colonist or the Christian missionary.

Another writer says: "The knowledge we possess of the western and eastern shores of Africa, in the region of the line, would lead us to suppose that the central country is mountainous, intersected with deep and extensive valleys, and large streams, whose banks have all the wild luxuriance of warm and rainy climates. All the interior of Africa between the tropics must be full of rivers, woods, and ravines, on account of the rains which inundate it during the winter season. Other travelers speak of the people. Their physical character and social condition were found to be superior to any other African races known. And more definitely yet do they speak of their civil condition. "On arriving at the three Wahuma kingdoms which inclose the western and northwestern shores of the Nyanza Lake," they say, " a remarkable state of social and political life arrests the attention. Two, at least, of these Wahuma kingdoms have the advantage of being ruled by a firm hand." Among the series of " strong kingdoms" which they met, particular mention is made of Uganda, which is described as a " most surprising country, in the order, neatness, civility, and politeness of its inhabitants." Our travelers were surprised at the " tidiness of the people, the manner in which they deported themselves, and the style of the native dress ;" which they said would " not disgrace a fashionable promenade in London. These people in Uganda are a superior people."

Nor should we overlook, in our estimate, the natural productions of these countries. The purest iron and the richest gold and silver mines in the world are found in Central Africa. The soil, too, is exhaustless ; and the resources of the forests and rivers are excelled by no other country. Natives constantly coming to Liberia, from the interior, tell of " lands exuberantly fertile, of large and numerous tribes, athletic, industrious ; not the descendants of Europeans—but black men, pure negroes, who live in large towns, cultivate the soil, carry on extensive traffic, maintain amicable relations with each other, and with men from a distance."

But the product which gives the great importance to these countries, now but recently revealed to the civilized world, is the almighty cotton. His majesty shows signs of a transfer of his throne from the dominions of Africa's white oppressors to the fairer regions of Ham's own sable sons. The capacity of the country for the growth of cotton seems to know no bounds.

We can not here too profoundly admire the hand of God in this very timely opening of that great cotton field.

The Southern States had well-nigh assumed the monopoly of this indispensable article of commerce. The negro must be enslaved—Africa be devastated by the demon of avarice—American soil be wet with tears of blood, that a few may riot in the great monopoly.

Discern we not the hand of God here? The thing that God has risen up to do, is to break the iron yoke that binds four millions of his oppressed ones in a bondage more cruel than that of Egypt. The cotton monopoly forged their chains, and would not let them go. Pharaoh wanted the Hebrews to make bricks, that he might consummate his great architectural schemes—perchance the construction of the Pyramids. Southern planters wanted the negroes to raise cotton, that they might grow rich and prosper, and rule the nation. The oppressed "sighed by reason of their bondage, and cried, and their cry came up unto God by reason of the bondage. And God heard their groaning, and came down to deliver them." How, in the exercise of his sterner judgments, he is, through the dreadful carnage of war, battering down every stronghold of slavery, it is not my province in the present connection to discuss. We are here only concerned to inquire how he does it in connection with the culture and traffic of cotton.

England must have cotton; 20,000,000 of spindles must be kept twirling, or millions of souls are sorely troubled. A civil war breaks out in America, and the supplies of cotton are cut off. Multitudes in England are thrown out of employment, and their families are brought to the verge of starvation. And vastly greater multitudes are troubled and perplexed for fear of the things that are coming on the earth. But what aileth thee, that trouble has taken hold of thee, and pain as of one that travaileth? Nothing—but that Sambo has dropped his hoe and retired from the cotton-field. Europe—the world in general—England in particular, is like a car thrown from the track, because King Cotton withholds his supplies. But the war goes on ; the cotton-fields are laid waste ; the cultivators have heard from afar the herald of freedom, and they will no longer stay.

What now can England do ? It is a question of life and death—of work and live, or be thrown out of employment and starve. Every mind is on the alert ; every nerve strung. Where shall we get cotton now ? The voice of God replies : it speaks through the opening cotton-fields, and the cheap labor, and the fertile soil, and the populous regions, and the great navigable rivers, of Central Africa. English capital, English enterprise and cupidity—much that is good and more that is bad, is engaged to open up a highway to the sources of the Niger and the Nile ; and to every great trading post in the interior. Lagos is already a great port of entry to this new cotton-field, and a great arena of commercial enterprise. Dr. Baikie strongly advises an English trading station on the banks of the Niger. He speaks of the mind of the Central African races as eminently practical, capable of appreciating advantages of trade, and ready to turn all proffered facilities to account.

England is appreciating the very great advantages of her trade with Central Africa. France is an active competitor. The contemplated railway from Algiers to Timbucto, and the sinking of artesian wells in the Great

Desert, by the aid of which every locality about a well becomes a fruitful field, are unmistakable intimations of the estimate which France puts on this newly opening field of commerce.

There is something truly noteworthy in the course of providential dealing at the present moment in connection with the existing slaveholders' rebellion in America ; and in its future bearing on Africa. It indicates, beyond all controversy, that the time has at length come when the mighty hand of God is engaged to recover, from the desolation of many generations, that great and singular continent, and a more singular race.

England must have cotton. Her great commercial machinery is deranged—the wheels stopped—the commerce of the world paralyzed the moment the supplies of cotton are suspended. Such a derangement, such a damaging restriction of supplies, has befallen Great Briton as a consequence of the present war. The derangements and devastations of this dreadful conflict have laid American cotton-fields waste, and scattered those who cultivated them to the four winds. England feels it to the quick, and loses no time and spares no pains to supply her lack. She is compelled to direct her search elsewhere, and Africa looms up before her as her most promising field. Every spindle in Lancashire now becomes a mute, unconscious advocate of the long-neglected race. Let us see if we can trace the lines of providential dealing in the matter in question :

In order to the renovation supposed, the following conditions would seem requisite, viz., natural capacities and resources of the country and of the people to be renovated, and the preparation of the agents who are to become the renovators. A sterile country, with no resources to be developed, is incapable of the ameliorations which we have supposed await Africa. And though she must supply the material (the raw material) for such a renovation, this material must first be wrought into shape and fitness, and be tempered to the work, before it can accomplish its assigned mission. This, we think, we can show in respect to the natural resource of Africa, and the two great classes of agents which are destined to work out her regeneration. We are at present more especially concerned to discover the *modus operandi*—the providential workings which are bringing about the purposes here supposed.

We have already spoken of the great natural resources of Africa in general, and the rapidly maturing of the instrumentalities which are preparing for the most efficient action in that direction. We have now to speak of the same in their present advanced condition. Central Africa has, within a few years, thrown open to the enterprise of commerce and philanthropy altogether new and more inviting fields. And, in correspondence with this, there has been as signal advance in the preparation of the human agencies.

We have seen how the explorations of Barth, Burton, Livingston, Speke, and Grant have revealed a new Africa to the world—regions of unsurpassed fertility—governments in advance of any thing heretofore known on the coast; peoples comparatively intelligent and refined; culing learning and favored with schools; acquainted with the useful and ornamental arts; with mining and the useful metals, and with much which goes to civilize and elevate a people. Persons not conversant with late explorations in Central Africa may not be prepared to believe that " schools, of different grades, have existed for centuries, in various interior negro countries, and under the provisions of law, in which even the poor are educated at the public expense, and in which the deserving are carried on many years through long courses of regular instruction.   Native languages have been reduced to writing, books translated from the Arabic, and original works written in them." Most erroneous and unjust is that judgment which forms an opinion of the hundred millions of men spread over the interior of Africa, from a knowledge of ten or twelve millions of sadly demoralized beings who are met on the coasts.

The significant developments referred to, doubly significant at this critical juncture in human affairs, indicate one of the interesting lines of providential dealing with Africa and her races, which characterize our times. What is discovered to exist in Africa, and what is doing for Africa, is rapidly preparing the theatre on which the great drama is about to be acted.   The agencies and actors are being prepared elsewhere.   And, in order to the fitting and bringing forth upon the great arena of action these agencies and actors, the most extraordinary commotions are taking place.

The true, legitimate renovators of Africa have, in their respective generations, been more than two centuries fitting for their mission.   In the rice-fields of the South ; in every department of useful labor ; in the hard school of unrequited bondage ; and in the scanty, though to them blessed, religious privileges, which, in spite of their " durance vile," the hand of Heaven's mercy has brought them, they have been fitting themselves to act an important part in the redemption of their fatherland.   With a faith unwavering, with a patience unequaled, with a childlike confidence and prayer that takes hold on the promises with all the simplicity and trust of a child, they have waited the time of their deliverance, till at length God came down and bade their oppressors to let his people go. The great American Rebellion which shakes the nation to its centre and vibrates in ominous sounds throughout Europe, is simply a mad and organized resistance to this mandate of Heaven.

One of the first felt results of the war, is to lay waste the cotton-fields, and to cut short supplies for Europe. This was a seeming, and for the time being, a real calamity. It has retarded or suspended the busy wheels of the great manufactories of Europe and America, thrown multitudes out of employment, and brought their families to the verge of starvation. It has made itself as a living calamity in the exorbitant prices of all cotton stuffs the wide world over. All this seemed decidedly calamitous. But when we look at the final cause—its bearings on the great continent of Africa, the seeming calamity appears but incidental and temporary; the final result, lasting and worthy of Heaven's great King.

Cotton, the great Babylon of the commercial world, is fallen—is fallen; and the kings of the earth who have lived deliciously with her, lament for her, and bewail her, when they see the smoke of her burning; and the merchants of thee arth weep and mourn over her, for no man buyeth their merchandise any more. The merchants, who were made rich by her, stand afar off, weeping and wailing—for in one hour so great riches are brought to naught, and every shipmaster, and all the company in ships, and sailors, and as many as trade by sea, stood afar off. But shall the mighty, onward rolling wheels of commerce and civilization stop because Hea-

18

ven will no longer allow the unpaid toil of Africa's sons to freight her ships, and to fatten their oppressors. Amid thunderings and lightnings and a great earthquake, which shakes two continents, the magical king, is transferring his sceptre to a third continent, where he, who once rioted on the unrequited labors of the oppressed, will now, by a benignant rule, honor and bless a willing people. Again, kings, merchants, statesmen, premiers, lords of the treasury, travelers and explorers of every name and nation, have, willingly or unwillingly, come to the rescue ; never did wit and wisdom, interest and enterprise, more heartily combine to devise a remedy.

Africa was opening to an enlarged and lucrative commerce before. Large trading companies had been organized ; lines of steamers run between England and Africa ; large capital was employed in the trade ; and extensive explorations were made. But now a new impetus is given to the whole. Central Africa all at once holds out new attractions to commerce, because it opens the most hopeful and inviting field for an abundant supply of cotton, and at the cheapest rate. The time having come for the renovation of Africa, commerce is again made the entering wedge to civilization and Christianity.

But we should fail of any just estimate of the real magnitude of this providential movement toward Africa, if we did not take into the account the present enlarged and yearly enlarging amount of commerce with that country. And it is with no feelings of national pride that we are obliged to acknowledge, that this trade, so promising of great and lasting results to Africa, and so abundantly remunerative to the nation that shall prosecute it, is, to a great extent, in the hands of our commercial rivals. England has won the credit and reaps the benefit of this important and profitable trade. England, first moved by a laudable regard to her own interests, and now compelled by a stern necessity to repair, as best she can, the unexpected failure of the Slave States of America to supply the indispensable fabric, now forces her way up the Nile and the Niger—up the Senegal and the St. Paul, and seems in the way of accomplishing a destiny of which our people might justly feel proud.

Besides the British Companies organized to trade with Africa already named, as the West Africa Company ; the Manchester Commercial Association ; the British Cotton Supply Association, and others ; we have recently noticed the West African Steamship Company, with a capital of $1,250,000 ; the London and West African Bank, with a capital of $2,500,000 ; and the London and Liberia Banking and Commercial Institution, with a capital of $1,000,000. We have here indicated the outlines of a commerce, the details and magnitude of which, as hastened on by the slaveholders' rebellion, hold out a presage for good to Africa hitherto unprecedented.

Statistics have here a peculiar interest, as indicating the progress of the great commercial revolution which is transpiring in favor of Africa. The following, though by no means complete, yet, as approximations, possess a significance worthy of notice.

We are indebted to an intelligent and ardent friend of Africa and her races, Wm. Coppinger, Esq., of Philadelphia, for the following statistics of English trade in Africa :

"In 1853, the export of palm oil from Lagos was 160 tons; in 1857, the declared value of this, with a few other articles, was £1,062,806. From Abbeokuta interior, a short distance from Lagos, the increase of raw cotton has been enormous. In 1852, nine bags, or 1810 pounds, were exported; in 1858, 1,819 bags, or 220,000 pounds; and in 1859, 3,447 bags, or 416,341 pounds. From the island of Sherbro, near the northern confines of Liberia, a cotton trade has sprung up in six years to the value of £61,000 for the last twelve months reported. Sixty thousand tons of palm oil are estimated as sent annually from the western coast of Africa, and the quantity that reached Great Britain during the year 1859 was 804,326 cwt.

The exports of British goods during the first six months of the three past years are stated as follows:

	1858.	1859.	1860.
To Gambia, Sierra Leone, and the Gold Coast, British	£95,404	£148,538	£139,643
To other parts of west coast of Africa	336,939	344,710	471,619
Total	£432,343	£493,248	£611,262

"This table shows an increase of nearly forty per cent. in quantity and value compared with 1859, and about fifteen per cent. in quantity and forty per cent. in value over 1858."

We may take this as an imperfect statement, and a beginning of a commerce which shall become an increasingly strong element in the civilization and moral renovation of Africa.

Do not passing events seem to indicate that the next great movement in the drama of human affairs will be in Africa? which, indeed, presents a broad and hopeful field for the exercise of the energies of all commercial nations ; and seems, too, to hold out the beckoning hand to the combined energies of philanthropy and religion, that they will hasten to the harvest of fields already white.

A single paragraph from the pen of an intelligent writer on Africa,* will confirm the view we have taken. Its chief interest and encouragement relate more especially to recent developments in Central Africa: "Its history, as to races, politics, learning, and religion, forms one of the most curious and interesting chapters in the world's annals. A better acquaintance would tend somewhat to abate the intense egotism of Caucasian ignorance, by leading us to contemplate the not improbable idea of savans of the eighth or tenth century discussing the probability of elevating the white barbarians of the North ; and questioning whether the Japhetic races were capable of civilization. But the prospects held out by this region, of mercantile profits and the conquest of trade, will interest a much larger class. Strangely enough, there is lying nearer to Western Europe than is any of the great fields of its foreign commerce, a country of vast extent and of almost boundless fertility, and accessible to sea-going vessels, that has been waiting through weary ages to pour its wealth into the lap of any who will receive it. Its agricultural resources excel those of India, and rival those of our own Mississippi Valley ; and the labor to develop these is at hand, ready to be employed at prices that would render American slave labor ridiculously expensive, and for which European fabrics would be

---

* Rev. Dr. Curry, in the "Methodist Quarterly Review," April, 1861.

received to any extent purchasable by such products. The whole region is one vast cotton-field, and the production of that staple seems to be easily capable of an infinite expansion, and there is no reason to doubt that that country alone would very soon be made, by native industry, to supply raw cotton to the whole of Europe. We are glad to know that Great Britain already has her hand, as well as her eye, upon that good land. We trust, before many years, her flag will wave along the Niger, the Bé-nu-we, and on the bosom of the Tchad; and that her strong and beneficent hand will bind the warring chiefs of Soodan in the bonds of a peaceful commerce, and so achieve the redemption of a great nation."

But what shall we say of the strange remissness of the American people to be first and foremost in a commerce which would seem so naturally to belong to her; and whose prosecution is so promising of large and lasting results? Every consideration would seem to urge this enterprise on the people of America; interest, honor, duty—the simple requital of great wrongs—the peculiar facilities Africa has, in respect to agencies and agents, to prosecute a stupendous commercial enterprise with Africa.

But it is time we draw this volume to a close. I shall avail myself, in conclusion, of the aid of a friend who has spent more than a quarter of a century in the service of Africa,* first as a missionary, and then in different departments of home labor. Passing events are now urging upon us the query: What shall be the coming destiny of this singular race? What shall we do with the negro—what do for him? We have said,

---

* Rev. A. A. Constantine, missionary to Africa.

do nothing for him, or with him—except to meet him in his present exigency as the good Samaritan did him that had fallen among thieves—stripped—wounded, and left half dead. Restore him to his God-given rights, as a man. Give him protection by law, and the opportunity to rise by his own merit and industry, and make his own position. Water finds its level. Let him go and come, buy and sell, in the full, free exercise of all his rights; do what he can, and make himself what, by his own well-doing and the suffrage of a free people, he may.

God's plans and purposes in connection with that whole African race are fast unfolding. As toward Israel in Egypt, his hand is visible in working out the greatest problem of the age. Grand results are already achieved. From a chattel the negro has already become a man, bearing arms in defense of his nation's flag. He is being educated in the best of schools to develop his manhood. The mandate for his redemption has gone out and must be obeyed, though the land be drenched in blood, and there be mourning in every family thereof. They have "cried unto the Lord, and their cry has come up unto God by reason of their bondage. And God has looked upon them, and had respect unto them." And through their redemption and elevation we confidently expect the renovation of the whole African family. Indeed, it will be but of a piece with the Divine procedure, should that race yet become, commercially, politically, and morally, a leading race among the nations of the earth.

Placed in the centre of the earth and capable of producing, in the greatest perfection and abundance, the products of the tropics and the temperate zones, America and Europe may be spared their long and perilous voyages around the Cape, and realize all the wants of commerce comparatively at their door. Africa can be made to supply the world with the great staples of commerce, cotton, sugar, rice, coffee, dyes, valuable oils, and precious metals. Her people, too, have all the natural aptitudes to realize such a result—quick perception, great power of endurance, love of home and fondness for agriculture, and a marked love of traffic.

Could the merchants of New York and Boston see Africa as she is, and as she shall be, they would not allow England to forestall them in a lucrative commerce. They would come in for their share, by organizing companies and placing lines of steamers to all important points on the coasts and up the rivers of Africa, manned by colored seamen. Congress should at once aid such companies, send out explorers, form treaties with the natives, and develop the resources of the country. This will be done, because the elements of commerce are there. A highway is thus opening to Africa, liberating and preparing a people to go and possess the land. Who does not see the hand of God in working out the destiny of that people?

From whatever standpoint we contemplate the destiny of the African race, in connection with the recent and peculiar intimations of Providence toward that race, we can not but look forward to a nationality in Africa as their only really hopeful prospect. And here we should fail to do justice to our own convictions if we did not indicate the " African Civilization Society" as incorporating, in its general features, modes of working and objects, the most suitable and hopeful agency to work out the final destiny of this people. With a

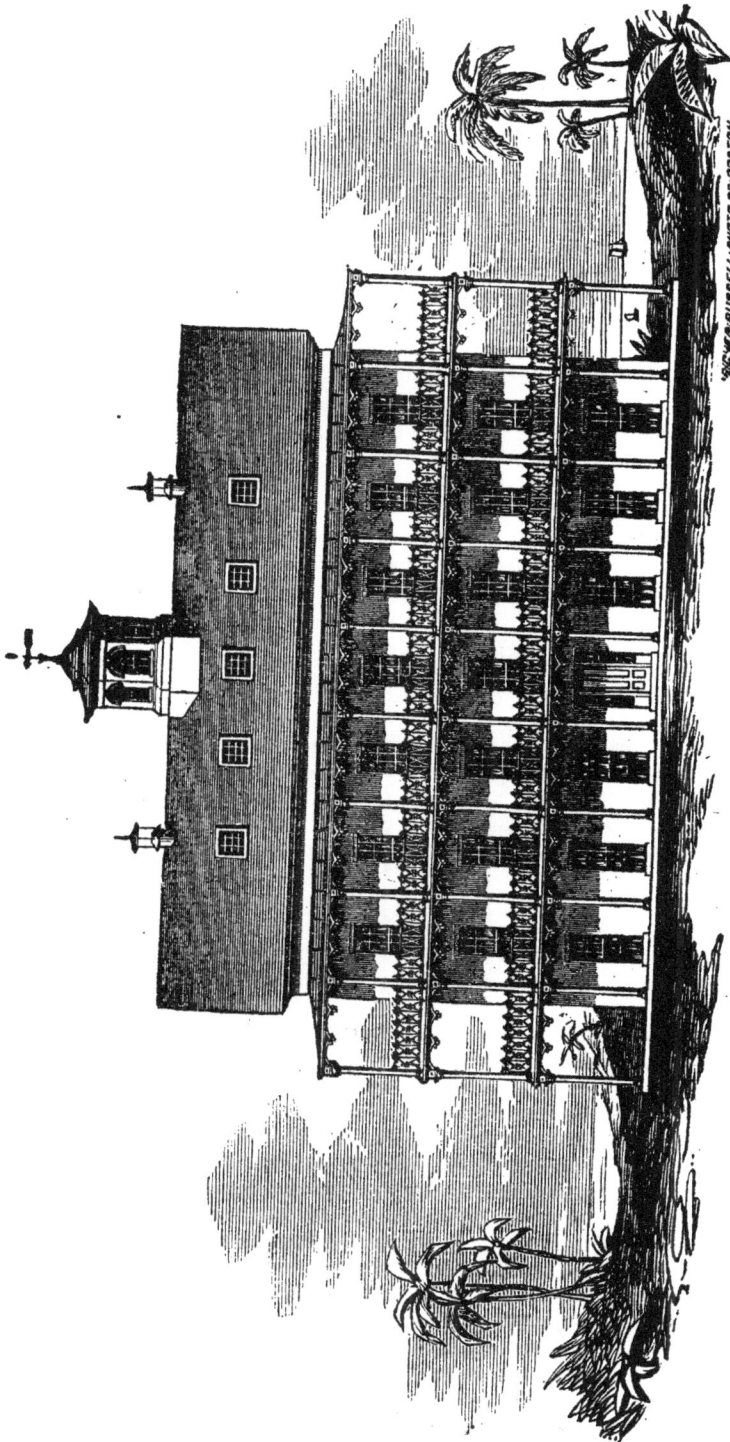

LIBERIA COLLEGE—See page 417.

working power of colored men, and a motive power—a guidance, encouragement, and co-operation of some of our most philanthropic and benevolent citizens, it promises a final success. The plan seems common-sense and practical. Small industrial settlements of selected colored families, composed of farmers, mechanics, teachers, and preachers, act as a civilizing agency, carry Christianity into the field and workshop, and thus make it practical and their missions self-sustaining. Each forms a nucleus about which the natives will gather, and each, in turn, become a radiator of the new light."

I have quite failed, in the foregoing pages, to give the deserved prominence to one of the most promising signs of Africa's coming renovation. I refer to the Liberia College. Nor can I do more—nor need I do more, than to recognize the fact of its existence. A college, a high literary institution, with a president, professors, and directors, patrons and pupils, who would do honor to any college, and yet of the lineage of Ham, is a speaking fact—a day-star risen upon that land of darkness and shadow of death. God bless it ; and may it cast its light far and wide over that long-benighted continent!

But enough. I have presented Africa in her waiting posture, ready to be delivered—her vast resources on the eve of development—Central Africa just at this juncture opening up to view elements of progress hitherto unknown, and a commerce inaugurating of equally gigantic dimensions ; the agents for this work preparing in the iron furnace of slavery, and the great slaveholders' rebellion brought about at the appointed time to loose them from their bondage and send them on their mission to their fatherland—England cut off from a supply of cotton, and compelled to seek a supply from Africa—

18*

how the war is carrying out the work of preparation begun by slavery, fitting for their mission warriors, statesmen, leaders, as well as merchants, mechanics, artisans, and scholars. Is there not good ground for the hope now taking hold of the philanthropic mind that the star of Africa is rising?

And what follows, but that the great heart of humanity should beat responsive to the mighty working of the Divine hand—that we should take the side of the oppressed and of God—meet our responsibilies—quit ourselves like men—lean on the everlasting arm—shake ourselves from the burden and bondage of the past— "up, sanctify ourselves," and put away the "accursed thing," praying with all prayer and supplication, with thanksgiving; work where and when God is working— throw ourselves into the current of providential working—as a nation, repent and humble ourselves before God, and put away the sins that have brought down upon us the sore judgments of God, and we shall see if God will not turn and smile upon us, and bless us more than before! "Though he hath torn, he will heal us; though he hath smitten, he will bind us up!"

www.ingramcontent.com/pod-product-compliance
Lightning Source LLC
Chambersburg PA
CBHW051440270326
41932CB00024B/3369